W9-CLB-075

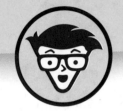

Adobe Photoshop® Lightroom® Classic

2nd Edition

by Rob Sylvan

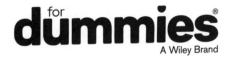

for dummies®

A Wiley Brand

Adobe Photoshop® Lightroom® Classic For Dummies®, 2nd Edition

Published by: **John Wiley & Sons, Inc.,** 111 River Street, Hoboken, NJ 07030-5774, www.wiley.com

Copyright © 2022 by John Wiley & Sons, Inc., Hoboken, New Jersey

Published simultaneously in Canada

For general information on our other products and services, please contact our Customer Care Department within the U.S. at 877-762-2974, outside the U.S. at 317-572-3993, or fax 317-572-4002. For technical support, please visit https://hub.wiley.com/community/support/dummies.

Wiley publishes in a variety of print and electronic formats and by print-on-demand. Some material included with standard print versions of this book may not be included in e-books or in print-on-demand. If this book refers to media such as a CD or DVD that is not included in the version you purchased, you may download this material at http://booksupport.wiley.com. For more information about Wiley products, visit www.wiley.com.

Library of Congress Control Number: 2022934235

ISBN 978-1-119-87321-1 (pbk); ISBN 978-1-119-87323-5 (ebk); ISBN 978-1-119-87322-8 (ebk)

SKY10033735_032122

Contents at a Glance

Table of Contents

Introduction

I t's been over 12 years since I wrote the first edition of this book on what was then Lightroom 2. Saying a lot has changed since then is a bit of an understatement. At the end of 2017 Adobe released two similar, but distinctly different, versions of Lightroom with the goal of addressing two similar, yet different, digital photography workflows. I've structured this book to help you understand the differences between these versions of Lightroom — one now called "Adobe Photoshop Lightroom Classic" and a new one now just called "Adobe Photoshop Lightroom" — so that you are prepared to choose the right one for your needs. Just be sure to read all of Chapter 1 to get a handle on that. That said, the primary focus of this book is on how to get the most out of Lightroom Classic. There are a few chapters to help a Lightroom Classic user get started with the new Lightroom on the mobile platform, but if you are using only the new Lightroom on all your devices, you'll want to check out a different book.

Back in 2007 when Lightroom 1.0 was released, it was considered a paradigm shift in the way photographers managed and edited their digital photos. Today we are witnessing a new paradigm shift thanks to the rise of the smartphone as digital camera with always-connected Internet (which is why there is this new Lightroom version). Although paradigm shifts offer new ways of doing things and the potential of improved workflows, they can sometimes be disorienting and frustrating to come to terms with at first. That's why Adobe still offers the original version, which is now called Lightroom Classic. My hope is that this book can serve as a resource to keep you out of trouble, on task, and moving forward as you take your photos from camera to storage to output, over and over again.

About This Book

I am more than just a user of both versions of Lightroom. Through my roles on the KelbyOne.com Lightroom Help Desk, as an educator, as an author, and my participation in various Lightroom groups, workshops, and forums, I've worked with tens of thousands of fellow Lightroom users over the last decade. I've tried to understand the problems they faced as I've helped them find solutions. I wrote this book with the intention of preventing you from encountering the same problems that others have stumbled on, while also sharing the collective wisdom I've gained to make your workflow as efficient as possible.

How This Book Is Organized

I organize this book with the larger Lightroom Classic workflow in mind, but each chapter — and even the sections within a chapter — represent all the smaller workflows that make up the larger whole. So although there's something to be gained from following the structure I lay out in the book, if you're new to Lightroom Classic, my hope is that you can pick up this book when you need it and jump right to the place in your workflow that you want to learn more about.

Because of the existence of two different versions of Lightroom, I've also structured the book with the goal of minimizing confusion about which version I am talking about. I explicitly refer to Adobe Photoshop Lightroom Classic as "Lightroom Classic" (as cumbersome as that is to read over and over again) and refer to the new Adobe Photoshop Lightroom as just "Lightroom" (along with references to it being *cloud-based* or part of an *ecosystem*) within a given chapter.

Note that up until the middle of 2019, both versions had the initials "CC" (for Creative Cloud) appended to the end of their respective names. Now that it is only possible to license any version of the Lightroom family of products through a Creative Cloud subscription, Adobe dropped the "CC" from the ends of both product names. For the sake of clarity, what was Lightroom Classic CC is now just Lightroom Classic, and what was Lightroom CC is now just Lightroom.

Lightroom Classic is a workflow tool by design, and within the macro workflow of capture to output there exist countless smaller workflows that cover all the micro tasks every photographer needs to complete. The very concept of a workflow implies that there is both a natural beginning and a finite end. I mean, you can't start editing a photo if you haven't first pressed the shutter, right?

Part 1: Getting Started with Lightroom Classic

If you're new to Lightroom Classic — or new to digital photography — you'll definitely want to spend some time in Part 1. I've seen too many people get off on the wrong foot with Lightroom Classic and lose time (and sleep) trying to get themselves back on track because they didn't get a few basic concepts under their belt first. I've helped quite a few folks get back on track, and I know some of the more common pitfalls, so here's your chance to benefit from my experience so you can spend more time productively working with your photos. In this part, I also explain the differences between the two versions of Lightroom and help guide you toward the one that best fits your needs.

Part 2: Managing Your Photos with Lightroom Classic

Managing data might be the least sexy part of a photographer's workflow; however, it's possibly the most essential. Considering that the volume of photos we photographers produce increases each year, this is an aspect of the workflow you have no choice but to get right. To be honest, this aspect of Lightroom Classic is where people have the most trouble.

Part 3: Working in Lightroom Classic's Digital Darkroom

This part is where you work to realize the vision you had the moment the shutter clicked. For some, it's as much fun as the capture, but for others, it's a chore to accomplish the greatest quality in the least amount of time. Lightroom Classic can meet the needs of both kinds of people.

Part 4: Sharing Your Work with the World

Unless you're satisfied with the process of only making photographs, you're going to require some form of output and sharing that extends beyond just your eyeballs. Lightroom Classic offers several options for output.

Part 5: The Part of Tens

You can think of this section as how to get started with the new Lightroom for Lightroom Classic users. I want to achieve three things with this part of the book: I want to prepare you for the option of using Lightroom Classic and Lightroom together; I want you to know the basics of organizing and editing in Lightroom on the mobile platform; and I want to teach you about my absolute favorite mobile phone camera app found in Lightroom for mobile.

Conventions Used in This Book

Lightroom Classic is wonderfully identical on both Windows and Mac operating systems. I use both operating systems, but I create the majority of screen captures on Mac because that's what I use most. However, I do include Windows captures where needed to highlight the few places where there are minor differences in the interface or dialog boxes, and there are a few captures from mobile devices where needed.

In the case of keyboard shortcuts (and there are many), I lead off with the Mac shortcut and always include the Windows shortcut in parentheses right after. All the shortcuts that don't require an additional modifier key are the same on both platforms. When I give an instruction for opening a contextual menu, I use the term *right-click* even though you may not be using an input device with a right-click button. For the Mac, right-clicking is the same as Control-clicking something to invoke the contextual menu, though you may have a mouse for Mac that has a right-click button too.

With regard to menu commands, I use the convention of separating each menu command with this cute arrow, ⇨. For example, I tell you to choose Lightroom Classic ⇨ Quit Lightroom (File ⇨ Exit for Windows) to quit. You can also quit the program by pressing ⌘+Q (Ctrl+Q for Windows).

Icons Used in This Book

Scattered throughout this book you find some nifty little icons that point out bits of information that are especially useful, important, or noteworthy.

TIP

You see this icon the most. I include many tips to help you get the most from each aspect of the program.

WARNING

There aren't many of these (fortunately). I only use them when there's a chance you might lose data if you aren't careful.

REMEMBER

Whenever a certain piece of information isn't particularly intuitive — but very important to keep in mind — I add this icon to help it stand out.

TECHNICAL
STUFF

This icon indicates a heads-up for those few places where I need to deal with some of the more technical aspects of the software.

Beyond the Book

Like every *For Dummies* book, this one comes with a free Cheat Sheet that brings together some of the most commonly needed information for people struggling with Lightroom Classic. Turn to this for a handy list of shortcuts, a closeup of what's included around image thumbnails, all the tools available on the Library Toolbar, and what to do when things go wrong. To get the Cheat Sheet, head for www.dummies.com and, using the Search box, search for **Adobe Photoshop Lightroom Classic For Dummies Cheat Sheet**.

Where to Go from Here

If you're just starting out, my advice to you is to visit Part 1 sooner rather than later. Beyond that, this book is intended to be a reference that you can rely on when you find yourself stuck or that you can use proactively to avoid the most common pitfalls before you go in.

Be sure to check out my website, https://Lightroomers.com, and my weekly Lightroom blog at https://LightroomKillerTips.com for the latest news, tips, and tutorials on both Lightroom Classic and Lightroom.

1
Getting Started with Lightroom Classic

Familiarizing yourself with the Lightroom Classic interface.

Understanding how catalogs work.

Using Lightroom Classic's most basic features.

Chapter **1**

Getting to Know Adobe Photoshop Lightroom Classic

When I wrote the first edition of this book, the only product available was "Adobe Photoshop Lightroom," and the iPhone had just been introduced. The intervening years have brought about a boon to camera technology, mobile technology, software capabilities, and the Internet. Adobe has responded to these advances by spinning off a new version of the original "Lightroom" (while adding "Classic" to the old version) in a way that leverages the ubiquity of mobile devices, cloud storage, and always-connected Internet. This has resulted in more choice but also a bit of confusion.

In this chapter, I aim to clarify the key distinctions between the two versions of Lightroom to help you choose the version that is right for you. I encourage you to go back and read the book's Introduction to get a big-picture view of how this book is organized and clarity on how I refer to the two versions of Lightroom throughout the book. To get some historical context on the evolution of Lightroom, I encourage you to read my blog post on Adobe's original announcement of the new version: https://lightroomkillertips.com/new-lightroom-whole-new-ecosystem.

The Two Versions of Lightroom

At the time of this writing, Adobe provides two separate but similar programs with the name *Lightroom* in the title. In a nutshell, the key differences are that

>> **Lightroom Classic** uses a catalog (more on that later) that is stored on your computer, which references photos that can be stored on your computer, an external drive, a network attached storage device, or any combination of those local storage options. It has been evolving since 2007 and will feel most familiar to anyone who has used a previous version of Lightroom. Lightroom Classic is the main focus of this book.

>> **Lightroom** stores everything (photos, information about the photos, and all adjustments) in the *cloud* (storage that is only accessible through an Internet connection and paid for through your Adobe Creative Cloud subscription), and by virtue of everything being stored in the cloud you can access all your work from any device (laptop, desktop, tablet, or smartphone) that runs Lightroom (available for the macOS, Windows, iOS, and Android platforms). Because everything is stored in the cloud, you can access your Lightroom photos through a web browser. Lightroom has fewer features than Lightroom Classic (although Adobe adds more all the time) and is designed for use in our always-connected mobile world. I introduce you to Lightroom in Part 5, where I explore how Lightroom on a mobile device can be a useful companion to Lightroom Classic.

This book focuses on Lightroom Classic because this version is the most mature of the two versions, has the most features, and doesn't require an Internet connection to access your photos. In my view, Lightroom Classic is the most powerful version of Lightroom and makes the most sense for most people looking to manage a growing photo library over time. It also provides the greatest variety of output possibilities (prints, books, slideshows, web galleries, and more). Lightroom Classic is what I use, and I will continue to use it into the foreseeable future.

I don't want you to think that I am not a fan of the new Lightroom; I am very excited about the opportunities it offers people who don't need everything Lightroom Classic offers, who want a simpler interface, and who place a premium on being able to access their photo library from any laptop, desktop, or mobile device. In fact, I devote three chapters at the end of the book to Lightroom to help you see its potential. That said, if you want to use just Lightroom on all your devices, this is not the book for you. Because Lightroom is new, simpler, and has far fewer features than Lightroom Classic, you can get by just fine using only the built-in guided tutorials (mentioned in Chapter 17) and the web-based training found on Adobe's website: `https://helpx.adobe.com/lightroom-cc/tutorials.html`.

Just about all of Adobe's software has moved from a pay-one-price perpetual license model to a new subscription-based model, which Adobe calls the Creative Cloud (often shortened to CC). Both versions of Lightroom are available only through a subscription plan. Let's dive into this a little deeper.

Understanding the Creative Cloud

Adobe coined the name *Creative Cloud* in 2011, but the term took on new meaning in 2013 when Adobe moved away from the old "Creative Suite" of products and made its flagship products (like Photoshop) available for licensing only through a monthly or annual subscription. All programs are still installed locally to your computer and function the same way they always had; the only difference with the Creative Cloud (CC) is how you pay for the software.

While paying monthly/annually for the use of software may seem like a drag, Adobe has made it pretty affordable for photographers through the CC Photography Plan (more on that in the next section). The subscription model offers a few benefits, including the following:

» Access to the latest version of included software the moment Adobe releases it, without additional cost

» Periodic updates, which include new features as well as new camera support and bug fixes

» Able to be installed on as many computers as you own, although you can be logged into only two at a time

» Cross-platform compatible, so no special hoops to jump through if you have both a Mac and Windows computer

REMEMBER

The Creative Cloud subscription model provides a few benefits. Notably, Adobe frequently releases updates that include new features, new camera support, and bug fixes. With the subscription service, you can access these features immediately instead of waiting 18 to 24 months to see new features added.

There are a few CC plans to choose from, and due to the somewhat fluid nature of how these plans evolve, I'm going to direct you to Adobe's website to read up on what's included and the various prices. Head over to `www.adobe.com/creativecloud/photography/compare-plans.html` to learn more.

Creative Cloud Photography Plan

Within the various subscription options, the plan that makes the most sense for photographers is the CC Photography Plan, which at the time of this writing goes for $9.99/month and includes the latest versions of Lightroom Classic, Lightroom, Photoshop, 20GB of online storage, and more (like a free online portfolio), so check the link in the preceding section to get the full details.

TIP

Adobe Photoshop is the prime tool to complement Lightroom Classic and, to a lesser extent, Lightroom. It gives you the most power and offers the greatest functionality and tightest integration with both versions of Lightroom. In fact, when you consider all the features in Lightroom Classic, you may find you don't need anything else for most of your work.

Adobe also offers a Lightroom plan, which is $9.99/month, and includes only Lightroom (it doesn't include Lightroom Classic or Photoshop) and 1TB of online storage (which is enough for hundreds of thousands of JPG photos). There are folks for whom this plan is a good fit, but the plan is not for everyone and is not the focus of this book.

From here, I assume that as a reader of *Adobe Photoshop Lightroom Classic For Dummies,* with a focus on Lightroom Classic, you have or will be getting the CC Photography Plan subscription. Note that apart from features added after Lightroom 6 was released, most of this book applies to Lightroom 6 users too. (Lightroom 6 is the precursor to Lightroom Classic.)

Figuring out whether Lightroom Classic is right for you

If you have used any older version of Lightroom in the past 10 years, you will feel the most comfortable in Lightroom Classic. Due to its maturity as a software product, Lightroom Classic has substantially more features and capabilities than the new Lightroom, and this alone may be the deciding factor for some people. For example, Lightroom Classic has an entire module devoted to printing, and Lightroom has no local print function at all.

Lightroom Classic is best used if you have a high volume of photos stored in your library and plan to continue adding photos to that library. Lightroom Classic stores all your photos locally, so this is a much more affordable option for anyone with over 1TB of storage. Hard drives are relatively cheap, so adding more space to store more photos is affordable and easy.

Lightroom Classic plays nicely with third-party plug-ins. Let's face it, there are a lot of really great photo editing programs out there from companies like On1, Topaz, DxO, and more. You can configure Lightroom Classic to send copies to these editors (and to Photoshop too!) and have those copies automatically added back to Lightroom Classic. Lightroom does not currently support third-party plug-ins (though it does have limited Photoshop integration).

If you like to create photo books, you will enjoy using Lightroom Classic's Book module. If you need to create slideshows, check out Lightroom Classic's Slideshow module. Lightroom Classic supports a high-volume workflow, so it has a greater array of output options for when you need to create copies for any reason.

Lightroom Classic and Lightroom share the same powerful editing tools used to make your photos look awesome, so there is no real compromise there. So what makes Lightroom compelling? Read on!

Knowing whether you need the new Lightroom

If I had to sketch out the type of photographer who would be the best fit for using Lightroom (at the time of this writing), I think of someone who primarily shoots with a smartphone and/or digital camera set to JPG mode, has a photo library that's less than 1TB of total data, and doesn't own an inkjet printer. That's not to say that someone who only shoots raw with a DSLR and prints every photo can't use Lightroom, but considering Lightroom's current set of features and cost, the raw DSLR shooter could find using Lightroom frustrating and expensive. I'm sure this will evolve.

Lightroom's greatest asset is that it makes all your photos available on all your devices, and it does that by storing the full-resolution photos in the cloud. This is an amazing feature! However, as I discuss in the Creative Cloud section earlier in this chapter, the Lightroom plan is currently $9.99/month for 1TB of storage. If you have less than 1TB of total storage needs, this is a pretty affordable way to have all your photos backed up, accessible, and combined with a state-of-the-art photo editor (and mobile camera app) with easy access to sharing on social media.

WARNING

Each additional 1TB of storage costs an additional $9.99/month. If you have a photo library that requires 3TB of storage, you are looking at $29.97/month to store that in the cloud in perpetuity. That's $359.64 per year, and I don't know many photographers willing to pay that much per year to store their photos in the cloud.

Now don't get me wrong; I love the direction Lightroom is heading, and I think it is a great match for people who fit well within its current feature set, but it just isn't for everyone. That said, Lightroom is a relatively new product as I write this. Who knows how things will change and evolve in the next 10 years? Nothing is static in the world of digital photography. However, keep in mind that Lightroom is also included with the CC Photography Plan with Lightroom Classic and Photoshop (and 20GB of storage), and in Chapters 16 through 18 I discuss how to use Lightroom Classic and Lightroom together.

If you're intrigued about Lightroom, jump ahead to Part 5 of the book for an introduction to using it on your mobile device. The remaining sections of this chapter look at the interface of the focus of the book, Lightroom Classic.

Introducing the Lightroom Classic Interface

Adobe built Lightroom Classic using a *modular* architecture, which means that Lightroom Classic comprises a set of unique applications that share a common interface and that access a common database (or *catalog*, as it is called). Each of the applications is referred to as a *module*, and Lightroom Classic has seven modules.

REMEMBER

None of these modules can function outside of Lightroom Classic. Although tightly integrated, they each have a set of unique menus, panels, and tools tailored to the specific function each module is designed to handle.

I drill down into the specific panels, tools, and menus in the chapters ahead, but for now, I'm going to do the overview thing by taking a stab at what makes each module unique and then showing you how to get the most out of the common interface.

Getting what makes each module unique

Lightroom Classic has seven modules — but the beauty of modular construction is that the potential exists for more to be added. Adobe has opened only limited aspects of Lightroom Classic's guts to third-party developers, and the outcome has been very positive.

The potential for extending Lightroom Classic's functionality in the future is something to look forward to, but there's already plenty of power under the hood. Here are the seven modules you find in Lightroom Classic:

>> **The Library module:** Your organizational hub, the Library module (see Figure 1-1), is where many of your Lightroom Classic sessions will start and end. Common Library module tasks include

- Keywording and metadata entry.

- File moving, deletion, and renaming.

- Finding, sorting, and grouping.

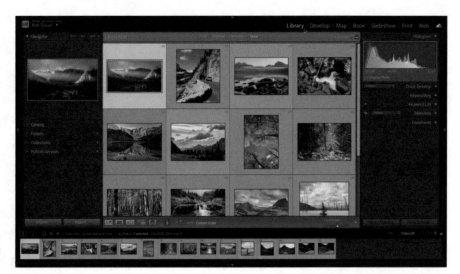

FIGURE 1-1:
The Library
module.

>> **The Develop module:** The bulk of your image processing takes place in the Develop module. Armed with a powerful array of image-adjustment tools, shown in Figure 1-2, common Develop module tasks include

- Setting white balance and tonal adjustments.

- Adjusting contrast and color.

- Reducing noise and adding sharpening.

- Cropping and adjusting crooked horizons.

- Removing red-eye and sensor spots.

>> **The Map module:** Shown in Figure 1-3, the Map module is for finding photos with embedded geolocation information on the map, or for manually placing photos on the map. The tools in this module allow you to

- See photos with geolocation data appear on the map.

- Manually place photos on the map.

- Use the geolocation data in the photo to apply location information (city, state, country) to its metadata.

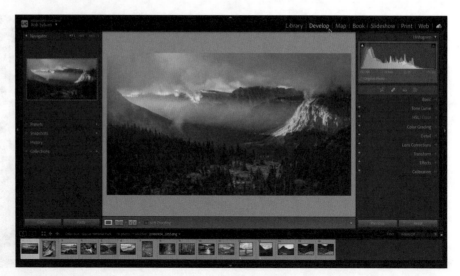

FIGURE 1-2:
The Develop
module.

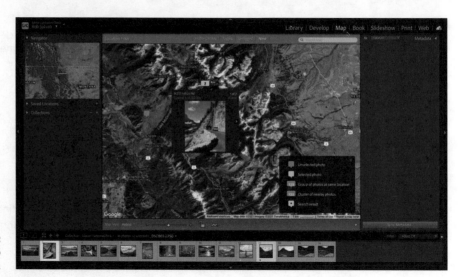

FIGURE 1-3:
The Map
module.

>> **The Book module:** Shown in Figure 1-4, the Book module is for creating book layouts that you can upload to be printed through Blurb.com. The tools in this module allow you to

- Adjust book page layouts.
- Create a cover for the book.
- Add text to individual pages.

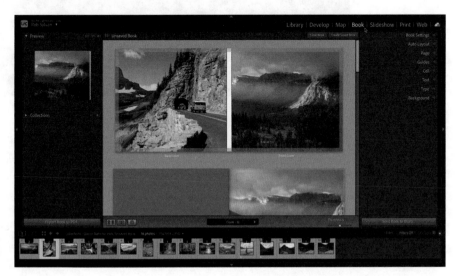

>> **The Slideshow module:** The aptly named Slideshow module, shown in Figure 1-5, is for creating presentations of your photos. The tools in this module allow you to

- Adjust slideshow layout.
- Adjust slide transitions.
- Set the show to music.
- Export a slideshow as a video, PDF, or series of JPGs.

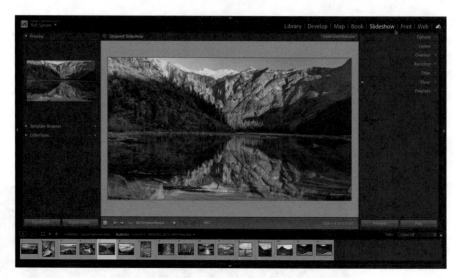

FIGURE 1-5:
The Slideshow
module.

>> **The Print module:** If you print photos, you'll soon find the Print module, shown in Figure 1-6, to be a valuable addition to your printing workflow. Here you find controls for

- Creating layouts and print packages.

- Using output-specific color profiles to ensure the best-looking prints.

- Printing to a local printer or to a JPG file.

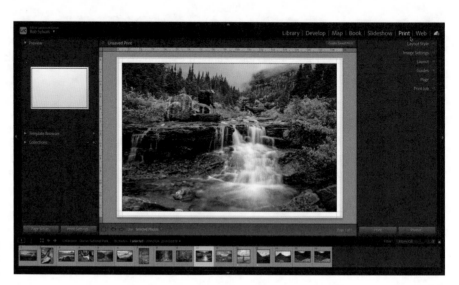

FIGURE 1-6:
The Print
module.

>> **The Web module:** Getting your photos online in some capacity is a requirement these days. The Web module, shown in Figure 1-7, allows you to manage your web presence by letting you

- Choose from various photo gallery styles.

- Configure the look and feel of your web gallery.

- Upload directly to your web server.

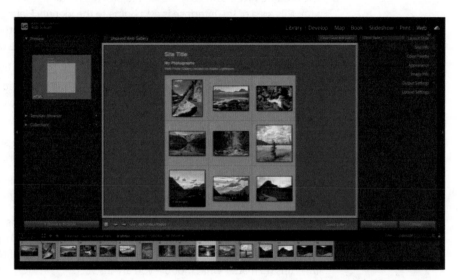

FIGURE 1-7:
The Web module.

What the Lightroom Classic modules have in common

Having all modules share parts of a common interface might make it harder (at first glance) to tell which module is which, but don't worry too much about that. Clarity will reign supreme when you have Lightroom Classic up and running. Think of it this way: A common interface is in fact one of Lightroom Classic's greatest strengths because keeping the same interface means you don't have to spend time learning seven different interfaces. The interface behaves the same and has the same basic structure no matter what you're using Lightroom Classic to accomplish.

Check out Figure 1-8 to see what I mean. The Library module shown there sports the following standard interface components that each module shares:

» **The Title bar:** Provides an at-a-glance view of the name of the catalog and the module you're in.

» **The Menu bar:** The go-to place for all the commands needed for each module's tasks.

» **The Module Picker:** An easy method to pick the module you want to work with. This area of the interface is also home to the Identity Plate on the left, which you can customize to insert your own graphic, as well as the progress meter that appears when Lightroom performs a task. (For more on the Identity Plate, check out Chapter 5.)

» **The Left Panel group:** Although the content varies with each module, the panels to the left of the interface are generally functions that involve accessing, grouping, and previewing photos and templates.

» **The Right Panel group:** The panels to the right of the interface also vary with each module, but this is where you find controls for adjusting and tweaking.

» **The Toolbar:** Each module has its own set of tools, but the Toolbar that appears under the main content area is a staple of every module.

» **The Filmstrip:** At the bottom of each module, you find the Filmstrip, which displays thumbnails of the image grouping you are working with. It also is home to a row of tools right there along the top that put a lot of things at your fingertips no matter what module you are in:

- *Main and Second Window controls.* Click and hold either of these window icons to access a number of shortcuts for controlling each window (more details on the second window function later in the chapter).

- *Jump to Grid View icon.* No matter where you are in Lightroom, one click takes you to Grid view in the Library module.

- *Go Back and Forward buttons.* Allow you to navigate between previously selected image groupings (folders, collections, searches) you have been viewing.

- *Filmstrip Source Indicator.* Provides an at-a-glance view of the current image grouping and active photo. Click the drop-down arrow at the end for quick access to the special collections found in the Catalog panel as well as a list of recently visited folders, collections, and favorites.

- *Filters.* When clicked, the Filter label expands to reveal ways to filter the current image grouping by flag, rating, or color label. The Custom Filter drop-down menu provides quick access to all of the Library Filter bar options. The last button on the right toggles filtering on and off.

I find a more convenient method for showing and hiding these screen elements is the keyboard shortcuts:

>> **F5:** Show/hide the Module Picker.

>> **F6:** Show/hide the Filmstrip.

>> **F7:** Show/hide the Left Panel group.

>> **F8:** Show/hide the Right Panel group.

>> **Tab:** Show/hide both the Left and Right panel groups.

>> **Shift+Tab:** Show/hide the Left, Right, Top and Bottom.

>> **T:** Show/hide the Toolbar.

When it comes to clearing the clutter and focusing on your photos, Lightroom Classic has one further cool trick up its sleeve. It's called Lights Out mode and has three states:

>> **Lights On:** The normal operating condition, where everything is visible.

>> **Lights Dim:** In this mode, your selected photos remain unchanged but the surrounding interface dims. Although dimmed, the interface is accessible and functional (if you know where things are).

>> **Lights Out:** Taking the dim view to the extreme, the entire interface is blacked out and only your photos are visible. The ultimate way to reduce clutter!

You can jump through each Lights Out mode by pressing the L key. You set the amount of dimming and the color the screen dims to in the preferences. (I cover all the preference settings in Chapter 3.)

Using Lightroom Classic's secondary display view

The ultimate way to gain more screen real estate is to add another screen! Lightroom Classic's approach to dual monitor support is the addition of a second window that you can move to your second monitor. The result is that you have the same primary Lightroom Classic window on one monitor (this is where you access all the modules and do your work) and then your secondary display window provides additional ways to view the photos you are working on. (Although it's possible to enable the secondary window on a single monitor system, it is limited in its usefulness because it competes for the same screen real estate as the primary window.)

The secondary display window functions in the same manner with all Lightroom Classic modules. Here are the options available in the secondary window:

- » **Grid:** By using the Grid option, you essentially extend the Filmstrip to the second window so that it provides greater access to all the thumbnails of the current group of photos. The secondary window Grid view functions the same as Grid view in the Library module (see Chapter 5 for more information on Grid view).

- » **Loupe:** Allows for viewing a single image in its entirety or zoomed in close within the second window. Loupe has three options:
  - ● *Normal:* Always displays the active photo selected in the primary window
  - ● *Live:* Continually displays the photo under the cursor as you move over photos in the main window
  - ● *Locked:* Allows you to choose one photo to display continuously in the second window while you view a different photo in the primary window

- » **Compare:** Allows you to compare two or more photos side by side. The secondary window Compare view functions the same way as Compare view in the Library module. (See Chapter 6 for more information on Compare view.)

- » **Survey:** Allows you to view multiple photos side by side within the secondary window. The secondary window Survey view functions the same way as Survey view in the Library module. (See Chapter 6 for more information on Survey view.)

- » **Slideshow:** Available only when you have the secondary window set to full screen (not possible on a single monitor system). This option allows you to run the slideshow on the secondary display.

There is one other cool option related to the secondary window called Show Second Monitor Preview. (It works only when the secondary window is in Full Screen mode.) When enabled, it provides a small preview window showing what's being displayed in the secondary window. Huh? It's intended for situations where you might have your secondary monitor facing away from you and toward an audience. This way you can be showing photos to an audience on the secondary display while you work on the primary display, and the preview window lets you have a peek at what your audience is seeing.

TIP

You can enable and disable the second window by clicking its icon on the Filmstrip or choosing Window ⇨ Second Window ⇨ Enable from the main menu.

Getting Up and Running

I'm sure you're champing at the bit for the opportunity to roll up your sleeves and start putting Lightroom Classic through its paces. I don't blame you! You're gonna love it. However, if you take the time to lay the groundwork so that you get all your ducks in a row, you're sure to start on the right foot (could I cram in any more metaphors?).

Preparing for installation

Don't think of an application installation as being a tiresome chore. Rather, think of it as a perfect excuse to do a little hard-disk housekeeping. What better time to do tasks like the following:

>> Freeing up disk space by deleting unused files, clearing caches, moving files to another disk, and emptying the Trash

>> Running an error-checking application

>> Running a defragmentation application (Windows only)

The best reason to clean house before installing is that it might just prevent problems that you'd likely blame on the new application you just installed. Save yourself some aggravation and run those programs now while you're busy reading this book!

I assume you've confirmed that your system meets the posted minimum requirements before you purchased Lightroom, but generally, it's always in your best interest to exceed the minimum whenever possible for best performance. Here's what matters most:

>> **RAM:** Maximizing the amount of installed RAM is probably going to give you the most bang for your buck. It's more than likely that you'll be running other applications alongside Lightroom, so the more RAM you have, the better for everyone.

>> **Processor:** Processing large volumes of huge files takes horsepower. Lightroom is able to take advantage of multi-core processors, so if an upgrade is in your future, put that under consideration.

>> **Disk space:** When working with digital images, you just can't have enough disk space. If you're shooting raw on a 10-, 12-, or 24+-megapixel camera, you don't want to worry about running out of storage space. Beyond storage, you need ample free space on your startup drive so that all your applications and

your operating system have enough elbow room to function. I like using 2+ TB external drives because they are relatively inexpensive, and easy to add and remove.

>> **Monitor:** You might think you're looking at your photos, but you are in fact looking at your monitor. (I actually don't want to think about how many hours in a day I spend basking in its glow.) For the benefit of your eyes and the quality of your editing, consider a monitor upgrade in your future. The truth is, the monitors that typically come bundled with most computers are better suited to word processing, web browsing, and email. This is probably a good time to call in a friend to help you shop if you're not sure where to start, but here are a few things to keep in mind:

- *Price:* Quality in a monitor doesn't come cheap. At the high end, you could look at models from Eizo and LaCie, although many people I know are quite happy on the higher end with Dell and Apple. The technology is improving, and prices are falling.

- *Size:* Bigger is usually better. Your monitor is your desk space. The bigger your desk, the easier it is to work. 24- to 30-inch monitors are pretty typically used for photo work.

- *Resolution:* A monitor's resolution is expressed by how many pixels across by how many pixels down it can display (such as 1600 x 900). The larger the number, the more pixels will be displayed, which means the more room you have to work.

- *Graphics card:* This is the part of your computer that drives the video display. You need to have a powerful enough graphics card to run your monitor at its native size. You don't want to cart home a monitor your system can't handle. Have all your computer's specifications with you when you shop, and ask for help.

You can read the minimum requirements here:

>> **Lightroom Classic:** https://helpx.adobe.com/lightroom/system-requirements.html

>> **Lightroom:** https://helpx.adobe.com/lightroom-cc/system-requirements.html

After you determine which version of Lightroom is best for you and install it, you are ready to take a closer look at this catalog thing that Lightroom Classic uses, which, as it turns out, is pretty important.

Chapter **2**

Working with Catalogs

When you install Lightroom Classic, it automatically creates an empty catalog file at the default location as part of the installation process. In fact, Lightroom Classic can't even function without one. You can open Microsoft Word without having a document open, and you can open Photoshop without having an image open, but you can't open Lightroom Classic without opening a catalog. The catalog is integral to Lightroom Classic's operation.

This chapter shows you how to work with the Lightroom Classic catalog. You will discover where on your system the catalog is located, how to keep it backed up, how to keep it optimized, the role of the associated preview cache files, and even how to transfer data between two catalogs.

Understanding How the Catalog Works

A key factor separating Lightroom Classic from a pixel editor like Adobe Photoshop and a file browser like Adobe Bridge is Lightroom Classic's use of a catalog file. The *catalog* in Lightroom Classic is essentially a database, and as such it is simply the repository for everything Lightroom Classic "knows" about your photos. Luckily, you don't need to know much about databases to use Lightroom Classic, but if you understand how this particular database fits into the big picture, you can work smarter when managing, organizing, processing, outputting, and safeguarding your photos.

The great thing about a database (unlike my own brain) is that it can recall everything you enter into it. Equally important to note, however, is that a database knows *only* what you enter into it. To ensure that the catalog remains "in the know," you should always use Lightroom Classic for basic file-maintenance tasks (such as moving, deleting, and renaming) of your imported photos (which I cover in Chapters 5 and 6).

WARNING

So instead of using Windows File Explorer, macOS Finder, or Adobe Bridge for file maintenance of your imported photos (use whatever program you want before they are imported), you'll want to use Lightroom Classic to ensure that your catalog remains up-to-date with the changes you make. If you perform file-maintenance tasks outside of Lightroom Classic, the catalog isn't updated as you move, rename, or delete files on your computer, and as a result, the locations of your photos within the catalog will be out of sync with the locations of your photos as they are actually stored on your computer. When this happens, your photos are considered missing or offline by Lightroom Classic, and you won't be able to edit in Develop or export copies until they are reconnected to the catalog. Take a moment to read an article I wrote about how to reconnect the catalog to missing or offline files (in case it happens to you): `http://missing.lightroomers.com`.

One catalog to rule them all

Before we go any further, I want to discuss the question of how many catalogs you should have. Ideally, and recommended by Adobe (and me), you would have only one catalog that serves as the master go-to location for accessing all your photography. After all, the catalog is nothing more than a database, and the more data (information about your photos) you put in it, the more you can leverage that database to find and organize your photo library over time. Lightroom Classic sets no hard limit on how many photos a catalog can hold, but performance can be impacted over time by having a very large catalog on a computer that is lacking in horsepower (see Chapter 1 for minimum requirements). My own master catalog approaches 200,000 photos, but I know others with much larger catalogs, and they experience no problems.

That said, I know of other photographers who feel that having multiple catalogs is the best solution for their workflow. They may feel that having one catalog per year, or per decade, or per event, or whatever grouping fits their shooting style and way of thinking, and that's fine, as long as it works. The thing you need to keep in mind about having multiple catalogs is that because you can't search across catalogs, you need to create an external system to organize your photo library so that you know which catalog you need to open to find a specific photo. Having one catalog per year sounds great until a few years go by and you can't remember which year you took a certain photo. My suggestion is to stick with one catalog unless you have a really good reason not to do so and you have a good system for staying organized.

Knowing where the catalog is located

By default, the catalog is stored in a folder named Lightroom within the Pictures folder on your system. Inside the Lightroom folder, you find the catalog file, which has a .lrcat file extension, and the file that holds all the previews of your imported images (called the *preview cache*), which has a .lrdata file extension. These two files work together to make Lightroom Classic operational. I cover the cache files contained in this folder in the section "Managing the preview cache files," later in this chapter. Note, there is a new file with a .lrcat-data extension for storing data related to the improved Masking functionality (see Chapter 9).

TIP

To store your catalog at a location other than the default (if your default drive is low on free space, for example, or if you prefer to keep all your photo-related files in a different location), use your computer's file management app to move the entire Lightroom folder to a new location on your computer. The catalog works fine from any (non-network connected) location — you just have to help Lightroom Classic find the catalog in its new location the first time you access it. More on that in a bit.

A couple of things to keep in mind regarding where a catalog can live happily:

>> **Local drive:** The catalog has to be kept on a locally connected drive (external drives are fine). Lightroom Classic can't access a catalog stored on a network drive (though it can access photos stored on a network drive).

>> **Free space:** Be sure to place the catalog on a drive that has a large enough amount of free space to store your work (as in hundreds or more gigabytes free). The size of your database and its companion preview caches (more on preview caches in the section "Managing the preview cache files") need room to grow as you import new images and process them.

REMEMBER

Chapter 4 covers where on your drive to store your photos in the sections that cover importing files. For now, keep in mind that photos are not physically stored "inside" the catalog file; they are stored, rather, on a drive of your choosing outside of Lightroom Classic. The catalog refers, or points, to the actual storage location of each imported photo.

If you move your catalog, you have to help Lightroom Classic find that catalog the next time you want to open it. Here's how that's done:

1. **Launch Lightroom Classic.**

   If Lightroom Classic can't immediately locate the catalog, it displays the dialog shown in Figure 2-1.

2. **Click the Choose a Different Catalog button.**

   The Select Catalog dialog appears (see Figure 2-2).

3. **Click the Choose a Different Catalog button in that dialog.**

4. **In the new file browsing dialog that appears, navigate to the location you chose as the new home for your catalog, select the .lrcat file, and then click Choose.**

   You return to the Select Catalog dialog, and the path to the catalog you selected appears prominently in the Catalog Location field.

5. **Click the Open (Select on Windows) button.**

   Lightroom Classic launches with the catalog at this new location and will remember it in the future.

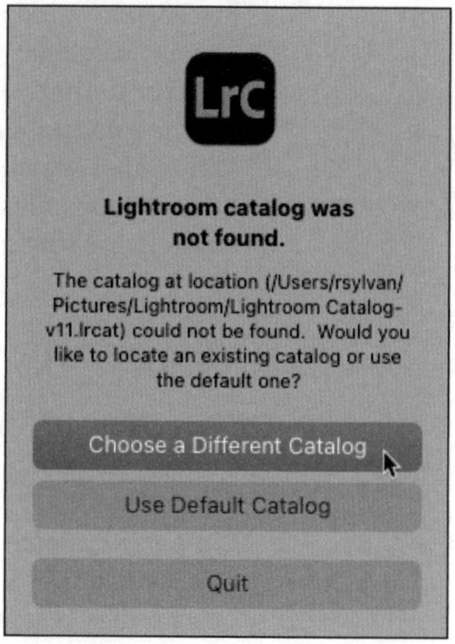

LrC

Lightroom catalog was not found.

The catalog at location (/Users/rsylvan/ Pictures/Lightroom/Lightroom Catalog- v11.lrcat) could not be found. Would you like to locate an existing catalog or use the default one?

Choose a Different Catalog

Use Default Catalog

Quit

FIGURE 2-1:
The Confirm dialog; the Lightroom Classic catalog was not found.

Choosing which catalog to open

Lightroom Classic stores the location of the catalogs you use in its Preferences file. You can configure which catalog Lightroom Classic opens upon launch by going to Lightroom Classic ⇨ Preferences (Edit ⇨ Preferences for Windows) and clicking the General tab, as shown in Figure 2-3. Clicking the Default Catalog drop-down menu reveals the following choices:

>> **Load Most Recent Catalog:** This is the default. Lightroom Classic simply opens the last catalog that was used.

>> **Prompt Me When Starting Lightroom:** The Select Catalog dialog box (refer to Figure 2-2) appears when Lightroom Classic is launched. From here you can choose to open any catalog or even create a new one.

>> **Other:** You can configure a specific catalog to always open when Lightroom Classic is launched.

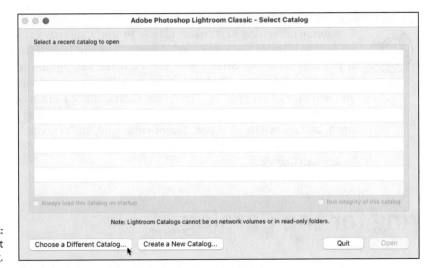

FIGURE 2-2:
The Select
Catalog dialog.

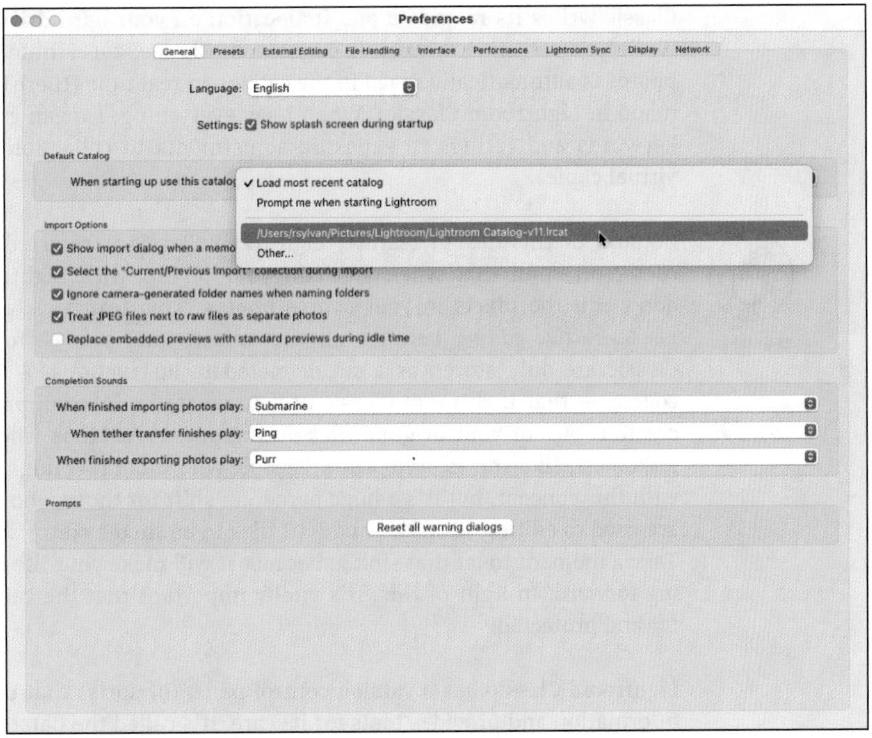

FIGURE 2-3:
The Default
Catalog
preference
setting.

TIP

I recommend setting Lightroom Classic to use a specific catalog when starting up so that it opens the same catalog every time you launch the program — even if you only have one catalog now (which is the best option for most people, as I recommend earlier). This will make your life simpler down the road because you will know that opening Lightroom Classic always means opening that specific catalog. It's easy enough to switch to another catalog using the File ⇨ Open Catalog or File ⇨ Open Recent command. In fact, you can even force the Select Catalog dialog to open by holding Option (Ctrl for Windows) and launching Lightroom Classic.

Caring for the Catalog

You initially enter information about your photos into the catalog with the help of Lightroom Classic's Import function. As each photo is imported, Lightroom Classic writes its metadata and its location on your hard drive into the catalog. While you continue to work in Lightroom Classic, everything you do with your photos is automatically saved in the catalog in real time (there is no "Save" command in Lightroom Classic). When I say everything, I mean everything — from keywords and ratings to exposure adjustments to collection membership and virtual copies.

REMEMBER

Because of this design feature, Lightroom Classic is referred to as a *metadata editor*, meaning that when you edit your photos with Lightroom Classic, you don't edit the pixels in your source photos. This feature is also referred to as *nondestructive editing* because all the adjustments you perform in Lightroom Classic are only stored as a set of metadata instructions — in the catalog, of course — that Lightroom Classic uses to create its internal preview files and to create copies of your original files during output (such as when exporting copies, books, slideshows, and prints). People who shoot raw might be more familiar with this concept, but it's a huge paradigm shift for those who shoot JPG, or who are used to editing JPG, TIF, and PSD files in an image editor such as Photoshop. Take a moment to let that sink in because it will make your life much easier moving forward. In light of this, it's vitally important that the catalog is well cared for and protected.

Lightroom Classic has a catalog control panel (of sorts) that displays important information and provides tools for its care. It's called the Catalog Settings dialog, and you can see it in Figure 2-4. Choosing Lightroom Classic ⇨ Catalog Settings (Edit ⇨ Catalog Settings for Windows) from the main menu gets you there.

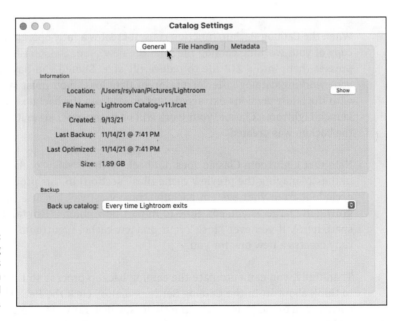

FIGURE 2-4:
The Catalog Settings dialog with the General tab active.

The General tab allows you to control the following:

» **Information:** Displays the catalog's location, name, creation date, last backup date, last optimized date, and file size. Click the Show button to open the folder containing the catalog in the Mac's Finder or the Windows File Explorer.

» **Backup:** Configures the frequency with which the catalog backup function is run.

TIP

Any long-time user might remember there was an optimize option on that panel. It has since moved to the menu under File ⇨ Optimize Catalog. Clicking Optimize Catalog performs a little database housekeeping on the catalog to reduce its size and improve performance, which is generally most helpful on very large catalogs (more on this in the section, "Optimizing your catalog"). Backing up and optimization are important enough topics to warrant their own sections, so I do the smart thing and provide them next.

Backing up your catalog

WARNING

Lightroom Classic's backup function does *not* back up your photos (because your photos are never in the catalog), but it can help protect you against data loss (meaning all the work you do in Lightroom Classic) by automating the process of creating backup copies of your catalog (or catalogs). A full computer system backup procedure outside of Lightroom Classic is still required to protect all your data (including your photos).

When the Catalog Backup function runs, it creates a fully operational and identical copy of your working catalog file (and the new .lrcat-data file), and then compresses them into a ZIP file to reduce file size. Should you have a problem with your working catalog (file corruption or data loss), you must swap the bad files with the latest versions extracted (unzipped) from the backup. The next time you launch Lightroom Classic, your work will be in the exact state it was in at the time the backup was created.

Note that Lightroom Classic does not back up the preview caches (more on these in the "Managing the preview cache files" section) in this process. I suggest you exclude it from your system backup strategy as well because the cache file will grow quite large as you continue to import new photos (I'm talking gigabytes of space here). If you ever "lose" your preview cache, Lightroom Classic automatically creates a new one for you.

Thankfully, you can automate the catalog backup process so that you don't have to think about it. In the Catalog Settings dialog, click the Back Up Catalog dropdown menu to see your scheduling choices, which range from Never to Every Time Lightroom Classic Exits, as shown in Figure 2-5. The first thing you might notice is that the backup can run only when Lightroom Classic exits. If you want to force a backup after a good day's work, set the backup to run Every Time Lightroom Exits; then close Lightroom Classic when you finish working to trigger the backup.

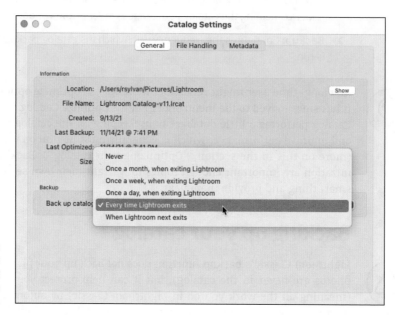

FIGURE 2-5:
The Back
Up Catalog
drop-down
menu.

TIP

When considering the frequency with which to schedule a backup, just imagine what would happen if your catalog went kerflooey. You want your backup catalog to be as fresh as possible, right? Setting it to run once per day is a safe choice. I personally have mine set to Every Time Lightroom Exits. It may seem like overkill, but the backup dialog you get on exit is equipped with a Skip button. The result is that I get a constant reminder to back up every time I quit Lightroom Classic and the option to skip if I haven't done much work since the last time I backed up. It also makes it easy to force a backup by simply closing the program after a big work session.

The next time you exit Lightroom Classic in the period for the backup function to run, you're greeted with the Back Up Catalog dialog, shown in Figure 2-6.

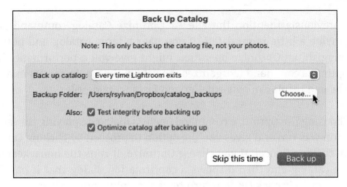

FIGURE 2-6:
The Back Up
Catalog dialog.

Here's how you handle the Back Up Catalog dialog:

1. **Specify where you want the backup catalog saved by clicking the Choose button and then navigating to your desired location.**

   I suggest having your backup saved to a different drive (if possible) than where your working catalog is located. The reason is that if you lose the drive containing your working catalog, you'll be very glad that you had a recent backup safely tucked away on a different drive. My laptop (refer to Figure 2-6) has only a single drive, so I save the backup copies to a local folder in my Dropbox account, which is then automatically synced to a cloud storage location.

2. **Check the Test Integrity Before Backing Up and Optimize Catalog After Backing Up boxes to have the backup process check for corruption in the database.**

   I know it adds a little time to the backup process, but it's time well spent.

3. **Click the Back Up button to begin the process.**

If you change your mind and just want Lightroom Classic to exit, click the Skip button to bypass the backup function. Note that you can change the backup schedule in this dialog as well.

REMEMBER

Each backup function creates a new copy without touching the existing backup files. It's up to you to manage the backup files so that they don't fill the destination hard drive. If you run your backups regularly without clearing the old ones, you might just have several gigs of hard drive space waiting to be recovered! I periodically delete all but the most recent two or three backup copies.

Optimizing your catalog

I previously mention the File ⇨ Optimize Catalog command and just want to provide a little more detail. If you have a large catalog and notice that it seems sluggish, an Optimize operation might give you a performance boost. Using the Optimize command reorganizes the data in the catalog and removes unused space. The end result can be a smaller and faster catalog file.

Choosing the Optimize command opens a dialog displaying the last time the operation was run and gives you the option to proceed by clicking Optimize or bail out by clicking Cancel. If you choose Optimize, it runs the housekeeping functions on the catalog and then displays a confirmation dialog that it has finished. All you have to do is click OK to return to using Lightroom Classic.

TIP

The whole Optimize process was originally put in place by Lightroom Classic's designers to speed up slow-pokey catalogs, but I've seen circumstances where Optimize has corrected problems ranging from catalog exports to identity plates, so I regularly include this as a troubleshooting step for people with strange catalog behaviors. If you are new to Lightroom Classic, you probably won't need this for a while, so just file it away for the future.

Managing the preview cache files

When you make your way through the options in the Catalog Settings dialog, you notice the File Handling tab to the immediate right of the General tab. The File Handling tab (shown in Figure 2-7) has options to help you manage the size and quality of the regular preview files that Lightroom Classic creates for all your imported photos, as well as a running tally of the size of the cache for the optional Smart Previews (which I cover in the upcoming section "Smart Previews").

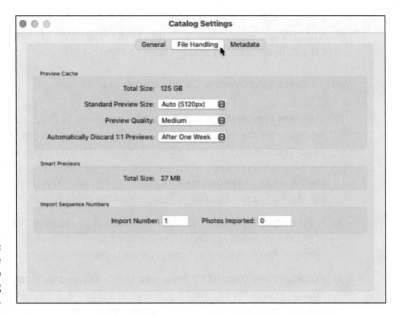

FIGURE 2-7:
The File
Handling tab
of the Catalog
Settings dialog.

Regular previews

Before I get into what the controls do, I'd like to talk about what previews are and what they do. I was once asked a great question by a new user who was trying to understand how previews work: "If my photos are never altered and never in Lightroom Classic, then what am I looking at when I'm working?" What a great question! The answer, of course, is preview files. You encounter two types of regular preview files in all modules except Develop (Develop needs to access the actual photos for its on-the-fly preview when you edit, so it doesn't use these previews):

>> **Standard:** These are what you see in all the modules except Develop. The size and quality of these previews are determined by the settings you choose on the File Handling tab.

>> **1:1:** These previews match the pixel dimensions of your source files. These are used when you view images at 1:1 view in the Library.

Therefore, you're almost always looking at a cached preview of your photos. While you make adjustments in Develop, Lightroom Classic re-renders previews on the fly to show you the effect of the adjustments (but never applies changes to the original photos). All these previews are stored in the Preview cache alongside the catalog file. Because Lightroom Classic renders the previews as needed, they're not essential files and are not included in the backup process. However, because they're rendered for every photo you import, they can require a significant chunk of disk space over time. This brings the discussion back to the File Handling tab of the Catalog Settings dialog (refer to Figure 2-7).

You can tweak your Preview Cache settings in three ways:

>> **Standard Preview Size:** Use this drop-down menu to choose a pixel size that best matches the resolution of your monitor, or let Lightroom Classic do it for you and just leave it set to the default of Auto. Lightroom Classic uses standard-sized previews when you view the image at Fit Screen, meaning you see the entire image on-screen. Because of this, you don't need to generate a standard-sized preview that is greater than the resolution of your monitor.

>> **Preview Quality:** This drop-down menu allows you to determine the amount of JPG compression applied to the standard-sized previews. The default setting of Medium is a good compromise between quality and file size.

>> **Automatically Discard 1:1 Previews:** Use this drop-down menu to configure how long Classic keeps the 1:1 previews in the cache. Because they're high-quality, pixel-for-pixel copies of your source files, such preview files can be quite large, so you might not want them lying about on your hard drive for too long. Lightroom Classic, of course, re-renders them if they're needed after having been discarded, but then you have to wait for the render to complete. Leaving the setting to After One Week is a good balance between performance and keeping a damper on the growing size of the cache.

TIP

You can force Lightroom Classic to delete 1:1 previews at any time by going to Library ⇨ Previews ⇨ Discard 1:1 Previews. Therefore, you're not entirely dependent upon that setting if you find your Preview cache is taking over your hard drive.

Smart Previews

OK, if those are regular previews, what are Smart Previews? Another good question. Smart Previews are basically a smaller version (2560 pixels on the long side) of the original that preserves many of the qualities of a raw file that make it useful for editing. This smaller version is saved as a special DNG file (I cover DNG in more depth in Chapter 7), which allows for a type of compression to make the file size in bytes smaller as well.

The original reason for the introduction of Smart Previews was to have a way to store a smaller, yet still editable, version of the original photo alongside the catalog file so that you could still perform tasks in the Develop module even if the original photo was inaccessible due to being offline. For example, I keep the majority of my photos on an external hard drive, which is not always connected. By creating Smart Previews of my photos (when needed), I can still edit them in the Develop module because Lightroom Classic is smart enough to refer to the Smart Preview when the original is not available, and then smart enough to switch back when I plug that drive back in. This has turned out to be a great compromise, because it just wouldn't be possible to keep my external drive plugged in all the time.

REMEMBER

The Develop module is a special case where it needs to access the original photo to be able to perform edits. If the original is offline, a Smart Preview, if created, can stand in to keep your workflow moving forward.

On a related but side note, the compact yet editable package of the Smart Preview became the key to keeping photos synced through the Adobe cloud when syncing with the new Lightroom ecosystem of apps for Mac, Windows, iOS, and Android (see Chapter 16).

Because not everyone needs Smart Previews all the time, or even at all, their creation is completely optional. You can create them from the Import process covered in Chapter 4, or afterward, in the Library module, accessed via the Library ⇨ Previews ⇨ Build Smart Previews menu. For now, you can see a running tally of how much space the cache is taking up on this tab of Catalog Settings. As with the 1:1 previews, you can manually remove them via the Library ⇨ Previews ⇨ Discard Smart Previews menu command.

Import sequence numbers

"But wait, Rob, what's this Import Sequence Numbers section doing at the bottom of the File Handling tab?" you might ask. Okay, this section's inclusion here might be Lightroom Classic's version of a non sequitur — at least in the context of talking about previews. However, because it is here and you're obviously looking at it (and no doubt wondering what it's all about), I tell you:

» **Import Number:** This is where Lightroom Classic tracks the number of imports for use in filename templates when renaming files during import using the Import# token. It only increments when that particular filename token is being used to rename files. You can change the number prior to importing to set it at a different value.

» **Photos Imported:** This is where Lightroom Classic tracks the number of photos for use in filename templates when renaming files during import using the Image# token. It only increments when that particular filename token is being used to rename files. You can change the number prior to importing to set it at a different value. The main use of this value is for when you want to number files incrementally across multiple imports.

I guess they had to put those two guys somewhere. Just keep them in mind when I discuss file naming in Chapter 4.

Exploring the Metadata options

Metadata is basically data about the data about your photos. It includes the data that comes from your camera (called *EXIF data*), the data you enter (such as copyright, location, and keywords), and all the settings for the adjustments you make when developing your photos — otherwise known as *Develop settings*). This metadata is stored in the catalog file and can be viewed on the Metadata panel of the Catalog Settings dialog (see Figure 2-8).

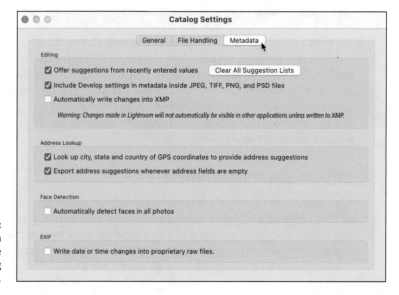

FIGURE 2-8:
The Metadata tab on the Catalog Settings dialog.

Here are the options that appear on the Metadata panel of the Catalog Settings dialog:

>> **Offer Suggestions from Recently Entered Values:** While you enter various metadata (such as keywords, titles, and captions), Lightroom Classic tries to help you by offering auto-complete suggestions after you type a few characters that resemble a previous entry. Uncheck the box to turn off this feature. Click the Clear All Suggestions Lists button if you want to keep the feature enabled but want to reset it.

» **Include Develop Settings in Metadata inside JPEG, TIFF, PNG, and PSD Files:** Okay, this setting and the next one are related. By default, Lightroom Classic stores only the work you do in the catalog. However, you might also want Lightroom Classic to write that information into each photo's own metadata as a form of redundancy. Leave this box checked if you want to include the Develop settings with all other metadata when you tell Lightroom Classic to write to each of these non-raw file type's metadata. If unchecked, the Develop settings reside only in the catalog file for non-raw photos even if you enable the automatic writing changes into XMP. One benefit of writing Develop settings to the file itself is that if that file is imported into another Lightroom Classic catalog, the settings carry over. The next setting in this list is for automating the process of writing from the catalog to each photo's metadata, but you can also do it manually by selecting photos in Grid view of the Library and going to Metadata ⇨ Save Metadata to File.

» **Automatically Write Changes into XMP:** When this box is checked, Lightroom Classic writes to each photo's XMP metadata space automatically and keeps it in sync with the catalog file. (XMP is short for Adobe's Extensible *Metadata Platform*, which simply defines how the data is stored in the file.) However, certain things cannot be written to XMP, such as collection memberships, virtual copies, and stacking (all of these are covered in Chapter 5), and develop histories (see Chapter 9). The benefit of writing to XMP is that you not only keep key metadata and settings embedded in the original photo's metadata space, but the information is accessible to programs outside of Lightroom Classic (Adobe Bridge and Camera Raw, for example). The downside is that the automatic process can include a performance hit (on slower systems) because Lightroom Classic works behind the scenes to write to each file.

» **Write Date or Time Changes into Proprietary Raw Files:** This setting comes into play only if you make a change to the capture date/time of a raw file (see Chapter 3 for more on file types). If the box is checked, Lightroom Classic will change the capture date/time inside the actual raw file. Some people prefer to keep their raw files completely unaltered, so if the box is unchecked (the default state), Lightroom Classic will write the change only to the associated XMP file, leaving the source raw file unchanged.

TIP

If you're noticing a drag on performance with the Automatically Write Changes into XMP option enabled, you can disable it and then manually tell Lightroom Classic to write to each file's XMP metadata by selecting the file(s) in Grid view and going to Metadata ⇨ Save Metadata to File or pressing ⌘+S (Ctrl+S for Windows). The result is the same, but you get to control when it occurs. The downside is that it's up to you to remember.

Although Lightroom Classic doesn't change the pixels in your source photos, these options do present an opportunity to have it change each photo's metadata (think of it as text stored within or alongside the original photo). Aside from performance issues related to using the Automatically Write Changes into XMP option, you might not want Lightroom Classic writing to each photo's metadata at all, in which case, leave those options unchecked.

Chapter 7 covers the Face Detection option.

Working with Multiple Catalogs

I often am asked about the circumstances under which it makes sense to employ a multiple catalog approach to working with Lightroom Classic. There's no absolute right answer, but if you understand the limitations of catalogs, you can make the best decision for your circumstances (however, for most people, just having a single catalog works best).

The single most important factor when considering the use of multiple catalogs is that Lightroom Classic cannot search across multiple catalogs. From a management perspective, if you want to access all your photos, it's far simpler to have them in a single catalog, which allows you to leverage all the power of Lightroom Classic's database to find, gather, and work with your photos. It's terribly inefficient to develop a manual (human) system for managing your catalogs just so you know which catalog is responsible for which photos. Yikes!

That said, if you have unique circumstances where groups of photos are so discrete that you might want or need to keep them separate from each other (for example, having a separate catalog for each client or job), a multi-catalog approach might make more sense. You still need a system for managing all these catalogs so that you can get your hands on the right image when you need it, though.

Some people are concerned about the size of a single catalog as a limiting factor, seeing that as a reason to have many smaller catalogs, but Lightroom Classic imposes no limit on the number of photos that you can import into a catalog. Your system components are a bigger limiting effect on performance when working with large catalogs. Generally, maximizing your RAM, maintaining ample free space on your startup disk (an SSD drive here is also a good idea), and using fast multicore processors all improve the performance of working with very large catalogs. I do know of many people working happily with catalogs in excess of 500,000 photos.

I can imagine one scenario, though, where multiple catalogs might make sense: when you're working with a laptop on the road and away from your desktop (and master catalog). Because this set of circumstances is probably common, I think it makes sense to look at what's involved in transferring information between two catalogs.

Transferring data between catalogs

Okay, in this scenario you have a desktop computer and it contains your master catalog. You do most of your image processing and printing from this workstation. The catalog on this computer is the hub through which all your work passes through. However, as the saying goes, you can't take it with you, so you also have a laptop for working offsite (or while watching TV).

Pretend you're leaving for a week of shooting at some exotic location (hey, you're imagining, so you may as well enjoy it). You need to be able to import and process the photos on your laptop while on location and then get all that work into your master catalog upon your return. In this circumstance, you must do the following:

>> Import and process new photos into the laptop while on the road.

>> Get all the work from the laptop to the desktop (and master catalog) upon returning.

Is this possible? Yes, by using Lightroom Classic's catalog Export and Import functions. The next two sections give you the blow-by-blow.

Exporting a catalog

Okay, you've returned from the trip with a laptop full of photos and the laptop's catalog full of data. The first part of your (imaginary) process is to get these photos and the catalog data from the laptop to the desktop computer. Here are the steps for one way to do it:

1. **Open Lightroom Classic on the laptop.**

   This opens your temporary working catalog from the trip.

2. **Expand the Catalog panel in the Library module and click All Photographs.**

   For this example, you'll want to export all the photos in the laptop catalog, and this is the easiest way to gather them up. You'll see the thumbnails of all imported photos appear in the content area.

3. **Choose File ⇨ Export as Catalog from the main menu.**

Doing so launches the dialog shown in Figure 2-9.

4. **Choose the location where you want the exported catalog and photos to be saved.**

The goal is to get the data from the laptop to the desktop. High-speed external drives are great for data transfers of this size. You can export across a network, but a high-speed external drive may be faster if you're moving a lot of data. I like using external drives so I can do the export before I get home and then simply connect the external drive to the desktop for transfer. The choice is yours.

5. **Enter a name in the Name field.**

6. **Configure the check boxes at the bottom.**

Figure 2-9 shows I am exporting a catalog with 1108 photos and 4 virtual copies (more on virtual copies in Chapter 5). By clicking All Photographs in Step 2, I told Lightroom Classic I wanted to export everything, so I don't want to check Export Selected Photos Only (this option appears only if one or more photos were selected before invoking the menu). The Export Negative Files option means that Lightroom Classic will include a copy of every imported photo along with the exported catalog, so that needs to be checked. (This is how you move the photos from the laptop to the desktop.) Including available previews is not required, but it will enable you to see the thumbnails when you import this catalog into the master catalog. There isn't a need to create Smart Previews now, so leave that unchecked.

7. **Click Export Catalog.**

Your export begins.

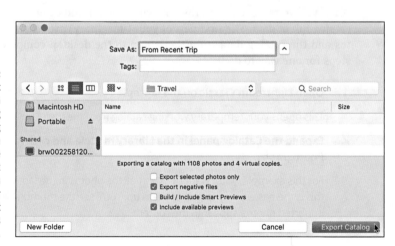

FIGURE 2-9:
The dialog that appears when exporting a catalog on Mac. In Windows, the dialog box looks like a File Explorer window but functions the same.

When the progress meter is complete, a copy of your catalog has migrated to the new location you chose. It's a fully functional catalog containing all the data the master catalog has on those exported photos. Look in the exported folder, and you see the folders containing the photos alongside the catalog file. Phase 1 is done. Time to connect that catalog to the one on your desktop computer.

Importing from a catalog

Now that you have a folder containing your exported catalog as well as copies of your photos, you need to make it accessible to the desktop computer. In my example, I used an external drive that I moved from the laptop to the desktop computer. Here are the steps to import from a catalog:

1. **Connect the external drive to the desktop computer.**

2. **Open the desired Lightroom Classic catalog on the desktop computer.**

   This opens the catalog you want to import the data from the other catalog into.

3. **Choose File ⇨ Import from Another Catalog.**

   A file browsing window appears.

4. **Navigate to the exported .lrcat file on the external drive, select it, and then click Choose (Open on Windows).**

   Doing so launches the Import from Catalog dialog shown in Figure 2-10.
   Note: The name of the .lrcat file you're importing from is shown on the Title bar of the dialog.

   If your photos aren't visible in the Preview section, select the Show Preview check box.

TIP

5. **Choose the Copy New Photos to a New Location and Import option from the File Handling drop-down menu.**

   The goal is to copy files from the external drive to the internal drive and store them with all your other photos.

6. **For the Copy To field, click the Choose button, navigate to a folder on the desktop computer drive where the photos can be saved, and then click OK.**

   The selected location is entered into the Copy To field.

7. **Click Import.**

   The import process kicks off. The data from the .lrcat file on the external drive is copied into the .lrcat file on the desktop computer. The photos are copied from the external drive to the desktop computer as well.

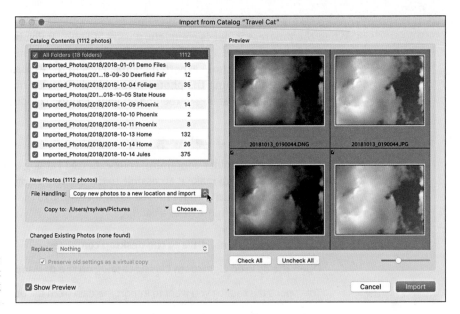

FIGURE 2-10:
The Import
from Catalog
dialog.

Once the progress meter is complete, you'll have successfully transferred a group of photos (and all the work that has been done to them) from the laptop to the desktop computer. (Time to congratulate yourself.) By using Lightroom Classic to perform the data handoff, you ensure that the program never loses track of the source photos and that all your work makes it back home.

Note that there is an option for importing edits made to existing photos under Changed Existing Photos. If you include photos from your master catalog when you first leave on your (imaginary) trip and then edit them on the road, you can import the changes back to the master catalog. In this case, I didn't have any existing photos, so there wasn't anything to import.

The other thing to keep in mind in this scenario is that once you have everything safely transferred to the master desktop catalog (and backed up), you should delete the temporary catalog and photos from the laptop and external drive used in the transfer to avoid confusion and duplication down the road.

Chapter **3**

Lightroom Classic Basics That You Should Know

Beyond the all-important catalog, there are a number of things, from key preference settings to color spaces, that every Lightroom Classic user should know before they dive in too deep. I also want to clarify what is meant by "the cloud" in the context of the Lightroom world. Let's start with the nitty-gritty preference settings you'll want to know.

Configuring Lightroom Classic Preferences

Lightroom Classic's default preference settings are good for getting you up and running, but that doesn't mean you can't make a few tweaks to suit your workflow better. You adjust the seat or mirrors in your car every now and then, right? You'll probably want to do the same here.

To see what's what with your default settings, first open the Preferences dialog by choosing Lightroom Classic ⇨ Preferences (Edit ⇨ Preferences in Windows) from the main menu. The Preferences dialog appears on-screen in all its glory, as shown in Figure 3-1. What you see here are global preference settings, meaning these preferences are in effect regardless of which catalog you have open. Although many of these preferences are self-explanatory (I'll skip those), a few are worth digging into. I do the digging for you in the next few sections.

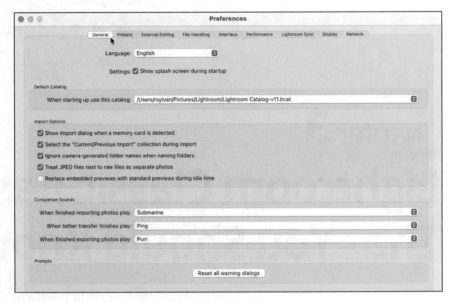

FIGURE 3-1: The Preferences dialog set to General.

General preferences

The General preferences tab is kind of like the catch-all drawer in the kitchen; it's got all the stuff that didn't fit neatly anywhere else:

>> **Default Catalog:** I cover this in Chapter 2, but it's important enough to repeat that you should choose a specific catalog instead of Load Most Recent.

>> **Import Options:** Controlling some things that happen at import:

- *Show import dialog when memory card is detected:* If you find it convenient to have the Import dialog open automatically, keep this option checked; otherwise, uncheck it.

- *Select the "Current/Previous Import" collection during import:* If you like to start an import and then select some other folder or collection to work on while the import happens in the background, uncheck this box; otherwise, when the import begins, Lightroom Classic shifts your view to this special collection found in the Catalog panel. I leave this checked because I like to see the new photos appear.

- *Ignore camera-generated folder names when naming folders:* Some cameras can be configured to create folders on the memory card. Check this box to ignore them.

- *Treat JPEG files next to raw files as separate photos:* Anyone shooting raw+JPG who wants to see both photos side by side in Lightroom Classic should check this box. By default (unchecked) Lightroom Classic treats the JPG as a sidecar file, and you only see the raw.

- *Replace embedded previews with standard previews during idle time:* Chapter 4 describes the import dialog options. In those options, you'll find a setting for previews called Embedded & Sidecar, which tells Lightroom Classic to use the embedded preview at first. This preference setting here tells Lightroom Classic to go ahead and replace those embedded previews with standard previews when you are not working.

➤➤ **Completion Sounds** (Optional)**:** Configure the sounds you want the program to make when it completes those tasks.

➤➤ **Prompts:** These are the warning dialogs that pop up when you attempt to do things like move photos or folders. Some prompts have a Don't Show Again option to disable them from appearing in the future, which is great when you find the warning prompts slow you down. However, they can help keep you out of trouble, so if you change your mind and want to enable them again, click the Reset All Warning Dialogs button to bring them back.

The Presets preferences

The Presets tab is one-stop shopping for all the settings that pertain to Lightroom Classic's default presets and templates, and is broken into three sections, as follows (I recommend leaving all default settings at first, so I didn't include a figure):

➤➤ **Raw Defaults:** Adobe revamped the process for customizing the default settings applied to all raw photos (visit the link below to see how it works). This gives you the power to define the starting point for your raw photos (non-raw photos do not have any settings applied by default) if you choose to take advantage of this feature. There's nothing wrong with using the Adobe Default when you are just getting started.

TIP

Check out my article on customizing your default settings: `https://lightroomkillertips.com/customizing-camera-raw-defaults-in-lightroom-classic`.

>> **Visibility:** A partially compatible preset is a preset that contains some settings not applicable to a specific type of photo. For example, perhaps you include a camera-specific profile along with other settings in a preset, so as a result that preset will only be partially compatible with photos that are not from that specific camera. When unchecked, you will not see presets in the Presets panel that are not fully compatible with the photo you are editing.

>> **Location:** By default, Lightroom Classic stores all your presets in a central location that's accessible to any catalog you might have open at the time (as well as the Camera Raw plug-in for Photoshop). This makes the most sense for most Lightroom Classic users. However, if you'd prefer to store your presets folder within the same folder as your catalog file, you can check this box, and Lightroom Classic will copy the default presets to the new location. Click the Show Lightroom Develop Presets Folder button for quick access to your preset files.

>> **Lightroom Defaults:** This collection of buttons serves a single purpose, which is to set each type of preset collection back to its default state. If presets ever seem to go missing, come back here and click the button that corresponds to the type of missing preset.

The External Editing preferences

If you have Photoshop installed, you'll see, as shown in Figure 3-2, that it's configured as your primary external editor. You can also configure other applications to have additional editors. However, if you don't have Photoshop installed, you'll only be able to configure the Additional Editor option because the first slot is reserved exclusively for Photoshop.

REMEMBER

The purpose of this dialog is to configure the default settings Lightroom Classic uses when you send a copy of a photo with adjustments to an external editor for additional work. Remember, Lightroom Classic doesn't alter your source photos, so if you want to take all the work you have done in Lightroom Classic and apply it to a file so that you can continue working in a different application, Lightroom Classic has to create a copy of that photo first. These are the settings Lightroom Classic uses to create that copy. You'll also configure what applications (if any) you want to use as an additional editor in this dialog.

All external editors have the same basic file-setting options (File Format, Color Space, Bit Depth, Resolution, and Compression) to be configured. You do need to configure both editors independently, but this gives you the opportunity to set up each editor differently. The options you choose are going to be determined by your own needs and the type of editor you are using. After giving you a closer look at

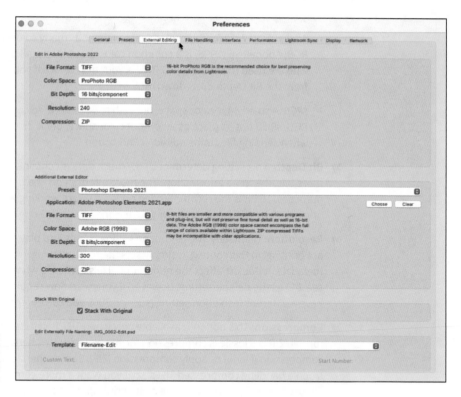

FIGURE 3-2:
The External
Editing
preferences.

the file options, I'll go over the steps for adding additional editors. Here are the
file options:

» **File Format:** You have two file format options to choose from — TIFF and
PSD. Both formats support layers, 16-bit files, and available color spaces. PSD
is Photoshop's native file format, but it's a proprietary format and not as
widely supported outside the Adobe family of applications. In light of this, my
preference is to use TIFF, but there's no wrong choice here.

» **Color Space:** You can find out more about color spaces in the "Understanding
color spaces" section later in the chapter, but in a nutshell, a color space is a
way to define a range of colors so that those colors can be accurately
reproduced on different systems. Lightroom Classic has an internal color
space that contains all the colors your camera can capture. Any time
Lightroom Classic creates an actual rendered copy of your source files, it
converts that file from Lightroom Classic's internal color space to the output
color space you've chosen. You have three color spaces to choose from:

  • *ProPhoto RGB:* A 16-bit color space capable of holding all the colors
    captured by your camera, ProPhoto RGB is very similar to Lightroom
    Classic's working color space, and therefore, I recommend this setting.

- *AdobeRGB (1998):* An 8-bit color space without as many colors as ProPhoto RGB, AdobeRGB (1998) is a common color space for digital photographers who are used to shooting JPG. This is your best choice if you choose 8 bits from the Bit Depth drop-down list.

- *sRGB:* Also an 8-bit color space, but with fewer saturated colors than Adobe RGB, sRGB has its place as an output color space, but it isn't a good choice when sending files to be edited in Photoshop.

» **Bit Depth:** This setting determines how much data is contained in a file. The more bits, the more information. The more information, the better for editing purposes. 16 bit is the recommended option if you're working with raw originals. 8 bit is recommended if you're working with JPG originals.

» **Resolution:** Ultimately, the resolution setting comes into play only when you are printing. In this context, it simply sets the resolution tag in the new file's metadata. It doesn't affect the number of pixels in the file whatsoever. You'll see 240 as the default setting; however, if your workflow requires that files have a different resolution setting (such as 300), you can enter that here.

» **Compression:** This option is available only when TIFF is selected as the file format. ZIP is a lossless compression format. Your choices here are to use no compression (None) or apply compression (ZIP). Some other applications have trouble handling compressed TIFFs, so if you want a more compatible choice, choose None. If you want to save a bit of disk space, choose ZIP.

Setting up additional external editors

In a nutshell, you choose an editor, configure its settings, and then save those settings as a preset. You can create as many presets as you need. Here are the steps:

1. **In the Additional External Editor section, click Choose.**

2. **Navigate to and select the application you want to use as an editor.**

   On Mac, look in the Applications folder. In Windows, look in the Program Files folder. Once selected, you'll see the name of the chosen application listed next to Application back in the Preferences dialog box.

3. **Configure all the file-setting options for the type of files you want to send to that editor.**

4. **Choose Save Current Settings as New Preset from the Preset drop-down menu.**

5. **Give the preset a name and click Create.**

You'll see this name listed under the Photo ⇨ Edit in the menu, so make it descriptive of both the application and file settings.

TIP

You can repeat those steps for any additional editors or multiple configurations of settings for the same editor.

When Lightroom Classic renders a copy to send to Photoshop, it appends an –Edit suffix to the copy by default. You can customize this suffix in the Edit Externally File Naming section at the bottom of the dialog box, but I'd say unless you have a real need to change the suffix, the default works just fine.

The File Handling preferences

Figure 3-3 shows the File Handling preference settings. Let's go through each section and make some sense of what can be done here:

» **Import DNG Creation:** These settings pertain to the Copy Photos as Digital Negative (DNG) on import. The medium-sized JPEG preview is a good compromise on file size. The default conversion method settings are great because they preserve the raw data and create a smaller file using lossless compression. The big choice is whether you want to embed the original raw file or not. You would want to embed the original raw file if you felt there may come a point in time where you might want to extract the original raw file so that you could process it in software that doesn't support DNG. The downside to embedding the original raw file is that you double the file's size because you will have the converted raw data (this is what Lightroom Classic will use) and then add the entire original unaltered file as well (which just sits untouched in case some day it is needed). I prefer to leave this unchecked. Keeping When Embed Fast Load data checked can help improve performance in the Develop module when editing DNG files with this information.

» **Reading Metadata:** It is possible to create structure or hierarchies in your keywords (that is, you might have a keyword "Animal" and then under it, you would nest all the types of animals in your photos). No single standard exists for what character must be used to separate hierarchical keywords when they are written into a file's metadata. Lightroom Classic automatically recognizes the | (pipe) character between two words as a means to denote structure, but if you use other programs that use either a . (dot) or a / (slash) as a keyword separator, check the respective boxes in the preferences; Lightroom Classic respects your choice during import so that your keyword structure is maintained.

>> **File Name Generation:** Different operating systems and even different applications can have problems with certain characters being used within filenames. The settings in the File Name Generation section allow you to configure how Lightroom Classic responds to these characters when it encounters them in a filename. Here's what I recommend for creating a consistent and bombproof approach to dealing with problematic filenames:

- Choose the largest set of characters to treat as illegal.

- Choose either dashes or underscores to be used as a replacement character when an illegal character is encountered.

- Don't sweat spaces in filenames (leave as-is).

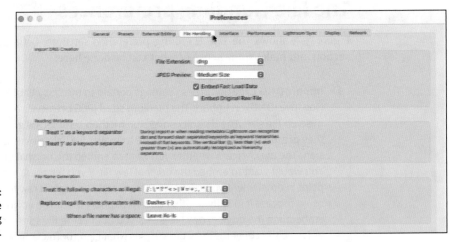

FIGURE 3-3:
The File
Handling
preferences.

The Interface preferences

Although some of the Interface preferences, as shown in Figure 3-4, are entirely cosmetic, other settings in this panel are really useful:

>> **Panels:** I'll leave the Panels End Marks decision up to your own sense of flair, but when this option is enabled, these little decorative icons will appear at the bottom of the panel groups in each module. For the most part you won't notice them after a while (set to none by default). In regard to panel font size, if you're finding the panel text a little on the small side, you can try bumping Font Size up a notch (will take effect the next time you start).

>> **Lights Out:** I go over the Lights Out function in Chapter 1, but here are its configuration settings. The Dim Level controls how much the Screen Color changes at the first level of dimming (at 80% you can just make out the interface). The defaults work well, but you can increase or decrease the first dim level amount by changing the percentage, or change the color used to hide the interface to different shades of gray.

>> **Background:** The area around the photo — but inside the panels — is called the background. The default color is medium gray because that's a neutral color that will have the least influence on how you perceive the colors in your photo. You might try different colors, but I think you'll come back to the default.

>> **Keyword Entry:** Choose to have keywords separated by commas or spaces. My suggestion is to use commas so that you can have multi-word keywords (such as *New Hampshire*).

>> **Filmstrip:** When it comes to the Filmstrip settings, I prefer to keep all these options checked. I like being able to see ratings, picks, and badges (small icons that appear if keywords, cropping, or develop settings have been applied to a photo) on the thumbnails in the Filmstrip. The Image Info tooltips are a great way to see the filename, capture date and time, and dimensions; just hover over an image with your cursor. The most helpful option is to check Ignore Clicks on Badges so that you don't inadvertently click a badge when trying to select a photo and end up jumping to the Crop tool or wherever the badge takes you.

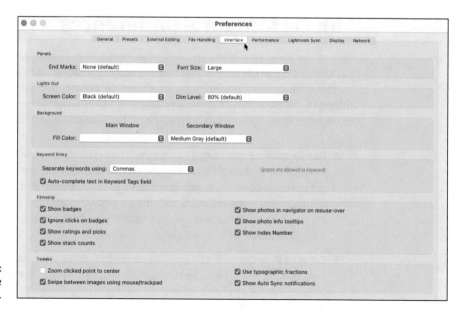

FIGURE 3-4:
The Interface preferences.

TECHNICAL STUFF

>> **Tweaks:** The Tweaks section is the one area of the Interface panel where you'll see a slight difference between Windows and Mac. On the Mac, you find an option to use typographic fractions, but if you wander over to a Windows machine, you find that such fractions aren't available. Therefore, Mac users can have their exposure fractions expressed in a much cuter manner. Don't take this as an unassailable argument for switching platforms, however; Windows users have a tweak that Mac does not — the Use System Preference for Font Smoothing option. What it means is that Lightroom Classic, in Windows, applies font smoothing (meaning it literally makes the edges of screen fonts appear smoother and rounder) independently of the operating system. If you intentionally turned off font smoothing at the operating system level (some people don't like the smooth look) and want Lightroom Classic to follow suit, check the Use System Preference for Font Smoothing box. Not to be outdone, a new option was recently added only to Macs, which is Swipe Between Images Using Mouse/Trackpad. This makes for one more (very fast) way to scroll the Filmstrip, and hardly one more reason to switch platforms. Uncheck if you find the speed too dizzying.

Both operating systems have a setting in common, though — Zoom Clicked Point to Center. When you check this option, Lightroom Classic zooms in and shifts the point you clicked to the center of the screen. I prefer to leave this option unchecked because when I click to zoom in, I want the point I clicked to remain under my cursor. When Zoom Clicked Point to Center is enabled, the point you click will instead zoom and shift to the center. Give it a test drive, but I think you'll agree unchecked is better.

The Performance preferences

One of the most requested areas of improvement in Lightroom Classic has been performance. To that end, Adobe makes pretty regular updates in this regard. Here on the Performance preferences, as shown in Figure 3-5, you can tweak a few things to get Lightroom Classic working at its best possible performance (be sure to click the More Performance Tips link embedded at the bottom of the panel too):

>> **Use Graphics Processor:** As long as you have recent hardware and have installed up-to-date drivers for it, you can leave this option set to Auto, but to get the most boost from your computer's GPU in Develop and even when rendering previews in Library, click the drop-down menu and choose Custom. However, if you notice weird display issues or performance slowdowns, set this to Off to see if that makes an improvement.

>> **Camera Raw Cache Settings:** The intended purpose of any cache is to store (usually temporarily) frequently accessed data to speed up the processes that require that data to function. In this case, Lightroom Classic shares a cache with Adobe Camera Raw, with the primary purpose of helping Lightroom

Classic reopen files in the Develop module faster. Keeping a cache size of 5-10GB strikes a good compromise between size of the cache and benefit from its use. If you have a drive with a lot of free space, you can click Choose and select a different disk.

>> **Video Cache Settings:** This setting can be left at the default.

>> **Enable Hover Preview of Presets in Loupe:** You can see a live preview of any preset as you hover your cursor over it in the Presets panel. Some people find it distracting or even a performance hit. Uncheck if the feature bothers you because the Navigator panel still shows the preview.

>> **Use Smart Previews Instead of Originals for Image Editing:** This is a tradeoff between improving performance and image quality when editing. On a high-powered computer, I would leave this unchecked, but if your machine seems to be struggling when editing, you might enable this setting to see whether it helps.

>> **Generate Previews in parallel:** If you have a quad-core CPU (or higher), you can check this box and have Lightroom Classic create multiple previews in parallel instead of just one at a time. In theory, higher-horsepowered machines should see much faster preview rendering.

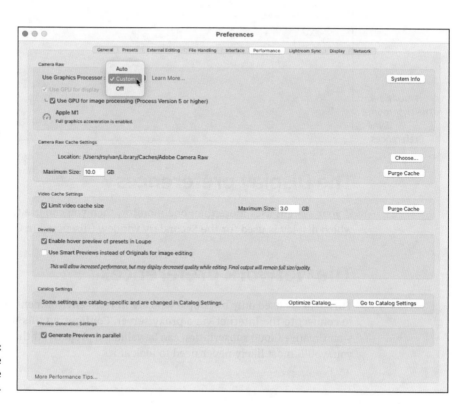

FIGURE 3-5:
The Performance preferences.

The Lightroom Sync preferences

The Lightroom Sync panel, shown in Figure 3-6, is used for those times when you use Lightroom Classic and the cloud-based Lightroom together, as covered in Chapter 16. If you're not syncing with the Lightroom ecosystem, you can ignore this panel completely. The main thing to remember is that you can come to this panel and configure where the photos synced back from Lightroom get stored locally on your computer. When sync activities are happening, you can see a live feed in the bottom of the panel.

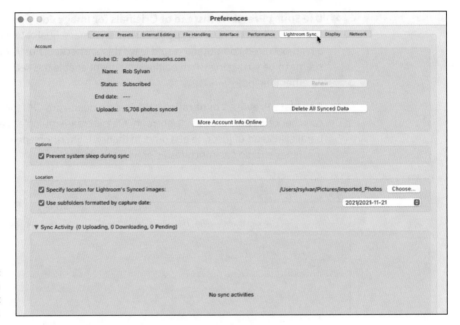

FIGURE 3-6:
The Lightroom
Sync
preferences.

The Display preferences

If your system uses more than one monitor, then you can use this panel to select which display is used for the Secondary window (discussed in Chapter 1).

The Network preferences

This panel is used only by people who are in work environments where they need to connect to the Internet via a proxy server. Configuring this panel ensures that your Creative Cloud subscription can be validated properly. If that doesn't describe you, you'll most likely never need to look at it.

Local Storage versus Cloud Storage

Let's talk about storage. Our digital photo libraries require an ever-increasing amount of storage. It is just too easy to keep taking more and more photos! Knowing the best place to store them is an ongoing challenge.

Local storage

I think it is safe to say that anyone using a computer or mobile device is already familiar with the concept of local storage, as that is the storage that comes with your actual device. Anyone who has ever gotten a mobile phone with only 16GB of storage is acutely familiar with managing local storage. When you're purchasing a new device, the size of the hard drive is usually within the top parameters that affects your decision to buy. Likewise, the size of that storage is going to affect the price of that device, and although the cost of storage has gone down overall, it is just a fact that the more storage you buy, the more the device will cost. My point is simply that there is a cost associated with storing our digital lives, and that cost increases over time.

Aside from the internal drive within the computer/device you are using, you are likely using additional storage in the form of external drives connected via cable and possibly even a network-attached storage device. No matter which type or combination of these storage options you are using, one thing they all have in common is that they are all under your local control. In other words, you purchased the actual drives, and they may be physically in your presence, or they are available on your local network. Anything that falls into these categories is what I mean when I refer to local storage throughout the rest of this book. Lightroom Classic can be used entirely with only locally based storage. In other words, no cloud-storage is needed to use Lightroom Classic. The cloud-based Lightroom ecosystem, on the other hand, has different storage requirements. The following sections discuss the Lightroom ecosystem and its associated cloud storage.

TIP

Adobe often refers to this family of Lightroom apps for each operating system (macOS, Windows, iOS, and Android) pointing to a central cloud-based storage as the *Lightroom ecosystem*. In the book's Introduction I discuss how I refer to the two versions of Lightroom throughout the text.

Cloud storage

In addition to all the local storage options you have at your disposal, you can store data on the Internet, in what has become known as *cloud storage* (think of it as remote storage maintained by a third party that you access over the Internet).

There are an ever-growing number of cloud-based storage options available these days, from services like Dropbox and Google Drive to Microsoft's OneDrive, and so many more. Some types of cloud storage can be free (usually in small amounts), some types may be included as a perk with some other service or subscription (like Microsoft's OneDrive), and others are completely integral to the actual service you are paying for, such as is the case with the Lightroom ecosystem run by Adobe.

The main benefit of cloud storage is that you can access the same pool of data from any Internet-connected device (with the right login information), which makes for a very flexible and useful storage solution. I've been a huge fan of Dropbox since 2009 and couldn't imagine doing business without access to an online storage service. That said, the downside of cloud-based storage is that it is not under your direct control, which means you need to put your trust in the institution behind the service. In addition, as connected to the Internet as we are these days, there are still plenty of times where we're faced with little or no connection, and in those situations relying on cloud storage can be problematic. There are tradeoffs in all things, and this is no exception.

In this age of always-connected mobile devices, Adobe recognized an opportunity to create a service (now just called Lightroom) that caters to people with large storage needs (such as for photos and videos) but who are using devices with relatively low amounts of local storage (mobile devices). Although the desktop version of the new Lightroom has the option to store copies of photos locally, for all intents and purposes you can (and should) consider Lightroom to be entirely dependent on cloud storage to work. In a Lightroom-only world, all devices point to the photos in the cloud as the primary storage location.

Though I have been mostly using the word "storage" in this discussion, there's actually more to Adobe's offering than just a parking place in the cloud for your photos. Because photos imported through Lightroom or synced from Lightroom Classic are sitting on Adobe's servers, Adobe leverages emerging technologies to analyze the contents of your photos to determine the subject matter they contain and then gives you the ability to use that information to more easily find and organize your photos without having to manually add keywords and names to them (refer to Chapter 17). Note that you can use the apps in the Lightroom ecosystem in limited ways while you are offline, but an Internet connection is required for full use.

What if I stop my subscription?

If you're using the latest version of Lightroom Classic or Lightroom, you must have a Creative Cloud subscription. Let me talk briefly about what happens if you cancel your subscription. If you are using Lightroom Classic, and you cancel your subscription, you retain the ability to launch Lightroom Classic and access all your photos. You can even still import new photos, as well as export copies of previously edited photos and make prints, web galleries, and slideshows. What you can no longer do is use the Develop and Map modules or sync to the Lightroom ecosystem. If you decide to renew your subscription at a later date, you get everything back.

If you are using the cloud-based Lightroom, and you cancel your subscription, you retain the ability to launch Lightroom and download your original files for one year, and that's about it. Adobe will keep your original files on its server for over a year, but if you are serious about canceling, I recommend that you download them as soon as you can. Should you decide to renew your subscription during that year, you regain all functionality and can pick up where you left off. If you cancel your subscription and need to quickly download all your photos in one go, check out the Adobe Lightroom Downloader tool: `https://lightroom.adobe.com/lightroom-downloader`.

Getting Familiar with File Formats

The Lightroom family of products is intended to be part of "the professional photographer's essential toolbox"; therefore, Adobe assumes its users are already fluent with a certain level of digital-photo-ese. Although that's certainly true for many users, it's been my experience (through helping many professional photographers with this application) that a person can be quite skilled in the art of photography without knowing a bit from a byte or an NEF from a CR2 or a DNG. I can tell you quite confidently that your experience with all versions of Lightroom improves significantly when you increase your working knowledge of a few fundamental digital photography concepts.

Some of these concepts are complex and involve new words and mind-numbing calculations (done by the computer, not you), and some subjects have entire books devoted to just that topic alone. I'm not going to get that in-depth. What I want to do is introduce you to these fundamentals and explain how they affect your Lightroom experience.

Digital cameras aren't just light-capturing devices, but image-processing computers as well. The act of clicking the shutter release *does* expose the sensor to light through the lens, but after that, the camera's internal computer takes over and creates a digital file. Your camera settings determine the type of file that is created and, depending on the file type, the image processing that happens to that file after it's captured. If you're scanning slides, negatives, or prints, you're using a different capture device (the scanner) to create a digital file. In the end, this digital file can move through Lightroom to any number of output destinations.

The file format choice you make has an impact on the amount of information contained in the file, the number and range of colors in the file, and its file size.

Supported file formats

Lightroom is a tool designed specifically for digital photography and as such supports only certain image formats. Image formats are largely known by their file extensions, but don't get too hung up on what the acronyms stand for, just understand the roles they play:

>> **JPEG:** The most common file format available on all digital cameras is JPEG (or JPG), which stands for *Joint Photographic Experts Group*. The JPEG format is popular because it can be opened in just about any application, and it can be saved at a range of file sizes. It achieves these various file sizes by compressing the original data contained in the file. The upside of this is that the more you compress an image, the smaller your file size becomes and the more pictures your memory card holds, and your camera can write the data to the card faster. The downside here is that the type of compression employed by the JPEG format is *lossy,* which makes files smaller by removing some of the original data. Too much compression results in too much data loss, which results in a degraded image.

>> **PNG:** Originally an alternative to the Graphics Interchange Format (GIF) file format for lossless compression of graphics, PNG (Portable Network Graphics) has emerged as a useful file format for screen captures and other graphics used in a photographic workflow.

>> **HEIC:** This is Apple's proprietary version of the High-Efficiency Image File format (HEIF), which is intended to be a better alternative for JPG when it comes to compressing photos to a smaller size and higher quality. HEIC has become the default image file format for mobile capture on Apple devices.

>> **Raw:** This file format is available on many digital cameras. The upside of shooting raw is that the image file contains all the data that the camera is capable of capturing, and it's saved without being processed by the camera (hence, "raw"). The downside is that the image has to be processed by software to be finished. Raw files come in many flavors (NEF, CR2, and ARW, to name a few) based on the camera maker. Lightroom Classic can also convert raw files to DNG (Digital Negative) that retains its rawness, but puts it in a more Adobe-friendly container (see Chapter 7 for more on this). Adobe releases periodic updates to include support for new cameras after they are released.

>> **TIFF:** Although TIFF (or TIF), which stands for *Tagged Image File Format,* is occasionally found as an option on some camera models, I don't recommend

using it, because the highest-quality JPG setting is almost as good but with a smaller file size. However, TIFF *is* a widely supported and versatile file format that provides either 8 or 16 bits per channel and supports all of Photoshop's features (layers, smart objects, and so on). TIFF can also apply a form of lossless compression (no data is lost) and is a great choice for scanning or for saving processed raw files that will be edited further in Photoshop or other image editors.

>> **PSD:** This is Photoshop's native file format (Photoshop Document). Although it obviously supports all of Photoshop's features, PSD is a proprietary format, so applications outside the Adobe family might not work with files stored in the format. Like TIFF, PSD files can be 8 or 16 bits per channel and are not lossy — they don't lose information like JPG files. PSD is a great format when you're working exclusively within the Adobe suite of products. Be sure to save these (and PSB) files in Photoshop with Maximize PSD and PSB File Compatibility enabled to work in Lightroom Classic.

>> **PSB:** If your PSD files end up being bigger than 30,000 x 30,000 pixels or 2GB in size, then you'll need to save them using Photoshop's Large Document format called PSB. Lightroom Classic supports PSB files up to 65,000 pixels on the long side and a maximum dimension of 512 megapixels (that's a lot of pixels!).

Note that you can import supported video files into Lightroom (for an in-depth discussion of the supported types, see `https://helpx.adobe.com/lightroom/kb/video-support-lightroom.html`), and Lightroom Classic can even perform a limited amount of editing (such as trimming, saving a still, and making color and tonal adjustments). For full video editing, you need to use a program like Adobe Premiere, but Lightroom can at least get the footage off the memory card and copied to your storage.

Making sense of bit depth

Numbers and math are part of any discussion of digital data — numbers are all that computers understand, after all. You don't need to understand everything that computers do with these numbers, but a basic conceptual framework of what's involved can help inform the decisions you make in your workflow. In the preceding section about file formats, I talk about how certain file formats can be 8 or 16 bits per channel. Let's dig a little deeper.

At its core, *bit depth* translates into how much data is used to describe a single color (and what could be more important than that?). Further, when it comes to color and Lightroom, you're only dealing with the *RGB color model*, which means that each color in an image is derived from a combination of three colors (called *channels*) — red, green, and blue. An integral concept to remember is that color is created only during *output* — when a color is displayed on your monitor or when ink hits paper. Cameras don't capture in color; rather, they capture various levels of grayscale data in the red, green, and blue channels. Computers combine the grayscale data from each channel to display the color you see on your monitor. The more grayscale data is used to describe each red, green, and blue channel, the more colors it can create. Okay, so if the color of every pixel is determined by the combination of data stored in each color channel, and you can't change the number of channels, the only variable you can control is the amount of data contained in each channel (the bit depth).

A *bit* is just a single unit of data, and in the digital realm, it has one of two possible values, 0 or 1, which you can think of as black or white. A single bit doesn't give much data to describe color, so how about using two bits instead? If one bit allows for 0 or 1, two bits allows for additional combinations. Doubling the number of bits (2x2) gives you four possibilities. This translates into white, black, and two shades of gray in between. That still isn't a lot of options to describe all the colors you want to capture, so how about jumping to 8 bits per channel? Now you have 2x2x2x2x2x2x2x2 possible combinations, which translates into 256 possible shades of gray for each channel (with white and black still being two of those possibilities). In an RGB image, that means 256 levels of gray for each red, each green, and each blue channel. When the three channels are combined, it allows for the creation of more than 16 million colors (256x256x256).

Cameras (and some scanners) can capture more than 8 bits per channel. In fact, if you are shooting raw, it's more likely that your camera is capturing 12 bits per channel. If 8 bits per channel meant you had 256 shades of gray, 12 bits per channel (2x2x2x2x2x2x2x2x2x2x2x2) means you have 4,096 shades of gray per channel. Clearly, that's a lot more data to work with! So if the camera is capturing that much data per channel, and you want to retain all that data for processing and editing, your only option is to shoot in raw format because the JPG format is limited to 8 bits per channel. You can also find higher-end DSLRs on the market that can capture 14 bits per channel.

I hope you are still with me, because all this number talk can get confusing. Keep in mind that 8 bits equals one byte. Data is stored only in full bytes, so this is why you only see the option to save files as either 8 or 16 bits per channel. Any file that has more than 8 bits of data is encoded in a 16-bit space. Think of 16 bits as simply a bigger container to hold data. When you have more data than will fit in an 8-bit container (that is, 10, 12, or 14 bits), it has to be put in the next size up, which is 16. Make sense?

Understanding color spaces

In the previous section, I mention that both versions of Lightroom deal only with the RGB color model, and I show that the number of gray levels that can be expressed by each channel determines the number of possible colors that can be represented. All great info, but none of it tells what actual color any combination of red, green, and blue will represent. To do that, the computer needs to know what color space is being represented. A *color space* defines the range of colors (called its *gamut*) an image can contain within a given color model (in this case, RGB) and assigns each color within that range a specific numeric value. You will encounter the following color spaces in camera settings and software when you deal with digital photos:

» **sRGB:** Contains the narrowest range, or gamut, of colors between these three color spaces. However, this narrow gamut is closest to the range of colors that most display devices are capable of reproducing. sRGB is also the color space best suited for photos being viewed on the web, which means this is most commonly used for JPG files.

» **Adobe RGB (1998):** Although it possesses the same number of colors as sRGB, Adobe RGB (1998) covers a wider gamut (meaning it has more colors at the more-saturated end of the visual spectrum than sRGB has). This color space was created to match the wider gamut of the offset press better. Adobe RGB (1998) is a more common choice for use with 8-bits-per-channel file formats because it contains more of these more-saturated colors than sRGB.

» **Display P3:** A newer arrival on the color space scene, Display P3 was created by Apple as an alternative to sRGB for displays. It contains a wider gamut than Adobe RGB, but where Adobe RGB has more saturated colors (compared to sRGB) toward the blue and green ends of the spectrum, Display P3 contains more toward the yellow and red ends. Newer devices like iMacs, iPads, and even devices in the Surface line from Microsoft have P3 displays.

» **ProPhoto RGB:** Primarily used with 16-bits-per-channel file formats, the ProPhoto RGB color space contains more colors (more shades of gray per channel) than 8-bits-per-channel files, and it has a significantly wider gamut than either Adobe RGB or sRGB — wide enough to contain all the colors your camera can capture.

2

Managing Your Photos with Lightroom Classic

Chapter **4**

Tackling the Lightroom Classic Import Process

Before you can do anything in Lightroom Classic, you need to introduce your photos to the Lightroom Classic library, which is referred to as importing your photos. In this chapter, you get up close and personal with the Import dialog, work through various importing scenarios, and even see how to configure Lightroom Classic to import photos while you capture them with your camera. By the end of the chapter, you'll have a firm understanding of the import process and be ready to customize this process to meet your needs.

Knowing How the Import Process Works

In a Lightroom Classic context, "importing" is commonly thought of as "getting your photos into Lightroom Classic," and on the surface, that appears to be what's happening. I use this conversational shortcut as much as anyone does, but it's not a literal description of what happens. What really happens is that Lightroom Classic writes data about your photos into your catalog file. The reason I make this important distinction — apart from its being true — is that it's been a source of confusion for many new users. Some people mistakenly think their photos are stored inside Lightroom Classic; this just isn't the case. With that in mind, *the import process* is where you introduce the catalog to your photos. During this introduction, Lightroom Classic learns everything it can about each photo. The way Lightroom Classic learns is by reading each photo's embedded metadata and copying that information into its catalog.

Based on your import settings and the location of the source files, Lightroom Classic might perform a few other tasks as part of the import process, including copying or moving photos to a new location and renaming them, applying user-generated metadata (such as your copyright), applying keywords, or even beginning the development process by applying a set of adjustments (called *Develop settings*). Importing is a powerful operation that's integral to working with Lightroom Classic. Put another way, you can't work on any photo in Lightroom Classic that hasn't first been through the import process.

Exploring the Import Dialog

Although the name doesn't appear on it anywhere, the dialog shown in Figure 4-1, which I refer to as the *Import dialog*, can be accessed by clicking the Import button in the lower left side of the Library module or by choosing the File ⇨ Import Photos and Video menu command. Depending on your Import preferences (see Chapter 3), the dialog may even open automatically when a memory card is detected. Note that depending on your system and what other software you have installed, some other photo program may open and try to assist with copying the photos from the memory card. You must close any other program that tries to access the memory card to keep it from interfering with Lightroom Classic. The Import dialog contains the following sections and controls, starting from the upper left side:

» **From/Select a Source:** Before you can import photos, you must select the location where the photos you want to import are stored. Lightroom automatically selects your memory card as the source if it is detected (as shown in Figure 4-1). If your computer doesn't have a memory card mounted, you will see the text *Select a Source* in the top left instead of *From*. This top left panel is actually a button you can click to select common sources (like the Pictures folder), but I find it easier to choose a folder for import from the Source panel.

» **Source panel:** If a memory card is detected, the Devices section appears at the top of the Sources panel. Below the Devices section is the Files section, which is the closest thing Lightroom Classic has to a file browser. You can navigate to any folder on your system to select a source, or you can choose a mounted device or memory card, as shown in Figure 4-1. If a memory card is selected, the Eject After Import check box appears and is checked automatically. To improve import speed, Lightroom should select the folder on your memory card in the Files section (make sure Include Subfolders is checked) rather than under Devices, but either method will work.

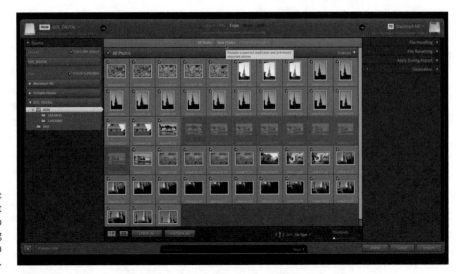

FIGURE 4-1:
The Import dialog set up for copying from a memory card.

>> **Center top area:** The four buttons at the top of the Import dialog tell Lightroom Classic what to do with the photos you are importing. It is critical that you make the right choice here.

- *Copy as DNG:* This method works the same as the Copy method covered in the next bulleted item, with the extra step of converting any raw photos to DNG after they are copied to the destination and added to the catalog. This increases the amount of time required for the import process, but some people prefer converting to DNG from the start. You can always convert to DNG after import (see Chapter 7 for more on DNG).

- *Copy:* You're most likely to use this method when you're importing from a memory card, but you can use it any time you want to copy files from one location to another and import at the same time.

REMEMBER

  Because you're copying files to a new location, you need to choose a location to copy them to as well as a means to organize the folders that are going to be created, which is handled in the Destination panel.

- *Move:* The configuration options for the Move method are the same as with the Copy method. The only difference is that Lightroom Classic *moves* the files to the location you choose instead of *copying* them. Move means the files are first copied and then deleted from the original location. I don't recommend using Move for this reason. Using Copy is safer, and you can manually delete photos from the original location after you are sure they are safely in the new destination.

- *Add:* This method simply notes where each photo is stored on your hard disk and adds each photo's metadata to the catalog. If your photos are already stored in the exact location where you want them to remain, choose this method (not available with a memory card for obvious reasons).

» **Main content area:** Smack in the center of the Import dialog, you see thumbnails of photos from the selected source. Above the thumbnails is a row of buttons you can use to change how those thumbnails appear. The meaning of All Photos is obvious, as is New Photos. If you choose Destination Folders, the thumbnails are grouped based on the folders they will be placed into (based on the settings you choose in the Destination panel). Below the thumbnails are buttons for switching between thumbnail and loupe view, checking/unchecking all photos for import, changing the sort options, and sizing the thumbnails. Below that is where you can save your Import settings as a preset.

» **To:** In the upper right corner of the Import dialog, the To area shows where your photos will be stored at the end of this import operation. For any Copy/ Move operation, you see the destination folder. When you use the Add option, however, you see only My Catalog. Like the From/Select a Source area in the upper left corner of the Import dialog, the To area is a button you can click to indicate where the photos are copied or moved, but I prefer to do that in the Destination panel.

» **File Handling:** This panel is home to controls for building previews, building smart previews, preventing the import of (suspected) duplicates, copying the photos to a second location for short-term backup, and adding photos to a collection. Let's dig in:

- *Build Previews:* Although Lightroom Classic renders previews on the fly as it needs to, you can configure it to begin rendering Standard-Size or 1:1 previews as soon as the import process is complete by choosing either option from the drop-down menu. The other two options — Minimal and Embedded & Sidecar — cause Lightroom to pull in either the low-quality or full-size previews (respectively) from the raw photos first to show you your photos faster. Lightroom will still eventually render its own previews after import. Embedded & Sidecar does provide the advantage of fastest import because Lightroom doesn't spend time building previews.

- *Build Smart Previews* (optional): If Smart Previews are part of your workflow (see Chapter 2), you can opt to have them created as part of the import process.

- *Make a Second Copy To* (optional): The primary function of this option is to provide a means to back up your memory card (in folders based on shoot date) when you copy and import from a memory card. Ideally, you would check the box and then choose a backup location on an alternative drive. Then, when the operation is complete, you have your imported files safely copied to two locations at the same time. After you verify that the files are unharmed, you can erase and reuse the memory card in good conscience. Once your photos are included in your full system backup, you can delete this temporary second copy.

- *Add to Collection* (optional): You can add all imported photos to a collection by checking the Add to Collection box and then choosing or creating the desired collection.

» **File Renaming:** When copying or moving files during import, you're given the ability to rename the photos. If you don't want to change the filenames, uncheck Rename Files. This panel does not appear when the Add option is selected.

» **Apply During Import:** With every type of import, you have the option to get a head start on editing, personalizing, and keyword tagging your photos. Keep in mind that any information you choose to apply at this stage is applied to all imported photos. These settings are also *sticky,* which means the choices you make today will become the default for the next import, so always double-check every field! Here are the options:

- *Develop Settings:* You can apply a Develop preset (saved Develop module adjustments) to all imported photos. You don't need to apply a preset during import, but it can come in handy if there are Develop settings you want to apply to all photos. I normally leave this set to None and edit later in the Develop module.

- *Metadata:* Even if it means adding only your copyright information, you'll do yourself a favor by including the metadata for your photos with every import. Click the drop-down menu to create a Metadata preset or apply an existing one (see Chapter 6 for more on creating a Metadata preset).

- *Keywords:* Only add keywords relevant to all the photos you're importing. After import, you can add additional keywords relevant to specific photos as needed. You might apply the keyword "beach" to all photos taken at the beach, but keywords like "ice cream" or "sandcastle" might not apply to all photos from that shoot. You can add "beach" during import and the more specific keywords later in the Library module.

» **Destination:** This is the most important panel on the Import dialog to consider when you copy or move photos. The location you choose here is where your photos will be saved. You've got to be in the driver's seat for this choice; otherwise, Lightroom Classic uses the Pictures folder by default. I review all the choices in the next section.

After you configure the options in the Import dialog to suit your needs, click the Import button to begin the process. At this point, the Import dialog closes, and the import process, based on your settings, begins. Clicking Cancel closes the Import dialog without importing any photos.

Importing Your Photos into Lightroom Classic

Okay, time to introduce Lightroom Classic to some photos! Unless you just happened to pick up this book, the Lightroom Classic software, and your new digital camera sometime earlier this afternoon, I'm guessing you already have some photos on your hard drive that you'd like to import. I'll go further out on a limb and assume that you will have new photos in the future to import from your memory card. The workflow is the same in both cases, but the options you encounter will have some subtle differences, so it wouldn't hurt to go over the basic process first and then step through a couple of examples.

Employing an effective import workflow

Things you want to keep in mind before you start the import process:

>> What import method are you going to use?

>> Are you going to back up your imported copies?

>> Do you know where you want your photos to go/remain?

>> Are there things like keywords or presets you want to apply?

>> Have you created a filename template for the file-naming convention you want to use?

When you begin the import process with all your ducks in a row, it saves a great deal of time down the road. Remember, the import process provides the opportunity to do more than just start looking at your photos in Lightroom Classic. To see what I mean, take a Big Picture look at an import workflow that takes advantage of the import process's full potential:

1. **Initiate the import.**

   You can initiate an import in several ways, but nothing happens without you taking the first step.

2. **Select the photos you want to import.**

   No matter where your photos originate, you have to choose which ones to import.

3. **Configure the settings to meet your input needs.**

   Having answers to the questions at the start of this section allows you to quickly set up the Import dialog and click that Import button.

With the Big Picture out of the way, time to sweat a few of the smaller details. The next few sections help you navigate the import process.

Initiating the import

The Import dialog is the gateway all photos have to pass through. You can open the door in several ways:

>> **Click the Import button in the Library module.** This method might be the most common way to launch an import because the big Import button in the Library module is easy to spot (and who doesn't love to click a button). It can be used when importing from any disk or device.

>> **Connect your camera or a memory card to your computer.** If you enable this feature in Lightroom Classic's Preferences file ahead of time, the Import dialog automatically launches whenever it detects the presence of a memory card — either solo or as part of a digital camera. This can be a real timesaver if the only time you connect a camera or memory card is when you want to conduct a Lightroom Classic import. For a detailed discussion of Preference settings, see Chapter 3.

>> **Choose File ⇨ Import Photos and Video from the main menu.** Use this option if you're importing files from a memory card or those already on your hard disk.

>> **Drag and drop.** You can drag and drop a folder of images from your file browser right onto the Library module to start the import process.

Selecting the photos you want to import

Although it may be true in most cases that you'll want to import every photo on the memory card, it's still worth your while to scan through the images to verify that you really want to import them all. The Don't Import Suspected Duplicates option on the File Handling panel is checked by default to ensure that you don't import the same photos twice, but when scanning the previews, you might find you just don't need to waste time importing some of the (bad) photos. Uncheck the check box on any photos that you don't want to import at that time. In some instances, you may find it easier to click the Uncheck All button at the bottom of the dialog and then just check the boxes for photos you do want to import. You can use faster methods to sort the wheat from the chaff in the Library module, but there's no need to import photos of the inside of your lens cap.

Configuring the settings to meet your input needs

Once you know which photos you want to import, it's time to make choices regarding how they're imported and whether you're going to multitask a little and process them on their way in the door.

Back at the beginning of this chapter, when I first discuss the Import dialog, I mention that the dialog gives you four options along the top center. The source you are importing from largely determines which options are available in the Import dialog. Let me explain.

REMEMBER

If you are importing from a memory card, Copy as DNG and Copy are the only available options. If you are importing from a drive, all options — Copy as DNG, Copy, Move, and Add — are available.

Here's why. If you're importing from a device (say, a memory card), you don't want the Add option because memory cards are only temporary storage devices. Lightroom Classic knows this and disables the option. Move also isn't an option, based on best practices for dealing with memory cards. First, you don't want to remove files from your memory card until you can visually verify that the files have been copied safely to at least one other disk (two if you want to be safe). The idea here is that you don't want to risk something going wrong in the moving process because you haven't yet created a backup. Second, it's better to use your camera to reformat the card when you're ready to erase the contents than it is to let your computer perform that task. When you reformat the card in-camera, the process is done in the best way for the camera, which means you experience less chance of corrupted data when the camera is writing files to the card in normal operation.

The Copy and the Move file-handling options include additional settings not found when using the Add option. The reason for this is that when you're only adding, you aren't changing anything about the photos. You're simply telling Lightroom Classic where the files are located and getting on with the business of importing their data. It would follow that if you're choosing to copy or move the photos and then import, you would need to tell Lightroom Classic where you want them to go and whether you want to change their names in the process. To that end, when you choose one of the Copy or Move file-handling options, you see the following options appear in the Import dialog:

>> **Destination:** Even though this option appears at the bottom of the Import dialog, I'm talking about it first because it is the most important. You do two things here: select the destination where the photos will go and control the folder structure that is created in the import process. You can choose three Organize methods (see the "Putting it all together" section for how I organize):

- *By original folders:* This option is useful when you're moving or copying from a disk and want to replicate the same folder structure on the destination disk.

- *By date:* The is the default option. Lightroom Classic provides eight date-based folder structures (YYYY/MM-DD, YYYY/Month/DD, and so on) to choose from. The capture dates from the photos are used to create the actual dates used, which is reflected in the space below the Organize field. The slash separating some of the date options means a folder and subfolder structure will be created.

- *Into one folder:* This option allows you to put all your photos into a single folder without regard for dates or original folder structure.

>> **File Renaming:** Provides the option to change the filenames when placed in the destination folder. Choose Filename from the Template drop-down menu if you want the filenames to keep the original names. An example of how the filenames will look appears above the Template field, using the selected template.

TIP

Lightroom Classic's file-renaming function is quite powerful and versatile. I feel it's a great option to have during import, but keep in mind that you can rename files later in the Library module. So don't feel pressure to do it at import. Lightroom Classic installs with a number of prebuilt filename templates for you to use, but its true power is unleashed when you use the Filename Template Editor, as shown in Figure 4-2, to create your custom templates. You access the editor by clicking the Template drop-down menu and choosing Edit.

The editor works by using what it calls *tokens* to represent various text strings that you can assemble into various configurations. There are tokens for image name data, image numbering options, date formats, metadata, and even custom text. The assembled tokens can be saved as reusable templates any time you want to rename files. (You'll use the same editor and tokens if you rename after import as well.)

TIP

Click through the various sections to get a sense of what data is possible to include in your filenames. I'd like to call your attention to two tokens in particular:

>> **Import #:** You can use this token to include the import number in your filename. The Import Number is managed from the File Handling tab of the Catalog Settings dialog box (see Chapter 2).

>> **Image #:** You can include this token when you want to number files incrementally across multiple imports. Controlled by the Photos Imported value, Image # is managed from the File Handling tab of the Catalog Settings dialog box (see Chapter 2).

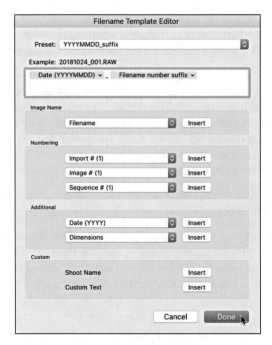

FIGURE 4-2:
The Filename
Template
Editor.

I bring these tokens to your attention because it can be hard to draw the connection between what they represent and the Catalog Settings dialog.

To see what I'm talking about, follow along as I walk through an example where I create a custom template that combines date information and part of the original, camera-generated filename (refer to Figure 4-2 to see what the template ends up looking like):

1. **Click the Template drop-down menu, and choose Edit.**

   TIP

   Doing so launches the Filename Template editor. When the editor opens, notice that the active template appears in the Preset field at the top of the editor and that the tokens that make up that template appear in the Editing field. Take a moment to click through the other templates and see how the tokens are constructed.

2. **Delete any tokens that appear in the editing field.**

   Start with a clean slate. Just click into the field behind the tokens and press Delete (Backspace for Windows). Notice the example above the field changes as you add or remove tokens to preview how the filename will appear.

3. **Click the drop-down menu in the Additional section of the editor, and choose the Date (YYYYMMDD) token.**

Just selecting from the menu adds the token to the editing field.

4. **Click the editing field behind the date token and type an underscore.**

TIP

You aren't limited to using just the tokens to build your filenames. You can type right into the editing field. Just remember that with filenames, you don't want to make them any longer than necessary, and you want to avoid all nonalphanumeric characters except for dashes and underscores to prevent potential problems down the road.

5. **In the Image Name section of the editor, choose the Filename Number Suffix token from the drop-down menu.**

This is the camera-generated file number. I use it because, when combined with the date, I know that because I typically use only one camera per shoot, it's going to produce a unique filename.

6. **Click the Preset drop-down menu at the top of the editor, and choose Save Current Settings As New Preset.**

Doing so opens the New Preset dialog. In case you haven't noticed, the folks at Adobe use the words *template* and *preset* interchangeably. Don't let that confuse you.

7. **Give the preset (template) a descriptive name, and click Create.**

I usually name my templates so that they mirror somewhat how the filename will look. In this case, I named it YYYYMMDD_suffix. After you click Create, you see this name appear in the Preset menu.

8. **Click Done.**

You're brought to the Import dialog with your new template selected.

Regardless of the file–handling method you use, you always have the option to apply three types of information to all the imported files via the Apply During Import panel:

>> **Develop Settings:** Although some prebuilt Develop settings are available to you out of the box, I don't recommend using any at this point. Applying a Develop setting to all photos at import can be helpful at times (such as when you're shooting in a studio and want to apply a custom white-balance setting), but the majority of your imports can do without Develop settings — which means you should leave this set to None.

>> **Metadata:** There's no reason not to apply a basic set of metadata to all imported photos. Create a preset (more on that later) that contains your basic copyright and contact information, and apply it every time.

>> **Keywords:** Keywords identify your photos and — when used consistently — provide a powerful means to find specific photos after your catalog grows. It isn't a sexy aspect of the import process, but do it, and you'll reap the rewards. During import, you only want to be careful about getting too specific because the keywords you enter here are going to be applied to every imported photo in the session.

The process for creating a Metadata preset is worth a closer look. You can create an unlimited number of Metadata presets, which can be applied during import or later in the Library module. I create a baseline preset (meaning information that I want on *all* photos regardless of subject, job, or location) containing all my relevant information (copyright, name, contact info, and so on). To create a basic Metadata preset, you do the following:

1. **In the Apply During Import panel of the Import dialog, click the Metadata drop-down menu, and choose New.**

Doing so launches the New Metadata Preset dialog (see Figure 4-3).

2. **Enter a name for your new preset in the Preset Name field.**

3. **Fill out all the fields in the IPTC Copyright and IPTC Creator fields.**

This is the basic information about who holds the copyright to this photo and how to contact them. Adding it here means it's written into the metadata of your exported files and can be written to the XMP metadata of your source files.

TIP

I often am asked how to create the © symbol so that it can be included in the Copyright field. If you are working in Windows and have a separate number keypad, hold down the Alt key and press 0169 on the keypad, and then release the Alt key. If you're on a laptop with a keypad overlay on your regular keyboard, hold down the function (Fn) key and the Alt key, and then press 0169. If you're working on a Mac, hold down the Option key and press G.

4. **Click Create.**

This saves the preset using the name you entered in Step 1 and closes the Metadata Preset dialog. You see the new preset in the Metadata field of the Import dialog.

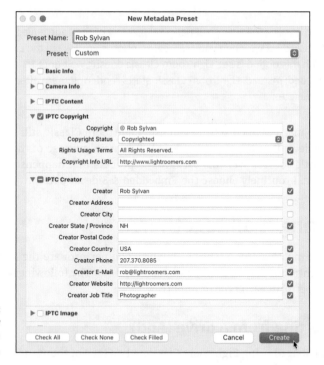

FIGURE 4-3:
The New
Metadata
Preset dialog.

The last setting to configure before clicking the Import button is Build Previews in the File Handling panel. I discuss the role of preview files in Lightroom Classic in Chapter 2, but the main thing to know here is that Lightroom Classic begins rendering the previews after the import process is complete. This setting determines the size of the previews it starts creating after import. Here are your options:

>> **Minimal:** With Minimal selected, the lowest-resolution previews are grabbed from each file as quickly as possible. Lightroom Classic renders its previews as needed when you are working.

>> **Embedded & Sidecar:** Some photos have a larger or full-size preview embedded within their files (or their companion metadata files). With this option, that preview is grabbed first, which may provide higher initial quality viewing over what you see if you choose the Minimal option. This is a great option for a fast import with the ability to check focus and separate the keepers from the deletions. I use this option almost all the time.

>> **Standard:** In Chapter 2, I discuss how to configure your initial settings for controlling the quality and size of the "standard" preview. This setting tells Lightroom Classic to go ahead and start rendering standard-sized previews based on those settings for all recently imported images.

>> **1:1:** This is a full-size, pixel-per-pixel preview of the source file that Lightroom Classic displays when you are viewing photos up close in the Library module. With this option is set, Lightroom Classic doesn't wait until 1:1 previews are needed; instead, Lightroom Classic starts rendering them after the import is complete.

Note: No matter which setting you use, Lightroom Classic still eventually renders the previews it requires when needed. The main purpose of the setting is to give you a little control over this background process that happens after the import is complete. I routinely choose the Embedded & Sidecar option.

Putting it all together

The two most common types of imports you perform are the Add (especially for new Lightroom Classic users) and Copy variants. The following sections show you how to perform each type of import.

Importing from a drive (Add)

When I started using Lightroom Classic, I had tens of thousands of photos already on my hard drive. I wanted to manage them all with Lightroom Classic, but I wanted to keep them right where they were on my hard drive. This scenario demands that you use the Add method. Here are the steps for adding existing photos to the catalog:

1. **Click the Import button in the Library module to open the Import dialog.**

    Note: To get to the Library Module, press G (for Grid) from anywhere in Lightroom Classic.

2. **In the Source panel, navigate to the top-level folder that contains your photos and select it, making sure that Include Subfolders is checked.**

TIP

I keep all my photos on a separate drive in a folder I call Imported_Photos. Within that folder, I have a subfolder for each year, and within each year, there's a folder for each day I was shooting (and then I add a one- or two-word description after import). I like this date-based approach because it's simple, Lightroom Classic can automatically generate the structure, and every photo is assigned a single permanent home. The problem I have with any type of categorical structure is that there's always the possibility that I might have a photo that could fit into more than one category. I don't want to duplicate a file, and I don't even want to waste time thinking about where to put it. Therefore, I use dates for storage, and I use keywords and collections to create and access my photos in Lightroom Classic. It works for me.

So in my case, I'd select the Imported_Photos folder. In your case, it might be the Pictures folder or whatever folder you use to hold all your photos.

3. **Click Add.**

4. **Leave all photos checked for import.**

   You can use Lightroom Classic's tools later to sort out and delete any less-than-perfect photos.

5. **In the File Handling panel, set Build Previews as desired.**

   This is a personal preference. As I said, I generally set it to Embedded & Sidecar.

6. **In the Apply During Import panel, set the Develop Settings drop-down menu to None, and choose your Metadata preset in the Metadata menu.**

7. **Apply any globally applicable keywords (doubtful that any would apply to all photos when you're first importing).**

8. **Click the Import button.**

After that final click, the Import dialog closes, and you see the progress meter advancing in the upper left corner of the interface as thumbnails start appearing in your catalog. Likewise, the Folders panel shows the imported folders. You can start working with photos as they appear, but I usually busy myself with other tasks until Lightroom Classic has completed the job.

Importing from a memory card (Copy)

TIP

After I import all my legacy photos, I tend to import all new photos directly from the memory card. I recommend using a card reader over directly connecting your camera. A card reader is cheap and portable, doesn't drain your camera batteries, and frees your camera to take more photos if you have multiple memory cards. Card readers often provide a faster data transfer rate than most cameras do. Card readers are so common these days that many laptops and monitors have them built right in!

Time to go through the steps for importing from a memory card — no matter how you connect the card to the computer. These steps are for the manual method and work only if you disable the Show Import Dialog When a Memory Card Is Detected preference setting:

1. **Connect your memory card to the computer, and click the Import button in the Library.**

2. **Verify that your memory card is selected in the Devices or Files section of the Source panel.**

3. **Confirm Eject after Import in the Source panel is checked.**

4. **Scan the previews, and uncheck any photos you don't want to import.**

5. **Choose the Copy option at the top of the Import dialog.**

6. **Go right to the Destination panel, and choose where you want the new copies to be saved.**

7. **Click the Organize drop-down in the Destination panel, and choose how you want the photos organized.**

   I made my case for a date-based structure in the previous section, but choose what suits your needs best.

8. **Confirm that Don't Import Suspected Duplicates in File Handling is checked.**

9. **(Optional) Check the Make a Second Copy To box in the File Handling panel, and configure a backup location.**

   This isn't a required step, but I highly recommend you consider a workflow that involves backing up your memory card during import.

10. **Set Build Previews as desired.**

    This is a personal preference. As I said, I generally set it to Embedded & Sidecar.

11. **In the File Renaming panel, choose a file-naming template from the Template drop-down menu.**

12. **In the Apply During Import panel, click the Develop Settings drop-down menu, and choose None.**

    You are free to choose one if it suits your needs, but I prefer starting from a clean slate in Develop.

13. **While you are in there, click the Metadata drop-down menu and select an existing preset or create a new one.**

14. **Apply any globally applicable keywords.**

15. **Double-check settings in the Destination panel.**

16. **Click Import.**

The Import process is now under way. After the progress meter is complete, it's safe to remove your memory card. Always visually verify that all the photos are where they're supposed to be before formatting that memory card!

Auto Import

On Lightroom Classic's File menu, you find an Auto Import option. Any time you can automate a repetitive process, it's a good thing! Lightroom Classic's Auto Import is handy when you're shooting *tethered* (meaning your camera is connected to your computer while you are shooting) with a camera that is not supported for tethering (more on that in a bit) or when you just want to set up a folder that will trigger Lightroom Classic to import files as soon as they appear in the folder (such as images you create while working in another application or using a scanner).

To open the Auto Import Settings dialog (shown in Figure 4-4), choose File ⇨ Auto Import ⇨ Auto Import Settings from the main menu. The Auto Import Settings dialog performs the same functions as the Import dialog, with the following exceptions:

>> **Watched Folder:** The idea here is to save/place the photos you take into this folder. As soon as Lightroom Classic sees a photo hit this folder, it initiates the Auto Import process. If you're shooting tethered, this is the folder where you should save the photos from your camera.

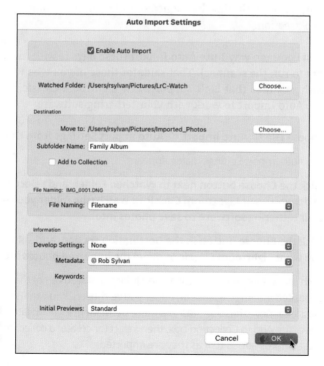

FIGURE 4-4:
The Auto Import Settings dialog box.

>> **Destination:** This location is where Lightroom Classic moves your photos during the import process. This keeps the watched folder empty. The Destination folder appears in your Folders panel after the import.

REMEMBER

When you use Auto Import, you don't see a preview; you must configure previews before you have photos ready to import. In fact, the watched folder needs to start empty for the process to function correctly.

Just as with a normal import, when you use Auto Import, you can configure your filename template and metadata template, add keywords, configure previews, and even apply a Develop preset if needed.

TECHNICAL STUFF

The next section is devoted to Lightroom Classic's built-in tethering function, but it supports only a limited number of camera models. If your camera is not supported for tethering, you can use third-party software in conjunction with Lightroom Classic's Auto Import function to bring the photos into Lightroom Classic. Some camera manufacturers bundle this type of software (or a limited version of it) with your camera, but others make you pay for it. (Check with your camera manufacturer.) The purpose of this software is to allow your camera to save photos directly to a specified location on your hard drive (that is, the watched folder) rather than on the camera's memory card. After you have that software installed and operational, you're ready to move forward with Auto Import. If your camera is supported for tethering by Lightroom Classic, jump ahead to the "Shooting Tethered" section.

The most common way I use Auto Import these days is with my scanner (and the software to run the scanner). That said, for those of you who want to shoot tethered with a camera that isn't supported by Lightroom Classic, here are the steps to set up Auto Import to work with your tethering software:

1. **Choose File ⇨ Auto Import ⇨ Auto Import Settings from the main menu.**

   The Auto Import Settings dialog appears.

2. **Click the Choose button next to Watched Folder, and select the empty folder you want Lightroom Classic to watch (the folder you've configured your tethering software to save photos into).**

3. **Click the Choose button in the Destination section, and select the folder you want Lightroom Classic to move the imported photos into.**

   Each photo that lands in the watched folder is moved out of that folder and deposited into the destination folder you've chosen. You can use Lightroom Classic to move these photos to a more permanent location later. (Optional) Check the Add to Collection box, then select (or create) a collection to have these photos added to it as they are imported.

4. Choose a filename template from the File Naming drop-down menu.

5. From the Develop Settings drop-down menu, choose a Develop preset, if applicable.

It's beyond the scope of this chapter to cover the creation of Develop presets, but check out Chapter 9 for in-depth coverage.

6. Choose a Metadata preset from the Metadata drop-down menu.

7. Apply globally applicable keywords to this import session.

8. Configure the Initial Preview setting.

9. Check the Enable Auto Import box at the top of the Auto Import Settings dialog.

10. Click OK.

At this point, Lightroom Classic is ready and waiting for that first photo to land in the watched folder.

11. Connect your camera to your computer.

12. Launch your camera control software, and configure it to save photos into the watched folder you configured in Step 2.

This process is going to vary with each camera-control software, but the goal is the same. Make sure your software is not configured for creating additional subfolders in the watched folder.

13. Take a test shot with your camera.

You should first see an indication from the camera software that the file is being transferred to the computer. After that, transfer is complete, and Lightroom Classic should automatically begin the import.

TIP

If your test shot was successful, you're ready to begin shooting your job. If the test was unsuccessful, double-check that you enabled Auto Import in Step 9, that the camera is actually saving photos to the watched folder, and that the watched folder starts out empty.

Shooting Tethered

Shooting with your camera tethered via cable to your computer is a powerfully efficient way to work. No, I'm not advocating you set up your laptop in front of a grand landscape in the great outdoors. Shooting tethered is ideal for photographers working in a studio or just working indoors. You can use your much bigger and better computer screen for evaluating the photos and have them imported into your Lightroom Classic catalog the moment they are created. What's not to love about that?

Well, there is one rub, which is that not every camera is supported by Lightroom Classic for tethering. To see if your camera made the cut, head over to Adobe's continually updated list: `https://helpx.adobe.com/lightroom-classic/kb/tethered-camera-support.html`.

TIP

Additionally, at the time of this writing, if you're using a Mac with an Apple Silicon chip, then you need to know that tethered shooting is only possible running Lightroom Classic in Rosetta mode. You can either choose to launch in Rosetta mode from the Adobe Application Manager, then start tethered shooting, or you can start tethered shooting and Lightroom Classic will prompt you that it needs to relaunch in Rosetta mode (with a handy Relaunch button). Once you've relaunched in Rosetta mode, you can shoot tethered using the steps that follow. Hopefully, support for shooting tethered natively on Apple Silicon will be addressed in a future update.

When ready, connect your camera to your computer with the correct USB cable for your camera and computer. (Wireless tethering is not currently supported, but you can use it in conjunction with the previously mentioned Auto Import.) Once the camera is connected, follow these steps:

1. **Choose File ⇨ Tethered Capture ([Your Camera Brand]) ⇨ Start Tethered Capture from the main menu.**

   This opens the Tethered Capture Settings dialog, as shown in Figure 4-5.

2. **Enter a name in the Session Name field, which Lightroom Classic will use to create the folder containing the photos.**

3. **Click the Template drop-down menu in the Naming section, and choose a filename template.**

4. **Click the Choose button in the Destination section, and select where you want this new folder to be created on your drive.**

5. **(Optional) Check the Add to Collection box to gain access to your collections or create a new one.**

6. **Select your metadata template, and add any globally applicable keywords in the Information section.**

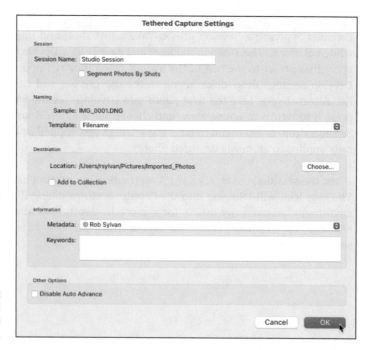

7. Click OK to close the dialog and begin the tethered session.

This opens the floating capture bar, which displays the name of the camera and relevant settings. You can change those values from within Lightroom Classic if needed, and you can click the Capture button to take the photo. At the bottom of the previously mentioned link showing cameras supported for tethering is a shorter list of cameras that are also supported for shooting in Live View. When using a supported camera, you will also see the Live button on the capture bar (as shown in Figure 4-6), which when clicked will open a window displaying the live view from your camera.

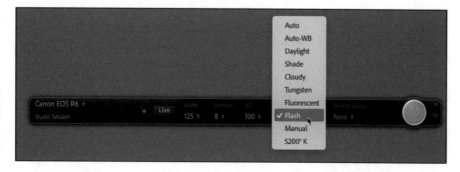

FIGURE 4-6:
The floating
capture bar
used when
shooting
tethered.

Consider applying a Develop preset. Take a test shot, and import it. Correct the white balance in the Develop module, and save it as a Develop preset. You could apply that preset to the rest of the images when they're imported by clicking the Develop Settings drop-down menu in the capture bar and choosing it from the list. Alternatively, take the first photo into Develop, set the white balance for it, press E to return to Loupe view, and choose Same as Previous from the Develop Settings drop-down menu to have the settings you applied in Develop automatically applied to all newly captured photos.

When the session is over, click the X on the floating capture bar to exit tethering. The gear icon will take you into the Capture Settings dialog if you need to tweak anything. Check out my article for a more in-depth look at shooting tethered: https://lightroomkillertips.com/a-look-at-the-latest-updates-to-shooting-tethered-part-1.

Chapter **5**

Viewing and Finding Photos in the Library

J ust like your local library, the Library module is the place you go to find and check out your photos. Except in this case, you're also the head librarian, which means you have the power to organize and manage the contents as well. The Library module is the hub — all your photos pass through here on their way to the other modules. Feel free to make as much noise as you want.

You can do a heck of a lot to your photos in the Library module — I hope good things, but you never know. This chapter focuses on the operations performed with the organizational panels. For help on sorting and applying various types of metadata to your photos, turn to Chapters 6 and 7.

Exploring the Library Module

When you first enter any building, you need to become oriented to the lay of the land. Although each of Lightroom Classic's modules contains tools and options that are task specific, the layout of the interface is essentially the same.

This common interface is designed to help you become acclimated to the modules as you move through them. More important, the common interface clues you in that you can modify many elements of the interface the same way across modules. Refer to Chapter 1 for a complete rundown of the interface controls.

Getting to know the panels and tools

The Library module, shown in Figure 5-1, is sure to become a frequent stop in your workflow. The top of the interface provides the means to access menus and move between modules. The left set of panels provides the main access route to your photos, whereas the right set of panels helps you mess around with your photos. Smack-dab in the middle is the content area, which is *the* place to get a closer look at your photos. As for the other elements, the following list details the ones you should probably spend some time getting to know. (For those following along using Figure 5-1, I'm starting in the top left corner and moving down.)

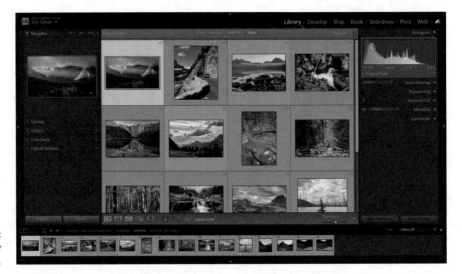

FIGURE 5-1:
The Library
module.

>> **Identity plate/Activity Center:** Also known as the *vanity plate,* this is a customizable component of the interface that you can use to make Lightroom Classic your own (see "Creating a custom identity plate," later in this chapter). If you hover your cursor over it, you'll see a white disclosure triangle that provides access to the Activity Center, where you can enable/disable address lookup, enable/disable face detection, and see progress bars for other activities taking place (like exports and imports).

>> **Navigator panel:** Displays a preview when you move over photos in the Filmstrip. Sets the zoom level in Loupe view.

>> **Catalog panel:** Contains a small set of collections for quick access to imported photos. In Lightroom Classic terms, a collection is just a special grouping of photos. The ones that appear in this panel are automatically created by Lightroom Classic. You can create your own using the Collections panel (discussed shortly).

>> **Folders panel:** Provides direct access to the folders that contain your photos on your drive(s).

>> **Collections panel:** Contains all your collections and provides tools for organizing and creating additional collections.

>> **Publish Services panel:** You can think of this as a way to create managed exports for different connected services (like Flickr or Adobe Stock) or even local folders.

>> **Filmstrip:** Displays thumbnails of all the photos in the current grouping.

>> **Library Filter bar:** Appears above thumbnails in Grid view of Library. Harnesses the power of the Lightroom Classic catalog to find and filter your photos based on a wide range of criteria.

>> **Content area:** Where your photos appear.

>> **Toolbar:** Below the content area, it contains a set of tools for completing organizational tasks — stuff like applying ratings, changing the sort order, and switching between Library module views (to name a few).

>> **Module Picker:** Allows for quick movement between various modules.

>> **Histogram:** Displays a graph of the tonal values in the selected photo.

>> **Quick Develop panel:** Allows for the application of Develop settings and presets while working with photos in the Library module. I cover this panel in greater detail in Chapter 7, but the real Developing tools are covered in Chapters 8 through 10.

>> **Keywording panel:** Provides a display of keywords applied to selected photos as well as a means to apply additional keywords.

>> **Keyword List panel:** Displays a list of all the keywords contained in your catalog as well as tools to create, edit, and remove them.

>> **Metadata panel:** Metadata is data about the data about a photo, if that makes any sense. Basically, we're talking about camera-generated information that gets recorded when you press the shutter (such as f-stop and shutter speed) as well as photographer-generated information to go along with it (such as title, description, and location). This panel provides a means for viewing, adding, and editing metadata.

>> **Comments panel:** Only used in conjunction with certain publish service connections and synced collections through the cloud-based Lightroom. Comments made by visitors to those connected services appear here.

Becoming familiar with the menu options

There's often more than one way to perform any single task, but the menu is usually the single location that contains all the options. What's more, the menu options provide the added benefit of displaying the associated keyboard shortcut (if there is one). Therefore, it's worth becoming familiar with the menus to get a good sense of what is possible in each module. The Library and Metadata menus are unique to the Library module, the Photo menu pops up in Library and Develop, but their siblings — File, Edit, View, Window, Help — appear in all:

» **Lightroom Classic (Mac only):** Contains the commands for opening preferences, catalog settings, identity plate, and watermarks setup. Windows users find these under the Edit menu.

» **File:** Provides access to all the import and export commands, controls for the Quick Collection (one of the special collections in the Catalog panel), as well as Library filters, the plug-in manager, plug-in extras, and more.

» **Edit:** You find the Undo and Redo commands here as well as all the selection commands. On Windows, this is where you go to access the preferences, catalog settings, and Identity Plate Setup.

» **Library:** Home to the commands for creating new collections and folders as well as advanced filtering options and preview controls.

» **Photo:** Go here if you want to do stuff to your photos, like opening them in your file browser or an external editor, stacking them with other photos, creating virtual copies of them, rotating them, applying flags, ratings or labels to them, or removing them from Lightroom Classic and your disk.

» **Metadata:** Here you find controls for adding and managing metadata, which also includes keywords.

» **View:** Commit this one to memory, because it contains the most used keyboard shortcuts for switching between various views across modules. Equally important are the view options for Grid and Loupe views (more on those later).

» **Window:** Use the Window menu to access commands for switching between modules, changing screen modes, and selecting options for the secondary display.

» **Help:** Here you find commands for accessing the Help file (both locally and online), checking for updates, and module-specific shortcuts.

TIP

You can access many of these same menu commands by right-clicking a thumbnail, which calls up a contextual menu similar to the one shown in Figure 5-2.

Creating a custom identity plate

In going over the menu options under the Lightroom Classic menu (or in Windows, the Edit menu), I mention an item called Identity Plate Setup that deserves more attention. This menu option controls the appearance of the Module Picker. Beyond the Module Picker, the identity plate can appear in a slideshow, in print layouts, or in web galleries.

In all cases, the identity plate provides you with an opportunity to personalize or "brand" both Lightroom Classic and the work you output from Lightroom Classic. In this section, I show you how to customize your Module Picker, but do keep in mind

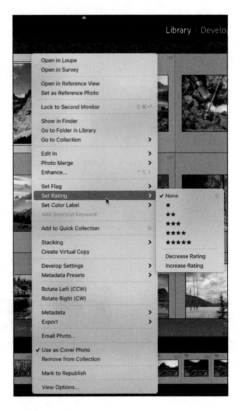

FIGURE 5-2:
Contextual menu options.

that the design you come up with here is going to show up in other places too. Basically, you have two types of identity plates:

>> **Styled text:** Allows you to enter the text you want to use and then configure the font face, size, and color.

>> **Graphical:** Allows you to include your own logo — image or text — that you design as a graphic in Photoshop. Keep in mind that you have only about 40 pixels in height to work with (41 pixels high on Mac and 46 pixels high on Windows), although it can extend behind the Module Picker buttons if that's what you want. Graphics can also contain transparency, which allows the black background to show through.

The first three steps for customizing the identity plate are the same for either styled text or graphical identity plates:

1. **Choose Lightroom Classic ⇨ Identity Plate Setup (Edit ⇨ Identity Plate Setup in Windows) from the main menu.**

   Doing so launches Identity Plate Editor, as shown in Figure 5-3. If you don't see the same, click the Identity Plate drop-down menu and choose Personalized.

2. **Click either the Use a Styled Text Identity Plate radio button or the Use a Graphical Identity Plate radio button, depending on your preference.**

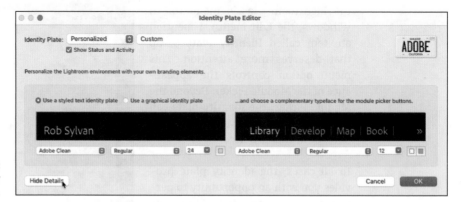

FIGURE 5-3: The Identity Plate Editor.

What happens next depends on the type of identity plate you create. If you're creating a text identity plate, you do the following:

1. **Still in the Identity Plate Editor, select the text in the Editor window.**

   The changes you make are going to affect only the selected text.

2. **Type the text you want to appear.**

3. **Reselect the text and then choose your desired font from the Font drop-down menu.**

4. **Choose the look for your font from the Font Style drop-down menu.**

   Some fonts have additional styles beyond Regular, such as Bold or Italic.

5. **Choose the font size you want from the Font Size drop-down menu.**

   You can also highlight the number and enter a new value.

6. **Click the color swatch to launch the Color Picker and choose the color of the text.**

REMEMBER

Because changes are applied only to the selected text, you can choose to style individual words (and even characters) with different colors and font faces. Mix, match, and experiment!

If you're creating a graphical identity plate, you do the following after clicking the Use a Graphical Identity Plate radio button:

1. **Still in the Identity Plate Editor, click Locate File.**

2. **In the dialog that appears, navigate to the location of the graphic you want to use.**

   Graphics in PNG format are your best choice here because they offer transparency, reasonable file size, and work equally well on Windows and Macs. Remember the 40-ish pixels height limit!

3. **Select the file and click Choose.**

After you have the identity plate looking how you want (either text or graphic), you can also modify the Module Picker buttons to better suit the look of your plate. Click the Show/Hide Details button at the bottom of the Identity Plate Editor to reveal the Module Picker button options, as shown in Figure 5-3. Here are the steps to modify the buttons:

1. **Choose your desired button font from the Font drop-down menu.**

   When you select a font, the preview in the Editor updates to reflect the choice. Select a new font if you're not happy with how it looks.

2. **Choose the look for your font from the Font Style drop-down menu.**

   Some fonts have additional styles beyond Regular, such as Bold or Italic.

3. **Choose a size for your font from the Font Size drop-down menu.**

4. **Click the left color swatch to open the Color Picker and choose the color of the active button state.**

   This color indicates the active module.

5. **Click the right color swatch to open the Color Picker and choose the color of the inactive button state.**

   This color indicates the inactive modules.

After you have the Identity Plate and Module Picker buttons looking how you want, click the second drop-down menu at the top of the Editor (where it says Custom) and choose Save As. Give this configuration a name and click Save. Click OK to close the Editor and apply the new look.

Choosing the Right View for the Task

You have a couple choices when it comes to seeing your photos while working in Lightroom Classic, but more likely than not the view mode you choose will be determined by the task you're performing. Expect to spend most of your time working with thumbnails in Grid view, with frequent dips into Loupe view to check focus at 1:1. That's how I use Lightroom Classic, at least.

Grid view and Loupe view work hand in hand, and a few important keyboard shortcuts make toggling between the two views rather seamless:

>> Press G to jump to Grid view from any module.

>> Press E to jump to Loupe view from any module.

>> From Grid view, select a photo and press Enter to jump to Fit Screen in Loupe. Press Enter again to jump to 1:1. Press Enter one more time to return to Grid view.

>> From Grid view, select a photo, and then press and hold the Z key to jump directly to 1:1 view. Release the Z to return to Grid view.

Working with thumbnails in Grid view

Grid view could also be called "Thumbnail" view because thumbnails are what make up the grid. Grid view is the workhorse of view modes, the place where you spend the majority of your time when you're performing common tasks like organizing, sorting, moving, and renaming your photos.

You do perform those tasks now and then, don't you? Whether you're watching a new import roll in, clicking into a folder or collection, or performing a keyword search of your portfolio, you're going to end up seeing thumbnails. The size of the thumbnails — and, by extension, how many thumbnails fit within the content area — can be changed with the Thumbnails slider on the Toolbar or by using the + and – keys on your keyboard.

TIP

If you can't see your Toolbar, press T to toggle it on (and off if you don't want to see it). Click the drop-down arrow on the right end to enable/disable the tools that appear on it.

Changing the look of the thumbnails

You have three different grid styles to choose from, all of which offer varying amounts of additional data to appear with each thumbnail:

» Compact Cells

» Compact Cell Extras

» Expanded Cells

You can cycle through each cell style by pressing the J key and can configure what information you want to appear in each cell style from the Grid View Options dialog. Here's how:

1. **Choose View ⇨ Grid View Style ⇨ Compact Cells from the main menu.**

2. **Choose View ⇨ Grid View Style and uncheck Show Extras in the menu.**

   You're now looking at unadorned thumbnails. This view is great when all you want to see are photos and nothing but the photos. If this strikes you as a bit too stark, keep reading.

3. **Choose View ⇨ View Options.**

   Doing so opens the Library View Options dialog, as shown in Figure 5-4, with the Grid View tab active.

   The reason I want you to go through Steps 1 and 2 here are that this is a live dialog, meaning that while you enable options in the dialog, you see them appear on the thumbnails. By entering the dialog from the most compact state, you see that all but two options are disabled. Those are the only options for Compact Cells with no extras. I recommend leaving them checked. Now you only have Compact Cell Extras and Expanded Cell Extras to configure.

4. **In the Library View Options dialog, check the Show Grid Extras check box.**

   Compact Cells should appear in the Show Grid Extras drop-down menu, and all the options are configurable. Notice that the thumbnails are now showing large index numbers behind them. You are now in Compact Cell Extras view.

5. **Using the Compact Cell Extras section of the dialog, configure Compact Cell Extras as desired.**

   How you configure this style is up to you, but the only change I make is to uncheck Index Number. The index number is a count of each photo in the grouping you're looking at. I find it to be useless and confusing because the number changes based on the filtering and sort order you're using. If you find it helpful, by all means, keep it. Otherwise, I recommend the defaults.

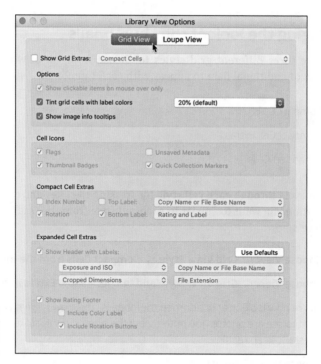

FIGURE 5-4:
The Library
View Options
dialog.

6. **Choose Expanded Cells from the Show Grid Extras drop-down menu.**

Note that the thumbnails change to Expanded Cells view style in the background.

7. **Using the Expanded Cell Extras section of the dialog, configure Expanded Cell Extras as desired.**

Again, Index Number appears as a default header label. Notice that the header label drop-down menus are arranged in the same way they appear within each thumbnail's header. Click each drop-down menu to choose the data you want to display. You have a wide range of metadata to choose from — you can even choose None, which is what I do in place of the Index Number.

8. **Click the dialog's Close button.**

Because the settings are applied while you work, there's no need to save them. After the dialog is closed, press the J key to cycle through each style and see if it works for you. Change as needed.

TIP

Refer to this book's Cheat Sheet for a complete diagram of a grid cell and all the icons, badges, and labels. You can find the Cheat Sheet by searching for **Adobe Lightroom Classic For Dummies Cheat Sheet** from the Search box on www. dummies.com.

Changing the sort order

How your thumbnails are arranged within the content area is the *sort order*. You can change the sort order with the controls in the Toolbar or by choosing View ⇨ Sort from the main menu. Capture Time is the most common sort order, but the others can be useful, too. The one that causes the most confusion is Custom Order, which is when you manually click and drag photos into a custom order — confusing because it only works under specific conditions. You can only apply a Custom Order when

>> **You're working within a collection.** Not collection sets or smart collections, though — only when working within a single collection.

>> **You're working within a single folder.** That folder cannot have any subfolders (even empty ones).

With that in mind, here's what you do to change the sort order manually:

1. **Click into a single folder or collection containing the photos you want to sort.**

If you want to sort photos that reside across a range of folders, you first need to put them into a single collection.

2. **Click the center of the photo you want to move and hold the mouse button.**

Although it's a photographer's natural tendency, don't grab the photo's frame (no need to worry about fingerprints here) because it won't work.

3. **Move the photo to the new location in the order you want and release when the separator line at that location darkens.**

Making efficient use of space with stacks

Stacking is a function that allows you to group photos into a virtual "stack" so that only the top photo is visible. This is helpful in situations where you have multiple shots of the same subject and want to group them under a single thumbnail, like when shooting for a panorama or HDR. (But really, any reason that works for you is fine — you don't have to justify anything!)

To stack photos together:

1. **Select all the thumbnails you want to group together.**

You can select multiple photos either by holding the Shift key and clicking the first and last photo in a series to select them all, or by holding the ⌘ (Ctrl key for Windows) and individually clicking each photo you want to select.

2. **Choose Photo ⇨ Stacking ⇨ Group into Stack from the main menu.**

Lightroom Classic brings the selected photos together into a collapsed stack. Note the other options under the Stacking menu command.

Stacked photos are identified by a bar on either end of the group of stacked photos, as shown in Figure 5-5 (note that the number in the upper left corner indicates how many photos are in the stack). You can expand and collapse the stack by clicking either of those bars, or by selecting one and pressing S.

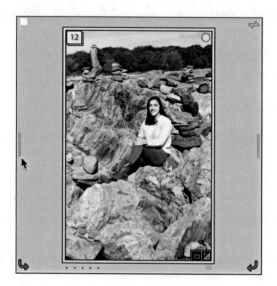

FIGURE 5-5:
Stacked photos
indicator.

Taking a closer look in Loupe view

When viewing a thumbnail isn't adequate for the job, it's time to switch to Loupe view. The easiest way to switch is to press E, which switches you to Loupe view at the Fit setting. The Navigator panel, as shown in Figure 5-6, is Loupe view's best friend in that it displays a thumbnail of the active photo. At the top of the panel are the various zoom levels you can use in Loupe view. The default zoomed-out state is Fit, which means the entire image fits in the content area, and the default zoomed-in state is 100%, which means actual pixel view. Click each zoom level to activate, or click the drop-down menu at the end to zoom in some more. When Fill is selected (under the Fit menu), the photo is zoomed in just enough to fill the entire content area.

The choice you make at the top of the Navigator panel will become the default zoomed-out and zoomed-in state. I find Fit and 100% to be the most useful.

When you zoom in beyond Fit, you can click and drag the photo to inspect different areas of the photo, or click and drag the white square in the Navigator panel to pan across the photo. Here's an alternative (and more efficient) method to inspect all areas of the photo when you zoom in beyond Fill:

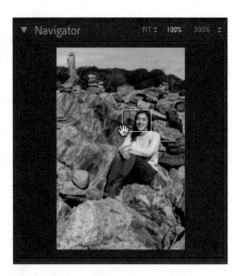

1. **Click the photo to zoom in.**

100% works very well for this.

FIGURE 5-6:
The Navigator panel.

2. **Press the Home key on your keyboard to jump to the upper left corner of the photo.**

On some keyboards there may not be a Home key (or Page Up, Page Down, or End), so the incorporation of the Function (Fn) key with your arrow keys may be required to achieve the same functionality. For example, on my Mac, holding down the Fn key and pressing the Left Arrow key is the same as pressing Home on my Windows machine. Fn+Up Arrow equals Page Up, Fn+Down Arrow equals Page Down, and Fn+Right Arrow equals End.

3. **Repeatedly press the Page Down key on your keyboard to move over the photo.**

Each press of the Page Down key moves you an equal amount until you reach the bottom, where one more press brings you back to the top but over to the right. You can continue to press the Page Down key until you've viewed the entire photo down to the lower right corner.

4. **Click the photo to zoom out.**

In practice, this process goes by rather quickly, and you're guaranteed not to miss one pixel of the photo this way.

Just like in Grid view, it's possible to display some important information about the active photo. Here it's called the Loupe Info Overlay, and two versions allow for different sets of information to be displayed (but not at the same time). You can cycle through each overlay and back to the Off position by pressing the I key. To set up your Loupe Info Overlay, choose View ⇨ View Options from the main menu to launch the Library View Options dialog. It should open to the Loupe View tab, as shown in Figure 5-7.

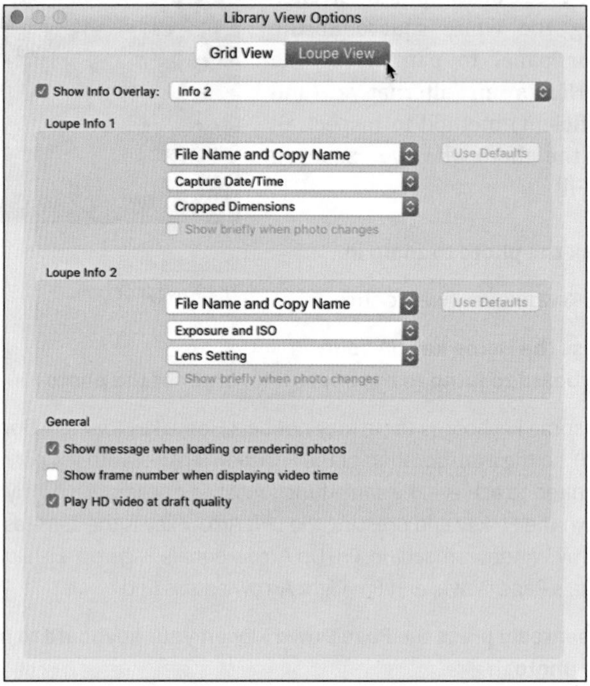

FIGURE 5-7: The Loupe View tab of the Library View Options dialog.

Each Info Overlay can be configured by clicking its respective drop-down menus and choosing the data you want to see. The check box in the General section toggles the display of the loading and rendering messages that appear in Loupe view. I find the messages to be a helpful reminder that there's something going on behind the scenes when first viewing a low-quality preview, so I leave that box checked — and recommend you do the same. The same goes for the default positions of the Show frame number when displaying video time and Play HD video at draft quality.

Using the Panels to Access Your Photos

The Catalog, Folders, and Collections panels provide multiple ways to view, organize, and access your portfolio. Each offers a unique set of tools to help you stay in control of your portfolio. Let's examine each panel in turn.

Getting the 20,000-foot view from the Catalog panel

The Catalog panel, shown in Figure 5-8, provides quick access to a few special collections of your photos:

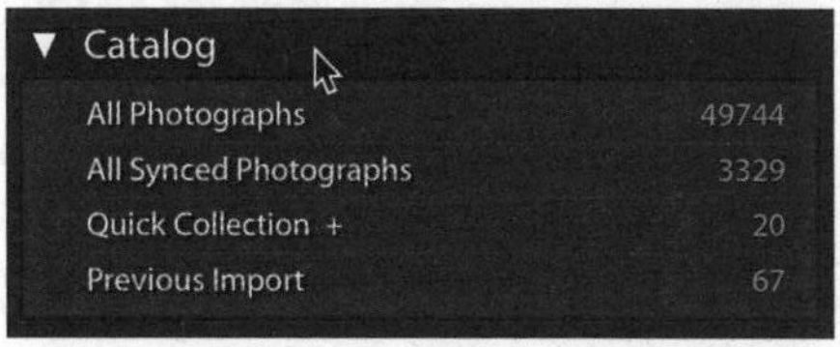

>> **All Photographs:** Provides quick access to all imported photos.

>> **All Synced Photographs:** Tracks the photos that are synced with the cloud-based Lightroom (see Chapter 16).

>> **Quick Collection:** A temporary holding place for photos. See the upcoming section on collections for more information.

>> **Previous/Current Import:** Shows the most recently imported photos. Each new import clears the last batch and adds the newest.

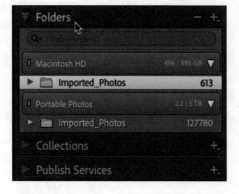

FIGURE 5-8:
The Catalog panel.

Using the Folders panel like a file browser

The Folders panel, shown in Figure 5-9, displays a listing of all the folders of photos that you've imported as well as the disk (or volume) where the folders reside. Volumes and folders can be expanded or collapsed as needed to access the contained photos. Volumes are arranged in the order in which they're imported, whereas folders within each volume are arranged in descending alphanumeric order — an ordering that cannot be changed.

FIGURE 5-9:
The Folders panel.

The *Volume Browser* — the bar that appears above your topmost level folder — indicates the name of the volume (disk) that your folders reside on as well as a number of other functions:

>> **Shows at a glance where your photos reside.**

>> **Can be configured to display disk space, photo count, or online status.** Mine is set to disk space in Figure 5-9. Right-click and choose the information to be displayed.

>> **Provides a color indicator (think dashboard warning light) of how much free space is on that disk.** Green means plenty of space, but it will turn to orange when it starts to get full, and then red when it is very low, and black if that disk is offline.

>> **Allows for all the folders on a given volume to be collapsed under one heading.**

If your imported folders reside on more than one disk, you see a Volume Browser for each disk. I have two disks showing in Figure 5-9.

Although the Folders panel looks a lot like your file browser (Finder for the Mac, or File Explorer for Windows), it's fundamentally different. The difference is that the Folders panel shows only the folders and photos that have been through the Import process. Your file browser, comparatively, simply browses the folder and shows its contents. That difference aside, the Folders panel reflects the reality of your actual folders in the following ways:

>> The actual folder names are shown in the Folders panel.

>> Changes made in the Folders panel are reflected on the actual folders.

WARNING

Unfortunately, changes that you make to the folder structure outside of Lightroom Classic aren't updated automatically in Lightroom Classic. This is an area where you can create problems for yourself. To avoid creating problems, only make changes to the imported folders (and photos) from within Lightroom Classic.

Adding new folders and subfolders to the Folders panel

Lightroom Classic shows only the folders that have been imported; therefore, you might decide at some point that you want the parent folder of one of your imported folders to appear in the Folders panel. The quickest way to bring the parent folder into Lightroom Classic is to right-click the child folder in the Folders panel, and then choose Add Parent Folder. The parent folder immediately appears in the Folders panel; however, any photos that it might contain will not be visible until they're imported.

Another option is simply to create a new folder entirely. The benefit of doing this in Lightroom Classic is that not only is the folder created, but it's also imported at the same time. You can either create a new folder inside of one of your existing folders (also referred to as a *subfolder*) or create a new folder in an entirely different location. Here's how the new subfolder thing works:

1. **Select the folder you want to use as the parent folder for the new subfolder.**

2. **Click the + symbol at the top of the Folders panel and choose Add Subfolder.**

   The Create Folder dialog appears, as shown in Figure 5-10. Note that in the Folder Options section, the name of the folder you select appears checked.

3. **Enter a name in the Folder field.**

4. **Click Create.**

   The new folder appears in the Folders panel under the previously selected folder.

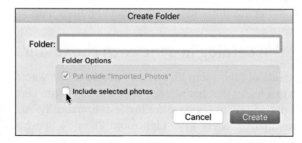

FIGURE 5-10:
The Create Folder dialog.

The process for creating a new folder in a new location is slightly different:

1. **Click the + symbol at the top of the Folders panel and choose Add Folder.**

   Doing so launches the Browse for Folder dialog.

2. **Navigate to the disk location where you want this folder to be created.**

3. **Click the New Folder button to create a new folder, give it a name, and click Choose (Select Folder for Windows).**

   The New Folder button appears near the top of the dialog in Windows, and near the bottom on Mac. The newly created folder appears in the Folders panel.

The most common reason for adding a new folder to Lightroom Classic is so that you can move photos or folders into this new location. Folders can be moved by clicking and dragging them to the destination folder of your choice within the Folders panel. You can also move individual photos by clicking and dragging them from Grid view to the destination folder in the Folders panel. After you drag a file or folder to a new location, Lightroom Classic prompts you to make sure you want to complete that action, as shown in Figure 5-11. Click the Move button to proceed.

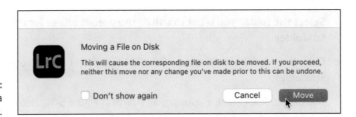

FIGURE 5-11:
The Moving a
File warning.

Along with adding new folders, you might feel the need to remove folders as well. If the folder you want to ditch is empty of photos and subfolders, right-click the folder and choose Remove. The folder disappears from Lightroom Classic as well as from your Mac hard drive. (On a Windows machine, that folder remains on your disk until you remove it via your file browser.) If you remove a folder that contains photos or subfolders, the folder is removed only from Lightroom Classic. (Both Mac and Windows machines keep such folders on their hard drives.)

Keeping the catalog in sync with the folders

If you're outside of Lightroom Classic and decide to use your file browser to add new photos to a folder that has already been imported into Lightroom Classic, the photos will not appear in Lightroom Classic automatically. All photos have to go through the import process first. Lightroom Classic's Synchronize command is great for making Lightroom Classic take a closer look at a given folder and, if necessary, opening the Import dialog to bring any additions into the catalog. Here's how it works:

1. **Right-click the folder you want to check.**

2. **Choose Synchronize Folder from the contextual menu that appears.**

   Doing so opens the Synchronize Folder dialog, as shown in Figure 5-12. Depending on the number of files contained in the folder, Lightroom Classic might take a couple minutes to compare what it knows about the folder to what is actually in the folder and to determine what action(s) need to occur to get the two in sync.

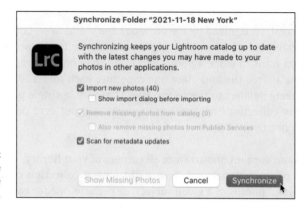

FIGURE 5-12:
The
Synchronize
Folder dialog.

3. **Check the boxes for each operation you want Lightroom Classic to perform.**

You can have Lightroom Classic

- Import new photos (with or without showing the Import dialog).

- Remove any missing photos from the catalog file — photos that were in the folder but might have been moved to another folder.

- Check for any metadata updates that might have occurred from editing in a different application (such as adding keywords via Adobe Bridge).

4. **Click Synchronize.**

Lightroom Classic closes the Synchronize dialog and performs the tasks you assigned.

Grouping photos into collections

The Collections panel, shown in Figure 5-13, is found just below the Folders panel. *Note:* I've created many custom collections over time, but by default you would see only a set of smart collections (more on those later). Although, on the surface, collections appear to function just like folders, they have a critically important difference; they don't exist outside of Lightroom Classic. You can open a file browser, navigate to a folder, and see what it contains, but you could search your entire hard drive and never find a collection.

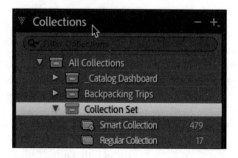

FIGURE 5-13:
The Collections panel showing collection sets, regular collections, and smart collections.

Folders are real, recognized by file browsers the world over. Collections are *virtual* folders, created out of thin air by Lightroom Classic for its purposes. In the real world, if you want to place a photo into more than one folder, you have to make copies of the source file and place one copy into each folder. With collections, all you do is create *pointers* to the source file. That way, a single photo can be placed into as many collections as you care to create without ever needing to duplicate the source photo.

Collections can contain photos from all corners of your library, which makes them a powerful organizational tool. You might have a collection containing all your best work, or all photos of a given subject, or perhaps one for each client. The purpose collections serve and how you might name them are entirely up to you. I find that they provide a very natural way to quickly access groups of photos around a specific theme.

You can create a collection a number of ways:

>> Click the + symbol at the top of the Collections panel and choose Create Collection.

>> Choose Library ⇨ New Collection from the main menu.

>> Press ⌘+N (Ctrl+N for Windows).

You can organize collections within the Collections panel by putting them into a *collection set.* (A collection set is simply a grouping of collections.) For example, if you shoot weddings, you might have a collection set for each client. Within that collection set, you might have a collection for the bride, another for the groom, another for the family, and so on.

To add a collection set, click the + sign at the top of the Collections panel and choose Create Collection Set from the menu that appears. After you give the set a meaningful name, it appears in the Collections panel. You can then drag and drop existing collections into it. Collection sets cannot contain photos, only collections and other collection sets, and are denoted with a box icon.

Quick Collection

The Quick Collection, a useful variation on the Collections idea, can come in handy when you just want to set some photos aside without putting them in a permanent collection. Quick Collection resides in the Catalog panel, and you place photos into the Quick Collection by doing one of the following:

>> Selecting the photos and pressing the B key

>> Clicking the tiny Quick Collection indicator that appears in the upper right corner of each thumbnail

This indicator is visible only when you place your cursor over a thumbnail. (I take that back: You can also see the indicator on photos you've already included in the Quick Collection.)

>> Choosing Photo ➪ Add to Quick Collection from the main menu

Those same options also work in reverse to remove photos from the Quick Collection. You can clear all photos from a Quick Collection by choosing File ➪ Clear Quick Collection. If you decide that you want to make a Quick Collection permanent, you can save it by choosing File ➪ Save Quick Collection. After you give the collection a name, it appears where all well-behaved collections end up — in the Collections panel. Here's a cool tip for taking the Quick Collection to the next level with a Target Collection: https://lightroomers.com/target-collection.

Smart collections

Smart collections are a great example of how to leverage the power of a database to do work for you. True, you already have all kinds of ways to group your photos by virtue of data they have in common — just think of the Filter bar. However, smart collections take that power to the Collections panel. A gear icon tells you it is a smart collection.

Now, instead of having to manually select photos and put them in a collection, you can create a smart collection that automatically pulls photos into it based on the criteria you choose to include. You can think of smart collections as saved searches based on whatever criteria you choose. To get you started, Lightroom Classic comes installed with six default smart collections:

>> **Colored Red:** All photos with a red label

>> **Five Stars:** All photos rated five stars

>> **Past Month:** All photos containing a Capture Date within the last month

>> **Recently Modified:** All photos with an Edit Date within the last two days

>> **Video files:** All imported video files

>> **Without Keywords:** All photos with an empty keyword field

TIP

If none of these starter smart collections appeals to you, you can easily delete them. Just select one (or more) and then click the minus sign in the Collections header bar. Poof, they're gone. If you want to see the rules governing a smart collection, you can right-click any smart collection and choose Edit. Doing so launches the Edit Smart Collection dialog, which spells out in gory detail the parameters the smart collection is using. Feel free to tweak the settings to better fit your needs and then click Save!

You can create as many smart collections as you need — and you don't need to start with one of the default sets. You can create one from scratch. One smart collection that I use as a sort of safety net is designed to collect any photo not marked as copyrighted in its metadata. Even though I include the copyright setting in my metadata template when I import photos (see Chapter 4) there are times when some photos lose that setting or enter my library without it when synced from the cloud-based Lightroom; so this simple collection automatically collects any photos that would otherwise remain unnoticed. Here's how to set up that type of smart collection:

1. **Click the plus sign on the Collections header bar and choose Create Smart Collection from the contextual menu that appears.**

Alternatively, you can choose Library ⇨ New Smart Collection from the main menu. This launches the Create Smart Collection dialog, shown in Figure 5-14.

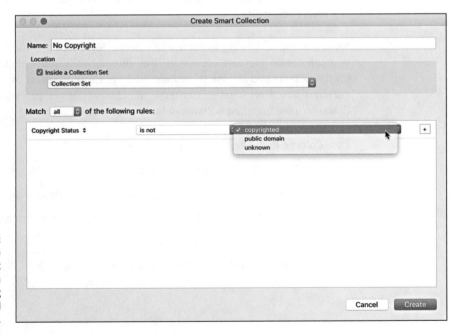

FIGURE 5-14:
The Create Smart Collection dialog showing a finished example.

2. **Enter a descriptive name in the Name field.**

3. **Choose a Collection set to put the collection in.**

4. **Select All from the Match drop-down menu.**

   The idea here is that a photo has to match all the provided rules to be included in the collection.

5. **Choose Copyright Status from the drop-down menu on the first rule that appears — the menu directly underneath the Match drop-down menu.**

   After clicking the rule drop-down menu, drill down to Other Metadata to find Copyright Status. Your first rule is now about *copyright status*. When you make that first choice about what criteria you want to use for your rule, the contents of the subsequent drop-down menus update automatically with relevant criteria until the rule is complete. Next, you need to define what is it about copyright status that you want to take notice of. In this example, you want all photos not marked as copyrighted, so you'll change that in the next step.

6. **Choose *Is Not* from the bordering drop-down menu — the next part of your first rule.**

   Great, so now you need to answer the question "Is not what?" Which you'll do in the next step.

7. **Choose Copyrighted from the far right drop-down menu — the last part of your first rule.**

   So your smart collection is set to grab all photos whose copyright status is not copyrighted. Perfect, that's exactly what you want to happen.

8. **Click Create.**

   The new collection appears in the Collections panel.

This is just one example of the many ways you can make smart collections work for your needs. Click through each of the criteria options to see what's possible. Many of my smart collections involve a single criterion, but feel free to use as many criteria as you need to get the job done. Because smart collections are basically saved searches, they operate automatically and instantaneously. The only way a photo appears in a smart collection is if it meets the rules, and the only way it can be removed is if it no longer meets the rules. Check out my article on Lightroom Killer Tips for more smart collection ideas: `https://lightroomkillertips.com/building-catalog-dashboard`.

Creating Multiple Versions with Virtual Copies

Virtual copies are based on all Lightroom Classic adjustments being recorded as a set of instructions waiting to be applied at output. A *virtual copy* is essentially an alternative set of instructions that references the same source file as the original. Here's a simple example: You have a color photo and wonder how it might look in B&W, so you create a virtual copy and convert the copy to B&W. In Lightroom Classic, you see two versions of that source file, one color and one B&W. If you look in the folder where the source file is saved, you see only the original. The grayscale copy is simply an alternative set of instructions stored in Lightroom Classic's catalog waiting to be applied during output.

A preview version of the virtual copy was created and stored in the preview cache, but even at 1:1 size, the preview file requires far less disk space than your original file (especially if it was raw).

TIP

You can recognize a virtual copy in Grid view by the page curl effect in the lower left corner, as shown in Figure 5-15.

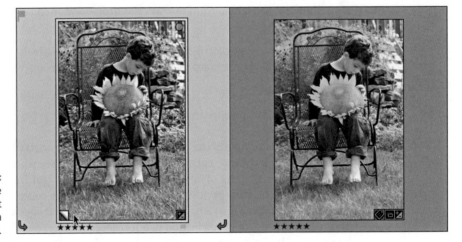

FIGURE 5-15: The page curl effect represents a virtual copy.

You can create a virtual copy three separate ways:

>> Choose Photo ⇨ Create Virtual Copy.

>> Right-click and choose Create Virtual Copy from the contextual menu that appears.

>> Press ⌘+' (Ctrl+' for Windows).

If you decide that you prefer the virtual copy to the original, you can make it the new master version of the file and make the old master into a virtual copy. With the virtual copy selected, choose Photo ⇨ Set Copy as Master. You see the page curl effect "jump" from one thumbnail to the other.

Chapter **6**

Getting Organized with the Library

O ne of the first tasks I perform when working with a batch of newly imported photos is to weed out the worst of the bunch. I keep anything that has at least some redeeming quality, but any poor exposures or photos with improper focus are sent straight to the trash. I do want to note that, even though photos I flag as rejected are deleted from disk, I do retain an archived copy of my original import as a fallback. This provides me with enough peace of mind to be a tougher critic of my own work, which I feel is integral to my own growth. That's one of the things I really like about Lightroom Classic: It gives me the tools I need to evaluate my work in an efficient manner.

An additional result of this tough-love editing process is that I don't have to spend time organizing, sorting, or applying additional metadata and keywords to photos

I don't plan to keep. But this is just *my* approach to this process. I've structured this chapter to reflect a common workflow scenario and illustrate how certain functions work, and I encourage you to develop and refine a workflow that best suits your style and needs.

Evaluating Photos

The Library module has five view modes — Grid, Loupe, Compare, Survey, and People. I covered Grid and Loupe — the workhorse view modes — in Chapter 5. You'll still be using them as you move between Compare and Survey (which I'll tackle in just a bit). People view is its own special case; I cover it in Chapter 7. Each view can serve a variety of purposes, but I find that when it comes to evaluating photos, the Survey and Compare views are the ones I reach for most. They still work hand in hand with Grid view and Loupe view, but they offer different ways to interact with — and see — your photos.

Survey view

Survey view, as shown in Figure 6-1, is great when you want to move from Grid view to look only at a small group of photos by themselves, and possibly reduce that selection further. To enter Survey view, just select the thumbnails that you want to look at together while in Grid view, and press N. Don't ask me why N is the shortcut, and don't ask me why it's called Survey view, for that matter. I'm just here to tell you what's what. As an alternative (there's always an alternative) you can enter Survey view by selecting photos and clicking the Survey view button on the Toolbar, choosing View ⇨ Survey View from the main menu, or right-clicking a selected photo and choosing Open in Survey from the contextual menu that appears.

Lightroom Classic automatically arranges the selected photos to fit within the available content area. The more photos you select, the smaller each photo appears; whereas the more screen real estate you provide to the content area, the larger the photos appear. For this reason, you might find it helpful to maximize the content area (if you're not already in full screen) by

» Pressing Shift+F to jump to full screen (and keep pressing to cycle back to normal).

» Pressing Shift+Tab to collapse all panels (and pressing again to expand the panels).

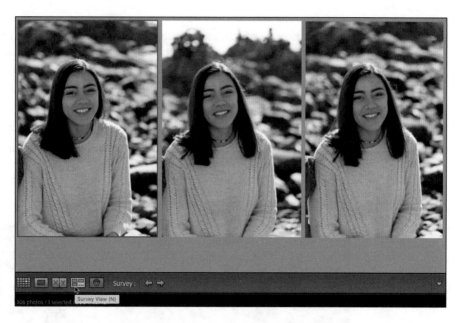

FIGURE 6-1:
Three photos
shown in
Survey view.

The photo with the border is the *active* photo (the one that any flags, ratings, metadata, or adjustments will be applied to). You can use the arrow keys on your keyboard to change the active photo or just click a different photo to make it the active one.

TIP

If you want to zoom in to take a closer look at any photo, click it to make it the active photo and press and hold the Z key to zoom to 1:1. As long as you hold the Z key, you can pan around the photo (by clicking and dragging) for closer inspection. When you're done, just release the Z key to return to Survey view. If you don't want to keep holding the Z key down, you can just press it once to jump to 1:1 Loupe view, examine the photo at your leisure, and then press the Z key to return to Survey view. Either way, Lightroom Classic provides you with a free round-trip ticket to Loupe view and back.

You can also remove photos from this view by clicking the X icon that appears in the lower right corner when you move your cursor over the photo or by ⌘+clicking (Ctrl-clicking for Windows) the photo itself. As photos are removed from view, Lightroom Classic adjusts the remaining photos to fill the newly available space. Removing from this view simply deselects that photo, so this can be a way to pare down a selection of photos to just the ones you want.

Compare view

The most useful view mode for side-by-side comparison of one photo to another is the aptly named Compare view. This view is best for situations where you have multiple shots of the same subject and you want to determine — after careful consideration — which one you like best. To get Compare view up and running, start out from Grid view, select the thumbnails you want to compare and then press C. (You can also enable Compare view from the button on the Library Toolbar, the main menu, or via the contextual menu.)

TIP

You can see an example of Compare view in action in Figure 6-2. Similar to Survey view, Compare view fills the available content area. The trick here is that Compare view limits itself to showing two photos at a time. Collapsing panels to maximize your content area allows the photos to be larger.

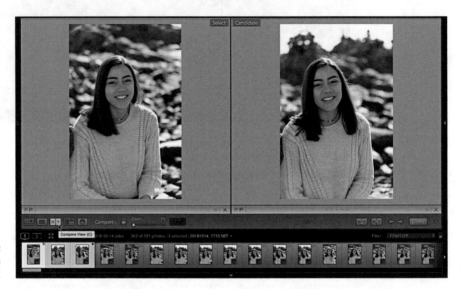

FIGURE 6-2:
Two photos in
Compare view.

The first photo you select before entering Compare view will be labeled the Select. The Select is the photo you are comparing against all the others. When the other photos appear in the content area, they're referred to as the Candidate. The Select is always on the left and the Candidate is on the right. You can see the Select and Candidate label appear as an overlay on the photos themselves. (Refer to Figure 6-2.) Additionally, the Select has a white diamond icon display on its thumbnail in the Filmstrip, whereas the Candidate displays a black diamond icon in the Filmstrip. The diamond icons are helpful visual cues when you have a large selection of photos to compare. You can use your arrow keys on your keyboard to swap other photos into the Candidate position.

TIP

The active photo has a white border around it in the content area. (The Select is active in Figure 6-2.) Click either the Select or the Candidate in the content area to set it as the active photo. When the Select is active, clicking another photo in the Filmstrip sets it as the new Select. Likewise, when the Candidate is active, clicking another photo in the Filmstrip sets it as the new Candidate. The active photo is also the one that can have flags, ratings, labels, quick develop settings, and metadata applied to it.

TIP

To aid the evaluation process, you can also zoom into each photo by either clicking into the active photo or by using the Zoom slider on the Toolbar. If the Lock icon on the Toolbar is closed, both the Select and Candidate zoom by the same amount. When the Select and Candidate are zoomed and locked, both photos pan in sync when you click the active photo and pan around. If the Lock icon is open, you can zoom and pan each photo independently. If you click the Sync button next to the Zoom slider, both photos zoom to the same section of each photo. The Z key shortcut I describe in the "Survey view" section works here, too.

You can have the Candidate become the Select and the Select become the Candidate by clicking the Swap button on the Toolbar, as shown in Figure 6-3. You can also promote the Candidate to become the Select by clicking the Make Select button on the Toolbar. (It's the button just to the right of the Swap button.) You can exit Compare view by either switching to a different view mode or by clicking the Done button on the Toolbar.

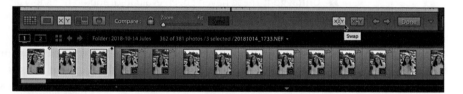

FIGURE 6-3:
The Compare view Toolbar buttons.

Flags, Ratings, and Color Labels

Having all the various view modes and their associated tools at your disposal won't do you a lick of good if you can't integrate them into your workflow in a way that makes the process of evaluating your photos more efficient. I've come up with my workflow model, but don't think of it as carved in stone. Perhaps you already have a system of, say, color labels or ratings that works for you. By all means, do what works. In these next few sections, I cover the available organizational tools and how they work in a typical workflow. Feel free to pick and choose the pieces that fit your needs.

Using flags to pick the winners and losers

Flags are a fantastic tool for quickly making a first-pass edit of your photos so that you can separate the shots you want to keep from the ones that no one else needs to see. You have three flag states to choose from, represented by the flag icons shown in Figure 6-4:

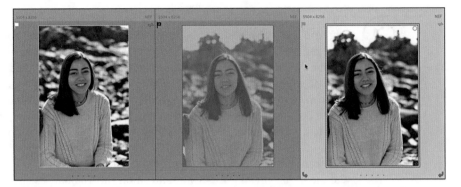

FIGURE 6-4:
Three photos
showing
picked,
rejected, and
unflagged
photos from
left to right.

>> **Pick:** These are your keepers and are marked with a White Flag icon.

>> **Rejected:** These are your rejects and are marked with a Black Flag icon.

>> **Unflagged:** These haven't been evaluated, and do not show an icon.

Flags (of each type) can be applied to one or more selected photos at a time. Unflagged photos do not show a flag, but if you position your cursor over an unflagged photo, you can see the outline of the flag icon. This clickable target can be used to set a flag. Click the icon once to set it as picked and click again to unflag. You can also apply flags by

>> Clicking either the Pick or Rejected Flag icon on the Toolbar.

>> Right-clicking a photo and choosing Set Flag and then choosing one of the three flag states from the contextual menu that appears.

>> Keyboard shortcuts: P for Pick, X for Rejected, and U for Unflagged.

>> Choosing Photo ⇨ Set Flag from the main menu.

TIP

The easiest and most efficient method to apply flags is to use the keyboard shortcuts. This process is expedited by choosing Photo ⇨ Auto Advance from the main menu (should be enabled by default). When enabled, focus automatically advances to the next photo after applying the flag.

Here's a real quick workflow using the Library Filter bar above the thumbnails in Grid view (which I cover in more detail later, in the section "Finding Photos with the Library Filter Bar") for making your first-round selections:

1. **Press G to jump to Grid view.**

2. **Press Shift+Tab to hide all panels and maximize content area.**

3. **Adjust the Thumbnail Size slider on the Toolbar as needed to get a good size for evaluating each photo.**

TIP

When you need to quickly see a 1:1 view of your photo while working in Grid view, press and hold the Z key to zoom. While holding the Z key, you can even click and drag the photo to inspect other areas. When you release the Z key, you return directly to Grid view.

4. **On the Library Filter bar, click the Attribute label to display the Attribute filters, and then right-click anywhere on the flag icons in the Attribute filter and choose Flagged and Unflagged Photos from the contextual menu that appears (see Figure 6-5).**

This sets a view filter that tells Lightroom Classic to display only photos that are either flagged as a Pick or Unflagged, which results in Lightroom Classic hiding (not deleting) any photos that are flagged as Rejected. This way, when you flag a photo as Rejected, it immediately hides from view and advances you to the next photo.

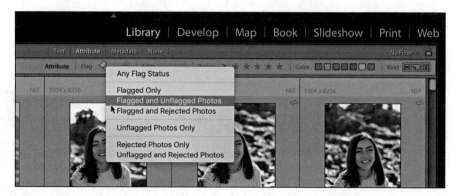

FIGURE 6-5:
The Filter bar showing the Attribute filters.

5. **Make sure Photo ⇨ Auto Advance is checked.**

6. **With the first image selected, evaluate and flag as a Pick or Reject.**

TIP

Press P for Pick and X for Rejected. Lightroom Classic automatically advances to the next thumbnail. If you just can't decide, press U (Unflagged) to advance to the next photo. I'll deal with unflagged photos in Step 8.

7. **Continue applying flags until you reach the last image.**

At this point, you should only see photos that are flagged as Pick or Unflagged. Skip to Step 10 if you didn't leave any photos Unflagged.

8. **On the Library Filter, right-click anywhere on the flag icons and choose Unflagged Photos Only.**

Now all picks and rejected photos are hidden from view, and you are left with only unflagged photos.

9. **Flag the remaining photos as either a Pick or Rejected.**

When photos are flagged, they're hidden from view because of the Unflagged Photos Only filter. You know you're finished when you don't have any photos left.

10. **On the Library Filter, right-click anywhere on the flag icons and choose Rejected Photos Only.**

Photos flagged as rejected are going to appear faded; this is normal and helps them to stand out when you see a mix of flag states.

11. **Verify that you're satisfied with your Rejected photos and change any to Pick if needed.**

12. **Press ⌘+Delete (Ctrl+Backspace for Windows) and choose Delete from Disk.**

This is the keyboard shortcut to delete rejected photos — you find the same command under the Photo menu.

13. **Press ⌘+L (Ctrl+L for Windows) to turn off all filters.**

You should now be left with all the photos you flagged as Pick!

Deleting photos from Lightroom Classic

Lightroom Classic is very careful (as it should be) in its approach to deleting photos from disk. You're always prompted with a confirmation dialog, as shown in Figure 6-6, before a deletion is allowed to take place. When prompted, click the Delete from Disk button to complete the deletion process and have Lightroom Classic move the selected photo(s) to the Trash (Recycle Bin for Windows). Clicking Remove removes the photo from the Lightroom Classic catalog only (and leaves the photo(s) on your drive).

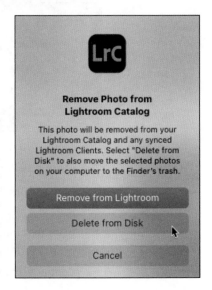

FIGURE 6-6:
The Confirm dialog appears when attempting to delete photos.

You can delete a photo from disk with the Delete key only when you're working in a Folder view. If you're working in a Collection view and press Delete, the selected photo(s) are removed from that collection only. (For more on Folder views and Collection views, check out Chapter 5.)

Using ratings to rank images

Ratings provide another means to sort your photos by subjective criteria. There's no hard-and-fast rule on what criteria correlates to any number of star ratings. It's entirely up to you to develop your system! Because I use a flag system to cull all the bloopers first, I don't use ratings to mark which photos stay or go. I find ratings helpful for quickly identifying the best of the best, while ignoring the photos that aren't so bad to warrant deletion but at the same time, just aren't good enough to do much with.

To prevent a lot of hemming and hawing over the difference between a 4-star photo and a 5-star photo, I typically use a 0–2 star scale. If I think it's a useable shot, I assign one star; if I think it's really good, I assign 2 stars; and if I can't decide, I leave it at 0. I find this helps me refine and focus my energy on processing rather than ranking.

As with most Lightroom Classic tasks, there's more than one approach to accomplishing the same result. After selecting the photo, you can apply ratings in the following ways:

>> **Press the number keys, 0–5, depending on the number of stars you want to apply.** Each number key corresponds to the number of stars.

>> **Click the appropriate star under each photo cell in Grid view.** Press J to cycle through Grid cell styles if you don't see rating stars.

>> **Right-click, select Set Rating from the contextual menu that appears, and then choose your desired rating from the menu.**

>> **Choose Photo ⇨ Set Rating from the main menu and then choose your desired rating from the menu.**

Applying color labels to photos

Color labels provide a visual that you can use to further sort and organize your photos. How these are used is entirely subjective, and perhaps you might not use them at all. They do offer some unique benefits:

- » Labels are very flexible.
- » Labels can be used as criteria in the creation of smart collections.
- » Labels can be used as a filter on the Library Filter.

I've seen people use labels to assign a different color to each photographer for easier sorting after an event with multiple shooters. I've seen others assign different colors to different states in the editing process (such as a color for Needs Keywords, another for Ready to Deliver, and so on). Maybe you'd find labels useful for labeling groups of photos that you intend to send to other applications for additional processing. However you use them, consider setting up a smart collection for each color label to provide quick access to those special groupings.

Instead of trying to remember what each color means in your system, you can create a Custom Label Set with names that make sense to you. Here's how to create your custom label set:

1. **Choose Metadata ➪ Color Label Set ➪ Edit from the menu.**

   Doing so launches the Edit Color Label Set dialog.

2. **Enter a name for each color in the set that you want to use.**

3. **Choose Save Current Settings as New Preset from the Preset drop-down menu.**

   The New Preset dialog appears.

4. **Enter a name and click Create.**

   The preset name appears in the Preset drop-down menu of the Edit Color Label Set dialog.

5. **Click Change to close the editor and begin using that set.**

REMEMBER

You can use only one color label set at a time, so when you change to this new set, you won't see any color labels applied with a previous color set. A color label is simply a tag in the file's metadata. When that label matches the color label set in use, Lightroom Classic displays the corresponding color. Changing the set doesn't change the label that's applied; you just won't see Lightroom Classic display a color. You can change color label sets by selecting them from the Metadata ➪ Color Label Set menu.

Applying color labels to folders and collections

A recent addition to Lightroom Classic is the ability to apply color labels to folders and all types of collections and collection sets. The colors you apply to folders and collections are not linked to the color label set you choose, and applying a color label to a folder or collection does not apply that color label to the photos within it. These color labels can be used to give you another visual cue for locating groups of photos based on the color label you assign. It is up to you to think of how this can be useful in your workflow, but for example, say you assign a yellow color label to all folders and collections you are currently processing to make those stand out from the rest. Or perhaps within a given shoot you assign one color to the folder or collection containing the originals and a different color to finished files for delivery. I do a lot of HDR, panos, and focus stacking, so I've assigned a different color to represent folders and collections containing those types of photos. There's no wrong answer, but only what helps you find and organize your library.

To apply a color label to a folder or collection, simply right-click the folder or collection in question, and then use the Add Color Label contextual menu to select the desired color. You can change or remove color labels the same way as your needs and workflow dictate.

Filtering folders and collections

Here's the real benefit to applying color labels to folders and collections though, you can filter the view of the contents of each panel based on the color label! At the top of both the Folders and Collections panels is an easy to miss field with a tiny magnifying glass icon that you can click the icon to access a menu of items to choose from for filtering the view of that panel. Additionally, you can type into the field itself and refine the filter further to only show folders or collections that match what you type. For example, if I want to only see folders with the yellow color label applied whose names include the word "falls" I can use the filter to show precisely that and nothing else (refer to Figure 6-7).

My example and corresponding figure shows the Folders panel, but the filter in the Collections panel works the same exact way. One way I've seen other people use these filters is when visiting with a client, they filter each panel to only show work that is relevant to that client, while temporarily hiding everything else. To clear each filter, click the magnifying glass icon again and choose All from the menu, then delete any text you typed into the field to restore all content back into view.

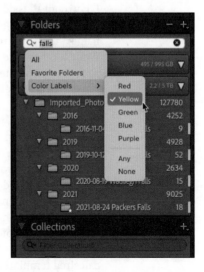

FIGURE 6-7:
Filter the contents of the Folders panel to show only what you want.

Filenames and Metadata

With every shutter click your digital camera creates a file, assigns it a name, and embeds all the settings used to make the capture into the file's metadata space. When you begin to work with your photos, you want to add additional custom metadata (such as your contact information) to your files. When doing so, you might discover that the camera-generated filenames don't particularly fit your needs. Lightroom Classic has an excellent set of tools to aid you in managing this aspect of your portfolio.

As described in Chapter 4, you can both rename and apply custom metadata during the Import process. However, that doesn't fit everyone's workflow. For some, the Import process is just getting photos off the memory card as quickly as possible, and everything else can come later. For others, it only makes sense to apply a minimal amount of custom metadata at import and then complete the job after the first round of edits, so that time isn't wasted working on files destined for the trash heap. Similarly, you might want to wait to rename all photos until after you remove the duds so you don't end up with any gaps in the filenames. Lightroom Classic allows for a flexible approach.

Batch renaming with filename templates

After you import your photos into Lightroom Classic, it's in your best interest to perform all your renaming tasks from within Lightroom Classic because Lightroom Classic stores each file's name in its catalog. If you were to rename files outside of Lightroom Classic, the data in the catalog wouldn't match the new names, and Lightroom Classic then would consider those files missing or offline. While it *is* possible to reconnect Lightroom Classic to the newly named files, doing so is an onerous task that I wouldn't wish on anyone. I can't tell you how many times I've seen people do this. Please don't fall into that trap!

Thankfully, the renaming function within Lightroom Classic is powerful, extremely configurable, and easy to use. Lightroom Classic comes installed with a number of file-naming templates that you can use as-is, or you can create custom templates to fit your needs (as explained in Chapter 4). Each file-naming template is comprised of *tokens* — little widgets that represent a chunk of data used to build your filename. These tokens include things like custom text, date/time values, sequence numbers, metadata elements, and parts of the original filename. As shown in Chapter 4, these tokens are assembled and arranged with Lightroom Classic's Filename Template Editor. Here's how to rename a batch of photos with a desired template:

1. **Select the photos you want to rename from Grid view.**

2. **Choose Library ⇨ Rename Photo from the menu (or press F2).**

   The Rename Photos dialog appears.

3. **Choose your desired template (or create one) from the File Naming drop-down menu.**

   Note that if your template includes custom text, you must enter that text before proceeding to the next step.

4. **Click OK to apply that template to the selected photos.**

Keep in mind that renaming photos in Lightroom Classic renames the actual photos on your drive.

Creating metadata templates to embed information into each image

The Metadata panel, located on the right side of the Library module, (see Figure 6-8) is great for displaying any metadata embedded in an image, but you can also use it to add new metadata, edit some existing metadata, or access other photos that share common data points. Because so much data about each photo can be displayed, the Metadata panel has a number of different view options accessible via the drop-down menu in the panel's header. This enables you to pick a view that shows only the type of metadata you're interested in, which makes work much easier.

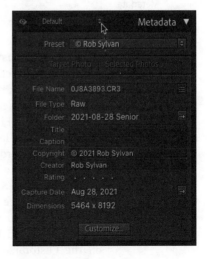

FIGURE 6-8:
The Metadata panel set to the Default view.

Within the Default view of the Metadata panel you have the ability to configure which metadata fields are visible, as well as their order within the panel. Click the Customize button to open the Customize Metadata Default Panel dialog, as shown in Figure 6-9. Here you can check the box next to any field you want included in the Default view or uncheck the box next to fields you do not want to see. There are a lot of potential fields to include, so be sure to scroll down to see the entire list. Note that including a large number of fields can impact performance, so go easy.

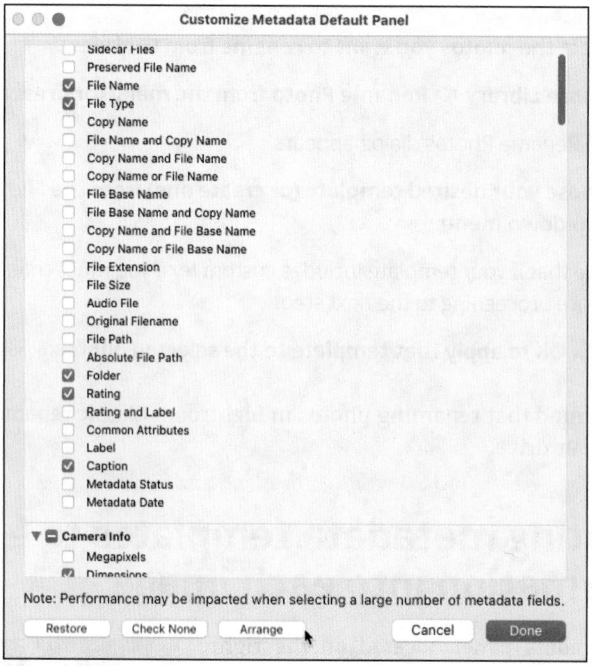

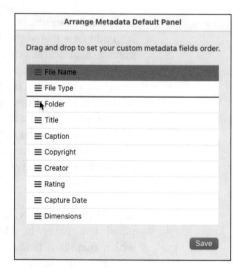

FIGURE 6-9:
The Customize Metadata Default Panel.

If you want to customize the display order of your selections after you have made them, click the Arrange button to open the Arrange Metadata Default Panel dialog (see Figure 6-10). Simply click the field's label and drag and drop it into the order you want to see the fields appear within the Metadata panel, then click Save to accept your changes and close all dialogs. If you do not want to customize the display order, you can click the Done button on the Customize Metadata Default Panel to accept your changes and close the dialog.

The Preset drop-down menu at the top of the panel gives you access to your custom metadata templates — as well as the controls to create *new* templates. Any templates you've created via the Import dialog are also accessible here. To create a new metadata template

FIGURE 6-10:
The Arrange Metadata Default Panel.

1. **Choose Edit Presets from the Preset drop-down menu.**

The Edit Metadata Presets dialog appears, and looks the same as the New Metadata Preset dialog you see in Chapter 4 during import. You can also access this dialog by choosing Metadata ⇨ Edit Metadata Presets from the main menu.

2. **Complete all applicable fields.**

Depending on your needs, you can complete as much or as little of the dialog before saving it as a template.

3. **Choose Save Current Settings as New Preset from the Preset drop-down menu.**

Doing so launches the New Preset dialog.

4. **Enter a name in the Preset Name field and click Create.**

The name of the preset appears in the editor's Preset drop-down menu.

5. **Click Done to close the editor.**

You can apply a preset by selecting your photos in Grid view, and then selecting the desired preset from the Metadata panel's Preset drop-down menu. Lightroom Classic prompts you with the Apply Metadata Preset dialog, where you can choose to apply the preset to just the active photo or to all selected photos. Select the Don't Show Again check box if you don't want to be prompted in the future. (The choice you make becomes the default behavior when the prompt is turned off.)

Keywording

I don't know anyone who loves the task of adding keywords to their photos, but I also don't know anyone who isn't glad to have well-keyworded photos when it comes time to find them. *Keywording* is your chance to describe the contents of your photos with words that aid you in finding them. By doing so, the words you use form a structure of their own inside your catalog. If you're thorough and consistent in the application of keywords, you'll reach a point where you can find all photos of a given subject with just a click (or two).

Although it's possible (and often helpful) to start keywording at import, you'll find the Library module is where you do most of your keywording activities. Both the Keywording panel and the Keyword List panel have supporting roles in this process.

The Keywording panel, shown in Figure 6-11, is made of three sections:

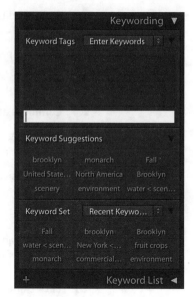

FIGURE 6-11:
The Keywording panel.

» **Keyword Tags:** The top section of the panel, Keyword Tags, provides a means to enter new keywords and to display the applied keywords of a selected photo. Use the Keyword Tags drop-down menu to access other options for displaying keywords.

» **Keyword Suggestions:** While you add keywords to your photos, Lightroom Classic begins generating a list of suggested keywords based on other photos that have similar keywords applied to them. Click any suggested keyword to add it to the selected photo.

» **Keyword Set:** This section is another keyword-entry aid. You can create an unlimited number of keyword sets of up to nine keywords in each. Lightroom Classic comes installed with three common sets that you can use or modify to fit your needs. Holding the Option key (Alt key for Windows) reveals the keyboard shortcuts for each word in the set. This makes for speedy keywording by selecting photos and pressing Option+number. Use the Keyword Set drop-down menu to access an existing set, or choose Edit Set to create a new one.

The Keyword List panel, shown in Figure 6-12, consists of the following:

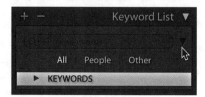

FIGURE 6-12:
The Keyword List panel.

» **Add/Remove keywords buttons:** Click the + or – buttons in the Keyword List header to add or remove keywords.

» **Filter Keywords:** Your keyword list can grow quite large. Enter a word (or part of a word) in the Filter Keywords field to display the keywords containing only that word (or part of that word). The disclosure triangle at the end will hide/show additional filter options by keyword type (more on People keywords in Chapter 7).

» **The master list of keywords:** The master list of keywords is all the keywords you've created in Lightroom Classic or that were imported along with photos that had been keyworded in another application before being imported into Lightroom Classic.

Adding and organizing keywords

You can add keywords to selected photos in the Library module a number of ways:

>> **Drag selected photos onto a keyword in the Keyword List panel.**

>> **Drag selected keywords onto selected photos.**

>> **Select photo(s) and enter keywords via the Keywording panel.**

>> **With the Painter tool (see the section "Using the Painter Tool," later in this chapter).**

You can't say Lightroom Classic doesn't give you choices! Just to narrow down the realm of possibilities, though, I walk you through *one* way — creating and applying a keyword in the same step:

1. **Select a photo to keyword from Grid view.**

In this example, I use a photo of my dog, Niko (see Figure 6-13).

2. **Expand the Keywording panel and then click into the smaller field at the top.**

Always use this field to add new keywords so that you don't accidentally delete keywords that appear in the larger field as you go.

3. **Enter a keyword and press Enter.**

In this example, I simply type **dog** and press Enter.

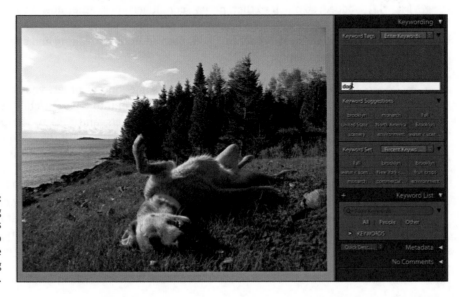

FIGURE 6-13:
Applying keywords to a photo using the Keywording panel.

At its most basic level, that's all there is to it (of course you can repeat that process and add as many keywords as you feel are needed). The keyword *dog* has been applied to the photo, and the keyword will appear in the Keyword List panel (or the photo will be applied to the existing keyword if applicable). If I have another dog photo, I can drag the photo onto the keyword (or vice versa) to apply the keyword to the photo. Alternatively, if I prefer to type the keyword, I can repeat the previous steps; however, as soon as I type **d**, Lightroom Classic kicks into auto-complete mode and displays possibilities from my keyword list that I can then choose from, as shown in Figure 6-14.

You can assign multiple keywords to selected photos by entering them into the active field in the Keywording panel, separating each word with a comma. For example, I could also type **pets, summer, Niko** and then press Enter. As more keywords are added to each photo, they appear in the Keyword List panel.

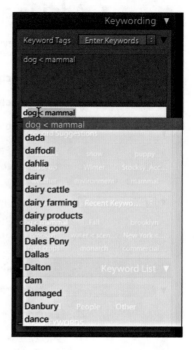

FIGURE 6-14:
Keyword auto complete example.

TIP

As you can imagine, the Keyword List panel keeps growing as each new word is added, so much so that, pretty soon, it becomes rather unwieldy. To maximize the effectiveness of your keywords, you might want to consider arranging them into a hierarchical structure that adds both additional meaning and organization to your keyword list.

To put your existing keywords into some kind of order, you can drag and drop keywords onto each other, which puts them into a parent/child relationship. For example, I originally added *summer, dog, pets,* and *Niko* to the photo shown in Figure 6-13. If I want to start building a structure with those words, I'd probably select *dog* in the Keyword List panel and drag it to *pets.* (I'm such a logical guy.) After releasing *dog,* it's nested under *pets,* and so on. Years ago I purchased a pre-made keyword list of thousands of words (from https://controlledvocabulary.com), as shown in Figure 6-15, that has helped me with my work, but may be overkill for some people. You can import a plain text keyword list like that one by choosing the Metadata ⇨ Import Keywords command. You can find free keyword lists at https://lightroom-keyword-list-project.blogspot.com.

Instead of creating your structure after you add words to your photos, you can reverse the process and create the structure first. This gives you the benefit of thinking about how you want to arrange your keywords beforehand and generally leads to a much more thorough keywording process. The Keyword List panel provides the tools to aid you in the creation of new keywords. For example, to continue building on the "pets" structure, I might want to add the keyword *cat* and nest it underneath *pets* in anticipation of future cat photos. Here's how:

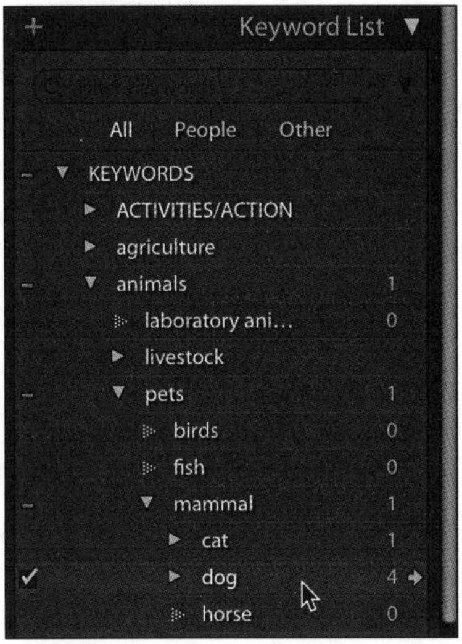

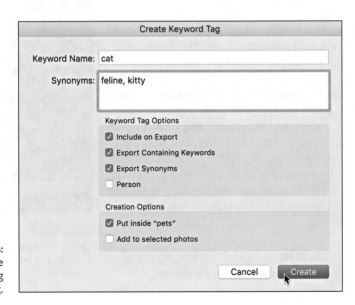

FIGURE 6-15:
Nested keyword structure.

1. Select the parent keyword.

In this case, I selected *pets* because I want to add *cat* as a child keyword.

2. Click the + symbol at the top of the Keyword panel to open the Create Keyword Tag dialog shown in Figure 6-16.

3. Enter the keyword in the Keyword Tag field.

4. Enter any synonyms.

Separate each synonym with a comma. Synonyms aren't searchable inside Lightroom Classic, but they can be included as a keyword in exported copies.

FIGURE 6-16:
The Create Keyword Tag dialog.

5. Note the Put Inside box is checked because I selected "pets" first.

6. Make sure the Add to selected photos box is unchecked.

In this case, I'm adding a keyword in anticipation of a future photo, not adding a keyword to any photos I have selected, so I uncheck this option. Of course, you can check it if you want to apply it as part of the process.

7. Check the Include on Export box.

If you want this keyword included in the exported copies, you need to check this box. If you just want the keyword to exist as an organizational aid in your catalog (such as a high-level category heading), leave this box unchecked.

8. Check the Export Containing Keywords box.

The parent keyword will also export. In this case, I want to ensure that *pets* exports as a keyword along with *cat*.

9. Check the Export Synonyms box.

10. Click Create.

My new keyword, *cat*, is now added to the Keyword List panel under *pets*. The process is the same for adding other new keywords while you flesh out a keyword structure.

Using the Keyword List to find photos

Now that you've added a few keywords and have begun creating an organizational struc-ture, you can use the Keyword List panel to jump right to a group of photos that share the same keyword. Figure 6-17 shows the Keyword List panel with my dog photo selected. Notice that the keywords pets and dog have a check mark next to them in the Keyword List. Those check marks identify all the keywords applied to the selected photo. Also, notice that the cursor is hovering over the *dog* keyword in the list. I want you to know about two important options:

>> **The check mark inside a box:** When you move your cursor over any keyword, you

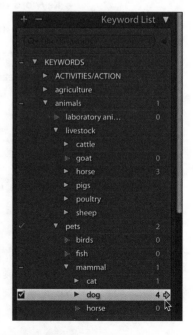

FIGURE 6-17:
The Keyword List panel showing explicitly and implicitly applied keywords.

see a check box appear. Unchecking a keyword removes it from the selected photo. Adding a check mark applies that keyword to the selected photo.

>> **The right-facing arrow next to the counter:** Clicking that arrow applies a Library filter that displays only the photos in the catalog that have that same keyword. Click None in the Library Filter to turn the filter off.

In my case, I have a large hierarchical keyword list, and you can see a — mark next to *mammal*, *animals*, and *Keywords* in the list. That mark means those keywords are implied by virtue of their children keywords *pets* and *dog* being explicitly applied. That means because I explicitly applied the keyword *dog,* my *photo* also gained *mammal* and *animal*, which is a real timesaver.

Before we move on to the often-mentioned Library Filter bar, there is one more cool tool I want to introduce you to that will make adding all these various types of flags, metadata, and keywords a lot more fun.

Using the Painter Tool

The Painter tool is the little spray-can icon on the Grid view Toolbar, as shown in Figure 6-18. You can use it to apply keywords, labels, flags, ratings, metadata, develop settings (the same Develop presets you saw in the Quick Develop panel), or photo rotations. You can even use it to assign a photo to a specific collection. It's quite simple to use if you prefer a more hands-on approach to adding the same piece of information to a large group of photos.

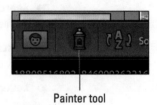

Painter tool

FIGURE 6-18:
The Painter tool on the Toolbar.

As a way to introduce you to a growing world of Lightroom Classic content I write besides this book, I invite you to learn more about the Painter tool by heading to the Lightroom blog I contribute to at https:// lightroomkillertips.com/painting-photos-information.

Finding Photos with the Library Filter Bar

Okay, you've invested a lot of time in managing your portfolio, so you may as well take a look at one of the ways you can start to get a return on that investment. Let me officially introduce you to the Library Filter bar, shown in Figure 6-19. The Library Filter is visible above the thumbnails only in Grid view. The Library

Filter bar display can be toggled on and off by pressing the backslash (\) key. This doesn't turn off any active filter; it just hides the bar to maximize the content area. Filtering is turned on and off by pressing ⌘+L (Ctrl+L for Windows) or by clicking None on the Filter bar.

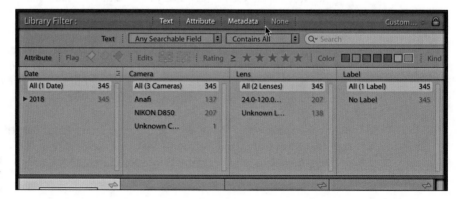

FIGURE 6-19:
The Library
Filter bar.

The Library Filter bar allows you to drill down into your portfolio as follows:

>> **Searching text fields:** Not limited to searching by keyword, you can search on filenames and metadata fields as well.

>> **By status indicators:** Clicking Attribute reveals the options for "refining" your view using flags, ratings, labels, and virtual copy status.

>> **Leveraging metadata:** Enabling the Metadata filter opens worlds of possibilities for gathering photos based on information about or embedded in each file, such as capture date, file type, aspect ratio, shutter speed, location, camera used, and more!

Filters can be used singly or in multiple mix-and-match combinations. I could have a hankering, say, for all TIF files with the keyword *flower* that were taken with my (very) old D200 and that have a rating of two stars or greater. Here's how I'd use a filter to satisfy that hankering:

1. **Select All Photographs from the Catalog panel.**

2. **Press \ if the Library Filter bar isn't visible and press G for Grid.**

3. **On the Library Filter, click the Text label.**

   The Library Filter expands and shows the Text filter.

4. Choose Keywords from the Search Target drop-down menu.

You could leave it set to Any Searchable Field because it's unlikely that *flower* would appear anywhere and not be a keyword, but I want to point out how specific you can focus your searches.

5. Enter flower **into the Search field.**

When you begin typing, the content area updates to show only those results that match the filter.

6. Hold ⌘ (Ctrl for Windows) and click the Attribute label.

The Filter bar expands and shows the Attribute filters.

7. Click the two-rating star.

Only photos with the *flower* keyword and rated two stars or higher are left in the results.

8. Hold the ⌘ (Ctrl for Windows) and click the Metadata label.

The Filter bar expands further to include the Metadata options. The Default Columns view appears, which does include the camera model, but I also want to limit the results to only TIF files. You can customize the metadata columns to show different data — would anyone like to change the Lens column to File Type?

9. Choose File Type from the drop-down menu located next to Lens.

I can change any column to File Type, but because Lens isn't criteria I'm concerned with in this example, I chose to ditch Lens. Now, I can see the file types as well as the camera models that represent the photos showing in the content area.

10. Click the TIFF label.

Now, only TIF files are showing.

11. Click the Nikon D200 label.

Now, only TIF files, shot with the D200, rated two stars or higher, that contain the *flower* keyword, are showing.

TIP

If this was a filter type that I thought I would use often, I could choose Save Current Settings as New Preset from the Custom Filter drop-down menu and give my new preset a name. It would then appear in the Custom Filter drop-down menu and be just a click away. Press ⌘+L (Ctrl+L for Windows) or click None on the Filter bar to turn off that filter and return to an unfiltered All Photographs. For a really deep dive into filtering what you can see, check out my article on that topic: https://lightroomkillertips.com/a-look-at-filtering.

Chapter **7**

Exploring the Library Module's Advanced Features

Although the Library module is packed with tasks primarily focused on managing your photo library over time, it does have a few additional superpowers you'll want to know about so that you can leverage them when the time comes. This chapter covers those, and wraps up with a look at the Map module, because its functions can help you organize and find your photos by location.

People View

If you're like me, you've got photos of people in your Lightroom Classic catalog. Wouldn't it be great to finally get names assigned to all the people in your photos so that you could find them easier down the road? Fortunately, Lightroom Classic has a facial recognition function that can churn through all your photos looking for faces and then grouping similar faces together for you to name. Let's look at how it works.

Finding faces

You can jump into People view, as shown in Figure 7-1, by clicking its icon in the Toolbar or pressing the O key while in the Library module.

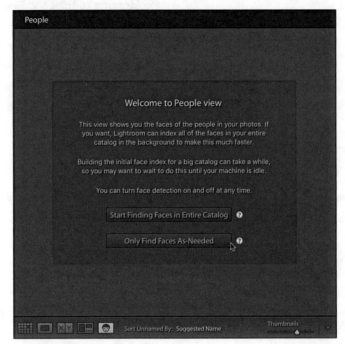

Welcome to People view

This view shows you the faces of the people in your photos. If you want, Lightroom can index all of the faces in your entire catalog in the background to make this much faster.

Building the initial face index for a big catalog can take a while, so you may want to wait to do this until your machine is idle.

You can turn face detection on and off at any time.

Start Finding Faces in Entire Catalog

Only Find Faces As-Needed

Sort Unnamed By: Suggested Name

Thumbnails

FIGURE 7-1:
You've got to enable facial recognition to begin.

As you can imagine, the process of going through all your photos is resource-intensive. The more photos you ask it to process, the longer it will take, and you may not want it to run while you are trying to do other work in Lightroom Classic. I suggest starting small by working on one folder at a time until you get a feel for what's happening. When you first enter People view, you'll see the welcome message, and I recommend clicking Only Find Faces As-Needed so that it only churns through the folder or collection you are currently viewing when switching to People view. If you ever decide you want Lightroom Classic to go through your entire catalog, choose Catalog Settings ⇨ Metadata, and then select Automatically Detect Faces in All Photos. You can pause/resume face detection via the Activity Monitor hidden in the ID plate.

Once enabled, Lightroom Classic starts to find what it thinks are faces and then groups similar faces together. These appear in the Unnamed People section as shown in Figure 7-2 with question marks under them.

As cool as this technology is, it isn't always perfect and needs our help to finish the job.

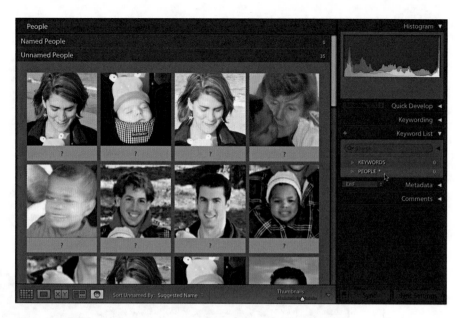

FIGURE 7-2:
Faces are
being found.

Tagging faces with names

Once you have some faces showing, you can start to tag the faces with their names. You can also remove any mistakes the facial recognition process makes and even manually assign face tags to photos that got missed by the automated process. The tags you apply to faces are similar to the keywords I discuss in Chapter 6, except that they are called *Person Keywords* (to make it easier to strip them out during export). Over time, as Lightroom Classic learns who is who, it pulls from the Person Keywords you create to suggest names for faces.

I'll go through a basic workflow to get you started, but feel free to improve upon my suggestions to tailor the process to your needs. Note that all names used here are fictional for privacy reasons.

1. **Select a folder you want to process and enable Only Find Faces As-Needed.**

2. **Create a parent tag to contain all your people tags.**

    While Lightroom is churning away, you can keep your Keyword List panel tidy by nesting your people tags under one parent. I created a new keyword tag, named PEOPLE, and disabled all export options (refer to Chapter 6 for a refresher on creating keywords). Then right-click that tag and choose Put New Person Keywords Inside this Keyword from the contextual menu (you'll see an asterisk on that tag).

3. **Add Person Keywords to unnamed photos by clicking the ? (question mark) under photos.**

   I decided to use a [*Last Name*] [*First Name*] convention for my person keywords to keep people with the same last name grouped together in my list, but use what works for you. The name you add will appear under the parent Person Keyword you created in the previous step, and it will begin suggesting that name on faces it thinks are that person.

4. **Approve names for correctly identified people.**

   As soon as you've added a few names, Lightroom Classic will start suggesting names for faces it thinks you've identified. It isn't 100 percent accurate, so you'll need to manually approve each suggestion, as shown in Figure 7-3. Enter the correct name for any mismatches to keep Lightroom Classic learning.

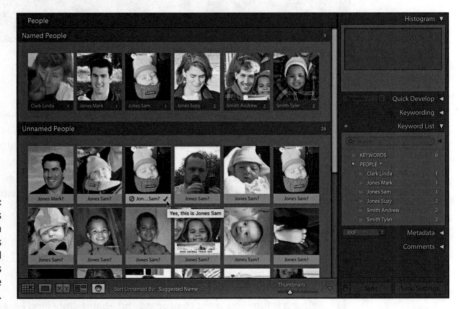

FIGURE 7-3:
Sometimes
Lightroom
Classic gets
it right, and
sometimes
it sees a face
in a foot.

5. **Speed things up by dragging a selection of unnamed faces onto the correctly named face.**

   Hold down ⌘ (Ctrl for Windows) and click all faces of the same person in the Unnamed section to select them, and then drag and drop them on the correctly named person in the Named section to apply that name in one go.

6. **Verify that all faces were found and manually add face regions if needed.**

Once you've successfully tagged all the people in your current view, you'll want to verify that no one got missed. Double-click the first thumbnail in the Filmstrip to see the entire photo along with the face regions Lightroom Classic assigned as shown in Figure 7-4. Use your arrow keys to move through the photos.

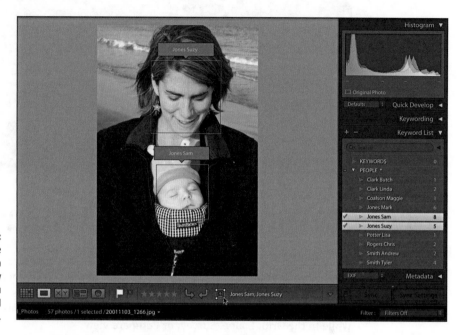

FIGURE 7-4:
Viewing the full photo in People view shows you the assigned face region.

7. **Draw face regions for any faces that were missed.**

If you find a photo where a face was missed, or if you just want to manually assign a Person Keyword to a non-person photo (such as one of your dog), you can draw out a region anywhere on the photo and then assign a Person Keyword to it, as shown in Figure 7-5. The Draw Face Region tool will be active when entering this view, so just click and drag to draw a region. You can also select an existing face region and delete it if it is a misfire. *Note:* Manually drawn face regions aren't factored into the algorithm Lightroom Classic uses to learn faces.

This process gets easier and easier the more you use it, but you definitely want to start small.

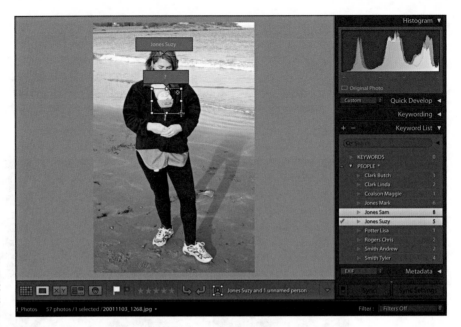

Adjusting Your Photos in the Library

Although not intended to take the place of the Develop module, the combination of the Histogram and the Quick Develop panels in the Library module can provide valuable information about your photos and allow for tweaks that can further inform your selection process. Quick Develop panel adjustments can be applied while in the Grid, Loupe, Survey, or Compare view.

Considering the Histogram

A *histogram,* in the digital photo world, is a graph representing all the tones in a selected photo. The left side of the graph represents the darker tones, and the right side represents the lighter. In the Lightroom Classic interface, the Histogram panel has a place of honor — first position — on the right.

The bottom of the Histogram panel displays the ISO, focal length, aperture, and shutter speed of the active photo to aid in that photo's evaluation. With all this information, you can use the tools in the Quick Develop panel to make adjustments without leaving the Library module. You see more about it when I cover the Develop module in Chapter 8.

Making adjustments with Quick Develop

The default rendering of your raw photos may not always be enough to judge the potential of a given photo. Perhaps a photo was slightly underexposed, or perhaps the wrong white balance was selected in-camera. Those issues (among others) can be corrected relatively quickly and should not be the cause for you tossing out an otherwise good photo. The Quick Develop panel, shown in Figure 7-6, gives you the tools to do some quick rehab work, and contains three subsections that can be collapsed or expanded by clicking the (very hard to see) arrow at the top of each subsection:

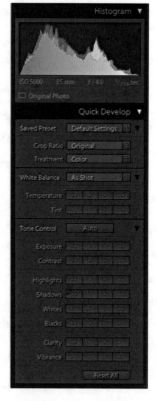

FIGURE 7-6:
The Quick Develop panel with all subsections expanded.

>> **Saved Preset:** Provides quick access to all Develop presets while also letting you crop to any aspect ratio and switch between color and B&W.

>> **White Balance:** White balance is the setting that compensates for the color of the light used to capture the scene so that subjects appear in the photo the way our eyes see them (our brains do this for us automatically). *Note:* The White Balance preset options are different for raw photos and rendered photos (JPG, PNG, TIFF, and PSD files). When working with raw data, an absolute white balance hasn't been "cooked" into the pixels, so it's possible to switch the absolute white balance value as needed. However, all rendered photos have a white-balance value applied to the pixels when the file is created, so all future white-balance adjustments are relative. When working with a rendered file, your White Balance preset choices are As Shot, Auto, and Custom.

>> **Tone Control:** This final subsection contains all the adjustments affecting the tonal range of the photo.

TIP

The Reset All button at the bottom of the panel removes *all* adjustment settings, including any adjustments made in the Develop module. However, you can reset any single Quick Develop adjustment by double-clicking the label of that adjustment.

You can apply adjustments to the active photo while in the Loupe, Survey, and Compare views. When in Grid view, any adjustments you make are applied to all selected photos (not just the active photo). This "one fell swoop" approach is handy during not only the evaluation process, but also a real timesaver when you want to apply the same adjustment to a lot of photos.

TIP

A good example of a bulk application of the Quick Develop panel is applying a new aspect ratio to a group of selected photos in Grid view. Here's how:

1. **Press G to jump to Grid view.**

2. **Select all the photos you want to crop to the new aspect ratio.**

3. **Expand the Saved Preset section of the Quick Develop panel.**

4. **Select the desired aspect ratio from the Crop Ratio drop-down menu.**

You see the thumbnails of the selected photos change to reflect the new crop ratio. When you apply the crop in this manner, you center the crop in each photo. Press R to jump to the Crop tool to tweak each crop for best composition. (I cover the Develop module's Crop tool in detail in Chapter 9.) The benefit of starting from the Quick Develop panel is that the aspect ratio is already set when you enter the Crop tool, which greatly speeds the process.

Along the same lines, if you adjust a single photo (whether using Quick Develop or the Develop module) and want to apply the same settings to multiple photos, you can use the Sync Settings button located at the bottom of the right panel group. Here's how:

1. **Press G to jump to Grid view.**

2. **Select the adjusted photo first.**

3. **Select the other photos you want to sync with the same settings.**

4. **Click the Sync Settings button.**

   Doing so launches the Synchronize Settings dialog, shown in Figure 7-7.

5. **Check only the boxes that correspond to the settings you want to apply to the other photos.**

6. **Click Synchronize.**

You see all the thumbnails of the selected photos update to reflect the newly applied settings from the first photo.

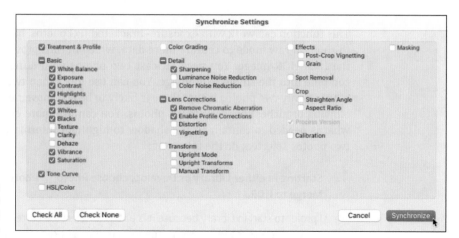

Synchronize Settings

FIGURE 7-7:
The
Synchronize
Settings dialog.

Merging Photos into HDR and Panos

One of my favorite features in Lightroom Classic is the ability to merge multiple raw photos into High Dynamic Range (HDR) images, panoramic (pano) images, or even HDR panos. The resulting merged file contains the cumulative data from the individual captures saved in the DNG format. What's DNG, you ask? Well, we'll dive into it later on, but it is essentially Adobe's version of a raw file format. This means if your original photos captured for the merge operation are all raw files, the resulting merged photo contains all that raw goodness when it comes to editing (such as changing the camera profile or white balance).

The key step in each situation is that you captured the set of photos with the intention of merging them later in your software. The capture of each type of these photos is beyond the scope of this book, but a simple Google search will yield a dizzying array of tutorials on the topic (check your camera manual too). So go out and create a few of each type; then come on back and we'll delve into how the merge function works.

Photo Merge to HDR

HDR photos often get a bad reputation due to how surreal they have looked in the past. I think the editing pendulum has swung in the other direction, because it is now possible to make extremely natural-looking HDR photos using the Merge to HDR function in Lightroom Classic. By *natural,* I just mean photographs that contain a lot more shadow and highlight detail than a single exposure can contain, just as our own eyes are able to see.

This function can work with exposure–bracketed JPG photos, but you ideally want to shoot in raw mode to capture more data, which in turn provides more data for the final HDR image. You need at least two photos with different exposures to combine into the single HDR image. You can use more than two, but one benefit of using only two photos is that there is likely to be less movement of objects (like blowing branches) between fewer photos. You can use more exposures if that is what is needed to contain all the shadow to highlight information. With at least two photos selected, do the following:

1. **Starting in either Library or Develop, choose Photo ➪ Photo Merge ➪ Merge to HDR.**

I prefer to start in Library because it is easier to select the correct photos. You can also access the Photo Merge menu from the right-click contextual menu.

This opens the HDR Merge Preview window (see Figure 7-8).

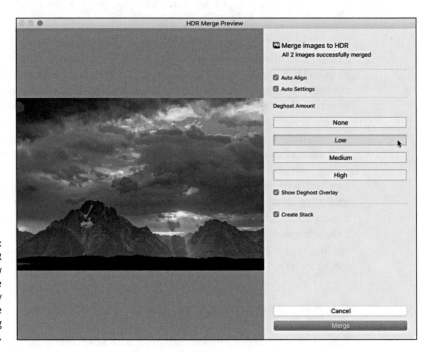

2. **(Optionally) Check the Auto Align, Auto Settings, and Create Stack boxes.**

These are optional but useful settings to consider. Auto Align will automatically align all the photos and crop out uneven edges, which is critical for the HDR merge to work. Auto Settings is a nondestructive (meaning you can change it later) way to automatically adjust exposure settings (more on this in Chapter 8).

Create Stack will stack the source photos with the final HDR image to declutter the view of the folder.

3. **Check one of the Deghost amount options if the source photos include something that moved from one photo to the next (such as moving clouds or swaying branches).**

    Deghosting works by filling in the area of movement with the information from just one photo rather than a merged composite from all frames. If the movement is slight, try the low setting; use a higher setting if that doesn't resolve the problem. Check the Show Deghost Overlay box to see the affected areas in the image in a red overlay.

4. **Click the Merge button to begin the process of merging the photos into one DNG file.**

    Once this button is clicked, you'll see the progress meter in the upper left corner. The merged result will have -HDR appended to the end of the filename. If you chose the stacking option, it appears at the top of the stack.

That's all there is to it. You can select the HDR image and press the D key to head to Develop to edit the photo just like you would any other raw photo. Because it is raw, you can apply a camera profile, change white balance, and apply lens corrections, and you'll notice the Exposure slider now has a range of +/- 10 stops (compared to the +/- 4 stops of a non-HDR image). I talk more about the Develop module in Chapters 8 through 10.

Note that after you get a handle of the settings, you may find that you don't need to see that dialog each time you want to merge. To start the merging process without invoking the HDR Merge Preview dialog, select the photos for the merge and press Shift+Control+H (same keys on both operating systems). This applies the last settings used. The progress meter indicates when the process has started. You can queue up multiple Merge to HDR processes this way.

Photo Merge to Panorama

As with the Merge to HDR, the coolest part of the Merge to Panorama function in Lightroom Classic is that it can merge raw photos into a final pano that is also raw. This feature has opened whole new worlds of capturing very high-resolution raw photos comprised of multiple individual frames. Yes, you can create the conventional very long horizontal panoramic views, but you can also create vertical panoramas, or even a very high-resolution wide field of view. For example, I once created a 137-megapixel raw photo by merging 60 individual frames using this function. Search using Google or another Internet search engine for tutorials on how best to capture images for a panorama merge. When you are ready, select the photos you captured for the panorama merge and follow these steps:

1. **Starting in either Library or Develop, choose Photo ⇨ Photo Merge ⇨ Merge to Panorama.**

   I prefer to start in Library because it is easier to select the correct photos. You can also access the Photo Merge menu from the right-click contextual menu. Note the keyboard shortcut that appears in the menu for future use.

   This opens the Panorama Merge Preview window (see Figure 7-9).

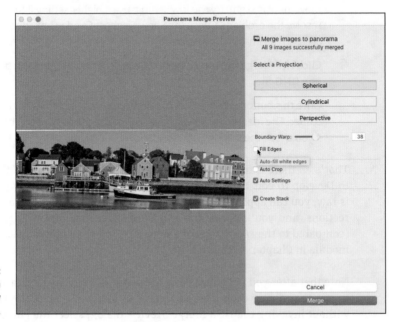

FIGURE 7-9: The Panorama Merge Preview window.

2. **Optional: Check the Auto Crop, Auto Settings, and Create Stack boxes.**

   These settings are optional, but they are useful settings to consider. Auto Crop crops out empty areas around the edges of the final image. Auto Settings is a nondestructive (meaning you can change it later) way to automatically adjust exposure settings (more on this in Chapter 8). Create Stack stacks the source photos with the final Panorama image to declutter the view of the folder.

3. **Choose a projection method.**

   Lightroom Classic creates the final image by mapping the frames using one of the three projection options. Using Spherical (a good choice for most merges), the individual frames are mapped onto the inside of a sphere, where they are then aligned and blended together. The Perspective option maps to a flat surface, which is good for keeping straight lines straight (such as in buildings). The Cylindrical option maps to the inside of a cylinder and does a good job of keeping vertical lines straight (try for really wide panoramas). You can click each one to see a live preview and then choose the one that looks best. I usually stick to Spherical.

4. **(Optional) Use Boundary Warp and/or Fill Edges.**

    Instead of using Auto Crop (or in conjunction with using it) try using the Boundary Warp function to warp the image to fill the empty areas around the edges. The higher the value, the more the image is warped to fill the space, so there's no one right answer. Alternatively, or in addition, check the Fill Edges check box to have Lightroom Classic create new pixels based on the surrounding pixels to fill in remaining white areas around the edges. Refer to Figure 7-9, where I used Boundary Warp a little and will use Fill Edges to finish the job.

5. **Click the Merge button to begin the process of merging the photos into one DNG file.**

    Once this button is clicked, you'll see the progress meter in the upper left corner. The merged result has –Pano appended to the end of the filename. If you chose the stacking option, it appears at the top of the stack.

Once the merged result appears, you can head off to the Develop module to edit just as you would any other raw photo. You don't need to edit the individual images before merging into the panorama.

Just like with the Merge to HDR process, once you get a handle on the settings, you might find that you don't need to see that dialog each time you want to merge. To start the merging process without invoking the Panorama Merge Preview dialog, just select the photos for the merge and press Shift+Control+M (same keys on both operating systems). Lightroom Classic applies the last settings used, and you'll see the progress meter when the process has started. You can queue up multiple merge-to-panorama processes this way.

Photo Merge to HDR Pano

Now you might be thinking, "What if I shot the individual frames of the panorama as a bracketed exposure so that I could use all the images to create an HDR Pano?" And you'd be in luck! The Merge to HDR Pano option takes all the goodness of the previous two options and gives you the ability to select an entire set of photos captured with the intention of creating a panoramic HDR final raw photo.

You do need to capture this set of photos with this intention, though — meaning that each bracketed set of photos must contain the same number of photos (three exposures is usually enough), each bracket should have the same +/- exposure offset (+/- 1 stop is often enough), and the entire set needs to be captured one after the other. So before you press the shutter for the first photo of your panorama, you'd want to dial in your auto exposure bracketing amount, capture the first frame of the pano as an HDR bracket before rotating the camera to capture the second frame of the pano, and so on until all frames of the panorama are captured.

Back in Lightroom Classic, select all the individual frames of the HDR panorama and choose Photo ➪ Photo Merge ➪ Merge to HDR Panorama to open the HDR Panorama Merge Preview window, which looks the same as the Panorama Merge Preview window in Figure 7-9.

It should not be a surprise that this dialog looks just like the Merge to Panorama window, because it does require the same options. On the HDR side, deghosting is set to off, so if your HDR brackets do require deghosting you'll want to merge the HDR brackets separately, and then you can funnel the merged HDR results into the regular merge-to-panorama function. Otherwise, follow the same steps as I outline previously for the Merge to Panorama option. The final merged result is a single DNG file ready to be edited in Develop.

Super-size it

Wouldn't it be cool if Lightroom Classic had a way to leverage the power of software magic to improve image quality and even increase the pixel dimensions of our photos? Good news, it does! Adobe utilized machine learning, a branch of artificial intelligence, which is a technology Adobe used to train an algorithm (using millions of photos) to enlarge a photo's pixel dimensions while maintaining important detail and reducing artifacts. (Read all about it here: https://blog.adobe.com/en/publish/2021/03/10/from-the-acr-team-super-resolution.) You can access this cool tech from the Photo menu, or by right-clicking the desired photo, and selecting Enhance. This opens the Enhance Preview window, shown in Figure 7-10.

There are two options available, depending on the file type of the selected photo, to choose from within Enhance. The first, called Raw Details, is, as the name suggests, for raw photos only. If you have a non-raw photo selected (like JPG, PSD, TIF, or PNG), that option will be unavailable, as shown in Figure 7-10. Raw Details was originally called Enhance Details when first released, and as that name implies its singular function was to create a copy (with the same pixel dimensions) of the selected raw photo with improved detail edge contrast, improved color, and fewer artifacts than the original. In my own testing, the improved results were minor and it is not a feature I have found useful in my own workflow. However, your results will depend on the camera used to capture the photo, and I encourage you to explore how it works with your own photos, especially any that you plan to print at a large size.

The second option, called Super Resolution, is the one that will create a copy of the selected photo, raw and non-raw alike, that has pixel dimensions twice as long in both height and width of the original photo. In other words, the pixel dimensions of the copy created by Super Resolution will be four times larger than the original.

This can be useful for instances where you needed to severely crop into a photo when you couldn't physically get closer to your subject or zoom in closer with your lens, or for simply enlarging the original photo to be printed at a larger size. In Figure 7-10, I used Super Resolution to enlarge a photo from my first 3-megapixel digital camera to be four times larger. The better the quality of the original the better your final results will be, but I've been pretty impressed with the results so far. If you start with a raw photo, the Raw Details function will also be applied when using Super Resolution for even better results.

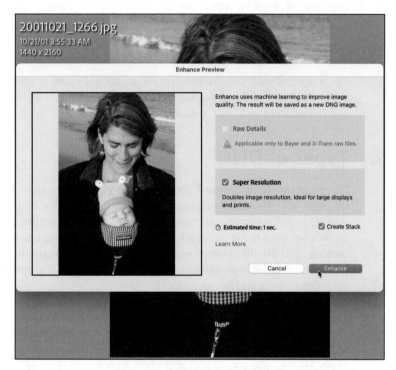

FIGURE 7-10:
The Enhance Preview window.

The copy created using either Raw Details or Super Resolution will have the word *Enhance* appended to the copy's filename, and it will have a DNG file extension. Give it a try!

What Is DNG?

As I mention earlier in the chapter, DNG is Adobe's file format for raw image data. In case you're unsure, DNG is an openly documented file format for holding raw data. Because the format is openly documented (unlike the proprietary raw file formats), third-party software developers can support the format (some do, some don't). This openly documented aspect is also valuable for those looking for an archival solution that lasts decades into the future. DNG creates an internal checksum value that can be used to validate the integrity of the image data, which is another key benefit. I've mentioned some advantages, so let's get the main disadvantages to converting to DNG out of the way. If you convert to DNG

>> You may not be able to open DNG files in some non-Adobe image editing software.

>> You may have problems with certain photo competitions if your camera does not have native DNG creation (always read contest fine print).

>> You may not feel it is worth the time to convert to DNG.

There are tradeoffs involved in every decision you make in photography, and this is just one more of those decisions that you must evaluate against your own needs and circumstances. There is no one right answer.

Types of DNG

There are two basic types of DNG files that you can create in Lightroom Classic. One uses a lossless compression algorithm (best quality option), and the other uses a "lossy" compression algorithm (similar to JPG compression). The key difference between these options is that with the lossy compression option, you can create a DNG file that is smaller in file size than with the lossless compression. In addition, with the lossy compression option, you gain the option of resizing the pixel dimensions smaller as part of the process.

The lossless compression type of DNG is the one that has been around since the start. This is intended to be an archival format for raw photos, so you wouldn't want to lose any image data as part of the conversion process. This lossless type of DNG is the only option available if you choose the Copy as DNG method on the Import window.

The lossy compression type of DNG is a relative newcomer, and it tries to find a middle ground between the reduced file size benefits of the JPG format and the editability of the original raw photo. In some ways you can think of it as a superpowered JPG that allows you to still edit things like camera profile, white balance, and lens profiles with the same options as a raw photo. You can find this as an option when exporting from Lightroom Classic, or choose Library ➪ Convert Photo to DNG to convert original raw files to DNG after import.

TECHNICAL
STUFF

To learn more about all the ways the DNG format appears in a Lightroom Classic workflow, download this free PDF I wrote for *Lightroom Magazine*: www. lightroomers.com/L4D/DNGinWorkflow.pdf.

Converting to DNG

One of the DNG benefits that has been of the greatest value to me over the years is its ability to compress raw data without any loss. This was the original flavor of DNG that was rolled out 14 years ago. I've leveraged the lossless DNG conversion to convert older raw photos simply to reduce file size (in bytes) and gain more space on my drives without losing any raw data. Yes, storage is (relatively) cheap, but I have a long list of other things I'd rather spend money on, and I can't tell you how many Help Desk problems I see every year related to managing multiple drive issues. Here's what I do:

1. **Select the source of the photos I want to convert to DNG in Grid view of the Library module.**

2. **Click the Metadata tab of the Library Filter bar and configure a column to display file type.**

   Click Raw to filter by only the raw photos in your source. You can skip this step if you know you have only raw photos in your source. Select all the raw photos. Refer to Chapter 6 for information on the Library Filter.

3. **Choose Library ⇨ Convert Photos to DNG to open the Convert Photos to DNG dialog, shown in Figure 7-11.**

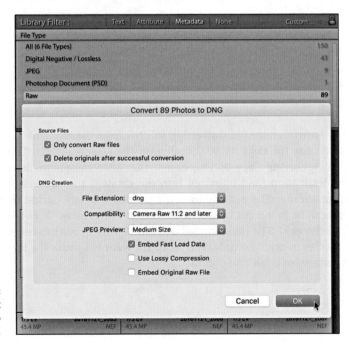

FIGURE 7-11:
The Convert Photos to DNG dialog.

4. **Check the box to only convert raw files.**

   Why bother with the Library filter if the dialog has this check box? Because I want to be in the driver's seat for what happens, and I want to know how many files will be affected before I start.

5. **Decide if you want to check the box to Delete Originals After Successful Conversion.**

   I understand this can be scary. Make sure you have a good backup in place before you do this. My reason for conversion in this instance is to reduce overall file size, so I am opting for deletion of originals after successful conversion so that I am left with only the DNG versions. You need to make the best decision for your workflow.

6. **(Optional) Check the box to Embed Fast Load Data.**

   This embeds a small preview in the DNG file that Lightroom Classic reads first to speed up slider activation in Develop.

7. **Choose your desired file extension and preview size (medium is a good compromise).**

   For this purpose, I leave Use Lossy Compression unchecked because I want to use only lossless compression and retain all my image data. I also opt to leave Embed Original Raw file unchecked because I want to end up with a smaller file size.

8. **Double-check your settings and click OK.**

As that DNG conversion runs you'll see your proprietary raw files replaced with a DNG version. I usually set this to run and walk away to do other things until it is finished.

If you are interested in converting to DNG from the moment of import, then you can choose the Copy as DNG option on the Import screen. This works just like the neighboring Copy option, except that once the photos have been copied to the destination (and imported into the catalog) the conversion to DNG begins automatically. The options to control what happens during that DNG conversion can be found at Lightroom Classic ⇨ Preferences ⇨ File Handling (Edit ⇨ Preferences ⇨ File Handling for Windows). This screen has fewer options because it applies to raw files only. You wouldn't want to choose the lossy DNG option at this stage, so it isn't an option.

Putting Photos on the Map

Having a GPS-enabled camera has become much more common in recent years (look no further than your mobile phone). Visualizing on a map where photos were taken can be both useful and interesting. The Library module has several options to help find and organize photos; location is just one more aspect of that. For that reason, I think of the Map module as basically an extension of the Library module, which is why I've included it in this chapter.

The Map module has two functions. It can show you where photos with geolocation data are located on the map, or it can be used to put photos without geolocation data on the map. Let's take a look around.

Getting oriented to the Map module

The Map module, shown in Figure 7-12, has relatively few panels compared to the other modules, so I just want to highlight what's different here:

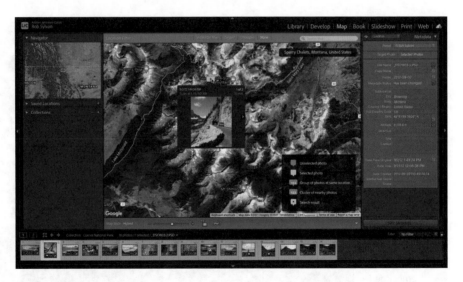

FIGURE 7-12:
The Map module.

>> **Navigator panel:** You can pan the map to move around by clicking and dragging.

>> **Saved Locations panel:** Allows you to quickly and easily apply saved location information to photos via drag and drop.

>> **Content area:** This is an interactive map of the world that requires an Internet connection to view. At the top is the Location Filter that can be used to control what photos are visible in the Filmstrip and allow searching the map for specific locations.

>> **Toolbar:** Provides controls for switching between map views, locking markers on the map, and working with a tracklog.

The Collections panel and Metadata panel are just the same as in the Library module and serve the same purposes. The Filmstrip will be populated with photos from the source you selected.

Map module basics

There are a couple of ways to access the Map module, and some start in the Library module. When looking at thumbnails of your photos in Grid view with thumbnail badges showing (see Figure 7-13), the badge showing a pin is a clickable button that takes you to that photo on the map in the Map module.

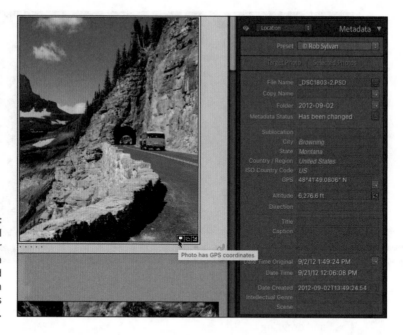

FIGURE 7-13: Thumbnail badge for photos with embedded geolocation data looks like a pin.

Alternatively, if you expand the Metadata panel and select a photo containing geolocation information, you see the coordinates appear in the GPS field. To the right of that field is a clickable arrow button that will take you to that photo on the map.

You can of course simply click the Map button in the Module Picker to switch to the Map module. When you do so, any photos containing geolocation information appear on the map. After you are in the Map module, you can drag and drop photos without geolocation information from the Filmstrip onto the map to apply location information to their metadata.

The Map module is pretty straightforward to use, and the best way to learn it is to see all of these features (and more) in action. Download this free PDF I wrote for *Lightroom Magazine*: `www.lightroomers.com/L4D/MapModule.pdf`. I even demonstrate how to use a tracklog to put your photos on the map if your camera doesn't have GPS functionality.

3

Working in Lightroom Classic's Digital Darkroom

Chapter **8**

Editing Photos in the Develop Module

Welcome to the Develop module! This is where Lightroom Classic's real magic happens. Since its release, Adobe has dedicated a lot of resources toward continually adding new tools and updating the existing features for editing our photos. So much so, the need to send photos to an external editor has been decreased significantly. Because this module has so much to offer, I split the coverage of the Develop module across this chapter through Chapter 10.

In case you are puzzling over the use of the word *develop* here, you need to keep in mind that Lightroom Classic was primarily designed to work with raw photos, which have not yet been processed for final output. So, Lightroom Classic approaches photos with the mindset that photos first need to be *developed* before they are ready to leave Lightroom Classic and face whatever comes next. That's not to say it can't work with non-raw photos, because it absolutely can do that as well. Aside from getting oriented to where everything is in the Develop interface, this chapter focuses on the most common, or essential, Develop tasks before digging deeper in Chapters 9 and 10.

Exploring the Develop Module

At first glance, it's easy to be a little overwhelmed by all the panels, sliders, and buttons in this module. Don't be! The layout is essentially the same as all the other modules. You find the Module Picker across the top; the left side holds the panels that pertain to saved settings (called presets) and different states of your photos; the right side contains all the adjustment controls. In the center, you find the content area and the Toolbar, and the ever-present Filmstrip runs along the bottom. Refer to Chapter 1 for ways to modify the interface to suit your needs.

Getting to know the panels and tools

To know the Develop module is to love it, so go ahead and get acquainted with the interface, shown in Figure 8-1. Here's an overview of what you can find lying about (I omitted elements covered in earlier chapters):

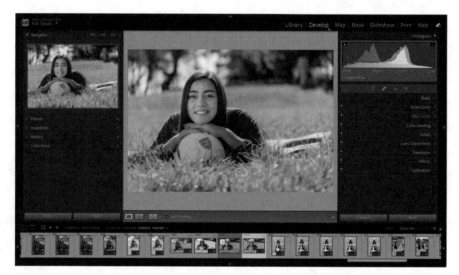

FIGURE 8-1: The Develop module interface.

>> **Navigator panel:** Displays a preview of your presets as you move the cursor over the contents of the Presets panel.

>> **Presets panel:** On the left side, the Presets panel contains all the preinstalled and (soon to be created) custom Develop presets.

>> **Snapshots panel:** A "snapshot" is a means to preserve a specific state in your editing process. Snapshots are great for creating multiple versions of a single file and storing them for easy access later.

>> **History panel:** Still on the left, the History panel records a running history of every tweak and adjustment you make to each photo. This allows for an unlimited "undo" because you can always step back through the Develop history to any point in time.

>> **Copy and Paste buttons:** Allow you to copy and paste Develop settings from one photo to another.

>> **Content area:** This is your workspace, which provides a live preview of the photo you're working on.

>> **Toolbar:** Just below the content area, the Toolbar contains the buttons for switching between view modes, along with additional tools available via the Toolbar drop-down menu for navigating between photos; playing an "impromptu" slideshow; controlling zoom level; and applying flags, ratings, and labels.

>> **Histogram panel:** Provides a way to visualize your image data through an interactive graph of the all the tones contained in the active photo.

>> **Tool Strip:** This is the collection of adjustment-tool icons nested under the Histogram, which include the Crop Overlay, Spot Removal, Red Eye Correction, and Masking tools (all covered in Chapter 9).

>> **Basic panel:** Why basic? Well, you touch these adjustments almost every time you bring a photo into the Develop module. You need to get these settings straight (such as White Balance and Exposure) before you can move on to other tasks.

>> **Tone Curve panel:** This is the best tool for putting the finishing touches on adjusting brightness and contrast.

>> **HSL / Color / BW:** Allows for the tweaking of individual colors as well as adjusting the conversion to B&W (note that the panel will only display BW when you switch the Treatment setting in the Basic panel from Color to Black & White).

>> **Color Grading panel:** Provides the ability to shift the color in the shadows, midtones, and highlights of your photos. This can be used for creative color modifications (on color or B&W photos) or neutralizing color casts.

>> **Detail panel:** Tools for increasing sharpening and reducing noise.

>> **Lens Correction panel:** Contains the options for enabling lens profile corrections and manual controls for removing that annoying purple fringe (that is, *chromatic aberration*).

>> **Transform panel:** The perspective distortion correction suite of tools.

>> **Effects panel:** Used for applying creative darkening (and brightening) to a photo's edges, as well as creative addition of simulated film grain.

>> **Calibration panel:** Provides the ability to switch process versions (the secret sauce for rendering raw photo data), as well as the legacy controls for tweaking your default rendering settings.

Becoming familiar with the menu options

The Lightroom Classic (Mac only) File, Edit, View, Window, and Help menus remain consistent across all modules, but the Develop module also has a dedicated set of menu options. Menus are certainly useful for accessing specific functions, but they also serve to remind you about all the options and their respective keyboard shortcuts. I cover all the functions in their context over the course of the three Develop module chapters, but here's an overview of what you find in the Develop module menus:

>> **Develop:** Contains the commands for creating new snapshots and presets, erasing the contents of the History panel, and navigating between photos.

>> **Photo:** This group of commands pertains to stuff you can do to the active photo, such as adding it to the Target Collection; showing its location; sending it to an external editor; creating virtual copies; rotating and flipping; applying flags, ratings, or labels; writing and reading the metadata stored in the photo; deleting; and more.

>> **Settings:** Provides access to all the commands for copying, pasting, syncing, and applying Develop settings, as well as converting to B&W and some cropping related settings.

>> **Tools:** Here you'll find commands for accessing various Develop tools and any related tool overlays (helpful visual guides).

TIP

You might find it more efficient in many cases to use the contextual menus that appear when you right-click various panels, settings, and photos. Don't be shy — click around and see what you find!

Understanding the view options

Working in the Develop module is obviously a visual process. You can scrutinize every nudge of every slider to get your photos looking how you want. Lightroom Classic offers three view modes (with multiple options) to help you see what you're doing and how far you've come:

>> **Loupe view:** This view is the default working view when you enter the Develop module and is where you will do almost all your work. You can zoom

in or out by clicking the photo, using the controls in the Navigator panel, or the Zoom slider in the Toolbar. You can jump to Loupe view in the Develop module by pressing D no matter where you are in Lightroom Classic.

>> **Reference view:** This is a special working view where you can compare two photos side by side while processing one (the Active photo) to look more like the Reference photo.

>> **Before and After view:** Allows you to switch out of Loupe view for a comparison between the work you've done and the photo you started with. There are several variations on how you can arrange views for comparison to give some choice over which might work best for a given photo. See the "The Before and After views" section in this chapter.

No matter which view you're working in, to cycle through the Info Overlay displays — that little summary of information about the active photo that appears in the content area — press the I key or choose View ➪ Loupe Info. To customize the information shown in the overlay, press ⌘+J (Ctrl+J for Windows).

The Loupe view

Just like in the Library module, the Navigator panel, shown in Figure 8-2, controls the zoom level. The default is Fit (the entire photo fits in the content area), with a zoomed-out level of 100% (as in actual pixel view). You can change the zoom level by clicking the labels in the Navigator panel. When zoomed beyond Fit view, you can pan around the photo by clicking and dragging in the content area or by clicking and dragging inside the Navigator.

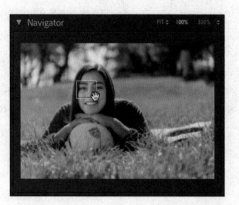

FIGURE 8-2:
The Navigator panel.

The Reference view

You may not use this view as often as the others, but file it away for a situation where you want to see two photos side by side, as shown in Figure 8-3, while you edit one (the Active photo) to look more like the static Reference photo. This could be useful if you shoot JPG + raw and want to compare the JPG as the Reference photo while you edit the raw photo to look similar; or perhaps you have a photo with a certain "look" and want to try to emulate that look on a different photo to give it a similar feel. This makes it easier to match white balance across a set of photos or perhaps create a preset that helps you achieve a certain look.

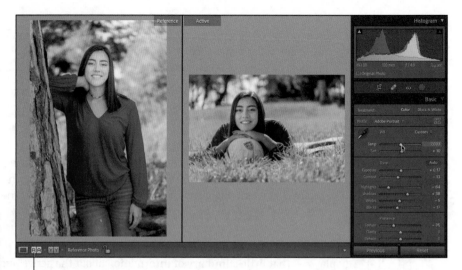

FIGURE 8-3:
The Reference
photo is on the
left, and the
active photo is
on the right. Reference View

Here's how to get started with Reference view from within Develop:

1. **Click the R A button in the Toolbar (or press Shift+R).**

This sets the selected photo as the Active photo. You can choose between Left/
Right and Top/Bottom reference views by clicking the drop-down menu on the
R A button.

2. **Drag and drop a photo from the Filmstrip to the Reference pane to set
the Reference photo.**

You can also right-click a photo and choose Set as Reference Photo from the
contextual menu.

3. **Make any desired adjustments to the Active photo.**

Use any of the adjustments possible to bring the look of the Active photo in
line with the Reference photo. Select any other photo in the Filmstrip to make
it the Active photo and adjust.

4. **Exit Reference view when finished by pressing the D key.**

While not something you're likely to use every day, Reference view is a handy
feature to have if you need it.

The Before and After views

Although much of your work happens in Loupe view, sometimes it's hard to
appreciate how far you've come until you look at where you started. You can compare Before and After views several ways:

>> **Left and Right:** Choose either a side-by-side view of the whole photo showing each state or a split view (shown in Figure 8-4) that shows the Before image on the left and the After image on the right.

>> **Top and Bottom:** Choose to have the Before image on top and the After image on the bottom, or a single photo split between the two views.

>> **Before Only:** This option is great for toggling between Before and After views for a quick peek by pressing the \ key.

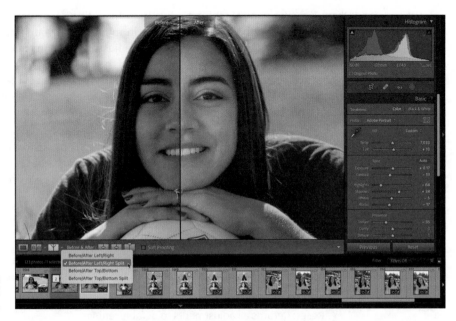

FIGURE 8-4:
Before and
After split view.

REMEMBER

These views aren't just for looking, though! All the adjustment sliders are still active and can be applied while looking at the Before and After views.

You can access all these view options from the button on the Toolbar (or the View menu). *Note:* When you're in Before and After view, three additional icons appear in the Toolbar. (Refer to Figure 8-4.) Here's what they do (from left to right):

>> **Copy Before's Settings to After:** If you want to start over, you can quickly revert your After state's settings to how they were before.

>> **Copy After's Settings to Before:** If you're satisfied with the After state, you can save it as the new Before state so that you can press on with additional edits and have this state to compare against (and revert to).

>> **Swap Before and After Settings:** This is handy if you want to create a new version that goes in a different direction from the original Before state and preserves the current After state for later comparison.

TIP

These commands are also accessible from the View menu and can be applied from the Loupe view, if needed.

Applying settings to other photos

Okay, I'm sure you're itching to dive in to the Editing tools (and you will!), but I really want you to have the big picture in mind before you start pushing sliders around. I promise you'll be knee-deep in adjustments soon enough.

I want to call your attention to the two buttons at the bottom of the left panel group and the two buttons at the bottom of the right panel group. (Refer to Figure 8-1.) Here's what they do:

>> **Copy:** Allows you to copy settings from the active photo so that they can be pasted onto other photos (one at a time). When clicked, the Copy Settings dialog opens (same options as the Synchronize Settings dialog shown in Figure 8-5), allowing you to choose which settings to copy.

>> **Paste:** Applies the copied settings to only to the active photo when clicked. For multiple photos, use Sync/Auto Sync, which I cover in a bit.

>> **Previous:** Applies all the settings from the last photo you worked on to the currently active photo. This button is visible only when you have a single photo selected in the Filmstrip.

>> **Reset:** Returns all adjustments to default settings.

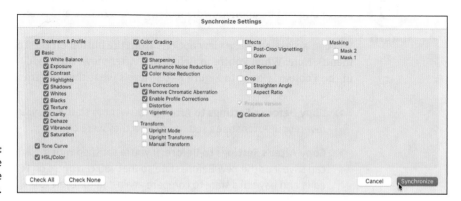

FIGURE 8-5: The Synchronize Settings dialog.

The Copy/Paste function is great when you want to keep a collection of settings ready to be pasted to any single photo when needed. However, when you want to apply a collection of settings across a selection of photos, you need to use either the Sync button or its alter ego, the Auto Sync button.

If you have more than one photo selected, either in the Filmstrip or if you are using the secondary window in Grid view, you notice that the Previous button has changed to Sync. When you click the Sync button, the Synchronize Settings dialog appears, as shown in Figure 8-5. This functions just like the Copy button in that it allows you to choose which settings in the active photo you want to apply, but in this case, the settings are applied to the other photos you select. After checking the boxes next to the settings you want to "sync," click the Synchronize button.

TIP

You can synchronize settings across any number of selected photos, which is most effective when you want to selectively synchronize a subset of settings across multiple photos. If you're in a situation where you have a grouping of photos that you want to process exactly the same way and in real time (almost), you want to change the Sync button to Auto Sync by holding ⌘ (Ctrl key for Windows) and clicking Sync, or click the little button to the left of Sync to flip it to Auto Sync. As soon as you press that key, you see Sync change to Auto Sync — clicking the button makes the transformation complete. After you turn on Auto Sync, every adjustment you make to the active photo is automatically applied to the rest of the selected photos. This is a huge timesaver!

REMEMBER

Here's the catch — once Auto Sync is on, it's on until you turn it off (just click it again without holding any key). I must tell you that I've accidentally autosynced a bunch of files more than once. Fortunately, there's that faithful Undo shortcut, ⌘+Z (Ctrl+Z for Windows)!

Development Essentials

Lightroom Classic's Develop module is both an image processor and an image editor. I'll tell you where I draw the line, but I'll be the first to admit that the distinction has blurred, thanks to Lightroom Classic. When your camera is set to capture in JPG mode, it takes the raw capture data and processes it by using the in-camera settings (such as contrast, saturation, and sharpening) to produce a rendered JPG version of the captured image data. The benefit of shooting JPG is that you're using the camera for both capture and processing, which can certainly be a timesaver. The downside is that the original *raw* capture data is lost after the JPG version is created. If you bring that JPG into Lightroom Classic's Develop module, you're not processing the capture data, but editing the rendered image data. Of course, with Lightroom Classic the actual pixels in the source file are never changed, so technically, only the pixels in exported copies are edited, but I hope you can see the distinction.

Here's why it matters. In contrast to JPG, when you shoot raw, you take the camera out of the processing business. The result is that the camera is primarily a capture device that saves the raw capture data to your memory card. That raw capture data needs to be processed by some type of raw-processing software. I'll assume you're using Lightroom Classic for that task. When you bring a raw photo into Lightroom Classic, you take over the image-processing tasks formerly performed by the camera in the JPG example. You decide how much contrast, saturation, and sharpening (to name just a few settings) are going to be applied to create a rendered version of the photo (during output). The benefit is that you can customize those settings to maximum effect on a photo-by-photo basis, and you never lose the original capture data! You can reprocess the raw data any number of ways. The downside is that you need to add that processing step into your workflow, which takes time.

The reason the line between processing and editing has blurred is that Lightroom Classic can perform a much wider range of adjustments on your photos than any camera could dream of performing. Red-eye removal, cropping, and spot removal used to be tasks that could be done only in a pixel editor (like Photoshop). With the introduction of the Linear Gradient, Radial Gradient, and Brush in earlier versions of Lightroom Classic (now all part of Masking), the line between processing and editing is almost erased.

That said, the place where the rubber meets the road (as far as each Lightroom Classic user is concerned) is that when you bring a rendered file (JPG, TIF, or PSD) into Lightroom Classic, you're working with processed data. Therefore, all the adjustments you make in Lightroom Classic are made relative to whatever processing decisions have previously been made. When you bring a raw file into Lightroom Classic, the adjustments are absolute settings — no prior processing has been done — giving you much more leeway in how you process each photo.

Using the Histogram panel

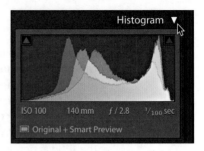

FIGURE 8-6:
The Histogram panel.

The Histogram panel, shown in Figure 8-6, is another way to look at your photo by displaying it as a graph of all the tones it contains. When this information is used in conjunction with the live view of the photo in the content area, it greatly informs the adjustment decisions you make.

Although the actual graph is the same as what is shown in the Library module, the Develop module's Histogram panel has a few additional features:

>> **It's interactive.** When you move your cursor over the Histogram, you see how each area of the Histogram relates to the tonal adjustment sliders in the Basic panel:

- *Blacks:* The far-left end of the graph showing the darkest shadows.

- *Shadows:* The tonal range between the darkest shadows and the midtones.

- *Exposure:* Covers the midtones, from the shadows to the highlights.

- *Highlights:* Moving to the right from the midtones are the brighter set of tones referred to as the highlights.

- *Whites:* The far-right end of the graph showing the brightest highlights.

Similarly, if you place your cursor over each of the tonal adjustment sliders in the Basic panel (except Contrast), you see the respective sections of the Histogram panel brighten. You can click and drag within the Histogram to make tonal adjustments, and when you do so, the respective sliders adjust in tandem. (This is not the best way to edit, but it makes the connection between the graph and sliders.)

>> **It has clipping indicators.** The arrows at either end of the Histogram are white when data in all three channels has been clipped or is a color when only one or two channels are clipped. (Clipping means that pixels in the image have exceeded the tonal range on an end of the Histogram — blacks or whites — and no longer contain any image data.) In some instances, this is okay, such as shadow areas you want to be all black, or bright highlights — reflections of the sun on chrome, for example. Other times, however, clipping isn't nice at all — such as when all the detail in a white wedding dress is lost due to overexposure.

In addition to the Histogram indicators, you can enable a visual clipping indicator that appears in your photo. Press the J key to enable the indicator (or just click the clipping indicator arrows). When enabled, areas that are clipped on the shadow end are shown in blue, and areas clipped on the highlights end are shown in red. Figure 8-7 shows an image with both shadow and highlight clipping.

>> **It's great for RGB readouts.** The photo you see in the content area is made from the image data contained in the Red, Green, and Blue channels of the photo. Lightroom Classic uses a scale that ranges from 0 percent (black) to 100 percent (white).

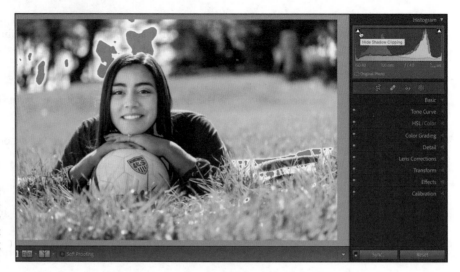

FIGURE 8-7:
An example
of shadow
and highlight
clipping
indicators.

The relationships between the Histogram, the basic tonal adjustments, the clip-ping indicators, and the RGB readouts make the Histogram an important tool for evaluating what's happening in your photos, which is why the Histogram panel remains visible at the top of the right panel group no matter how far down you scroll to the other adjustment panels.

Making basic adjustments

It's almost a given that you're going to be making certain kinds of adjustments to almost all your photos. These adjustments are grouped into five sections in the Basic panel, as shown in Figure 8-8:

>> **Treatment:** Choose between working on a color or B&W photo. All the controls in the Basic panel apply to B&W images as well. I cover B&W conver-sions in Chapter 10.

>> **Profile:** Choosing the profile is similar to choosing an in-camera picture style (such as portrait, landscape, vivid, and neutral) that can have a major impact on color and contrast rendering at a foundational level.

>> **White Balance:** Provides tools you can use to neutralize color casts or to creatively interpret the lighting conditions that existed at the moment of capture. White balance is subjective. Have fun with it.

>> **Tone:** Contains the controls for adjusting the range of tones in the photo. You can set highlight and shadow-clipping levels and adjust midtone brightness levels as well.

>> **Presence:** These controls have a big effect on how people respond to your photo. Texture is brand new and is designed to enhance (in positive amounts)

or smooth (in negative amounts) the contrast of medium-sized areas of detail (think of it as a specialized form of sharpening). The Clarity slider is essentially a midtone contrast adjustment (which can improve apparent depth and sharpness); Dehaze is another type of contrast adjustment (great at correcting atmospheric haze); and Vibrance and Saturation adjust the colors. I go over each in more detail a little further on.

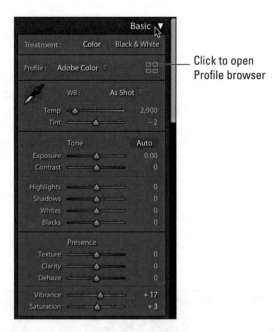

Click to open Profile browser

FIGURE 8-8:
The Basic panel.

With that overview in mind, make your way through the next few sections, where I delve deeper into the Basic panel.

Choosing a starting profile

If you've used previous versions of Lightroom, you might never have known that a camera profile was being applied to all your raw photos, because the setting was buried down in the Calibration panel. One of the first new features added when Lightroom was renamed *Lightroom Classic* was the relocation of profiles to the Basic panel (refer to Figure 8-8) and the expansion of how many profiles you had to choose from. Adobe added so many new profiles they had to also add in a Profile browser, as shown in Figure 8-9, to organize them.

You can open the Profile browser by clicking the button to the right of the Profile drop-down menu (refer to Figure 8-8) or choose Browse from the bottom of that same Profile drop-down menu list.

The contents of the Profile browser are dictated by what type of file (raw or non-raw) is selected, and if a raw photo, by what camera it came from. In Figure 8-9, you are seeing the profiles for a raw photo from a Nikon D850. The Profile browser is divided into at least three sections, but if you've installed third-party profiles, you'd also see a fourth section (in this case the profile group named Sylvanworks, but the name will vary based on who created the profiles). Those main three sections are

>> **Favorites:** You can customize what profiles are shown here, which also determines what profiles are shown in the Profile drop-down menu. Clicking the star on any profile will mark it (or remove it) as a favorite.

>> **Raw / Basic:** When you have a raw photo selected, the next section down will contain various raw profiles organized into subgroups with headings for Adobe Raw, Camera Matching, and Profiles. You may see more or fewer profiles in this area, depending on the camera used to create the raw photo. If you have a non-raw photo selected (PSD, TIF, JPG, or PNG) you will just see a group named Basic that has one profile for color and one for monochrome.

>> **Creative:** The section at the bottom containing groupings for Artistic, B&W, Modern, and Vintage appear for both raw and non-raw photos. These profiles provide for some very creative looks to try.

Amount slider

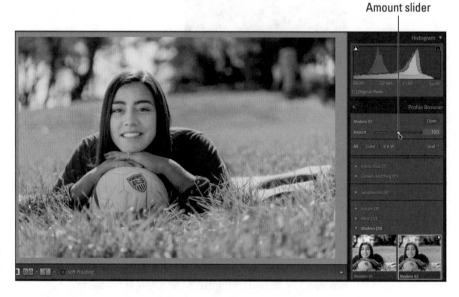

FIGURE 8-9:
The Profile browser.

If you are new to this part of Lightroom Classic, I strongly suggest that you check out all these profiles to get a feel for how they look on your photos. Try some with people photos, try some with landscapes, and try some with whatever other types of photos you have. You can always go back to the default Adobe Color at any time by selecting it or just clicking the Reset button to go all the way back to your default settings. Here's how to explore the Profile browser:

1. **Select the photo you want to edit.**

   Although you can change a profile at any time, you'll get the best results by applying the profile as one of the first things you do.

2. **Expand the Basic panel and click the Profile browser button to see its contents.**

   Remember, the file type of the selected photo will determine what profile groups and what profiles appear in the browser.

3. **Simply move your cursor over profiles to see a live preview in the content area without having to click a profile.**

   Expand each profile group to explore all the options.

4. **Click any profile in the creative group at the bottom to apply the profile and note the Amount slider that appears in the Profile browser (refer to Figure 8-9).**

   Each of the profiles in the Creative section comes with an Amount slider that allows you to tone down (or even turn up) the effect of the profile.

5. **Click the star icon on any profile you want added to the Favorites group.**

6. **Once you've explored all the options, click the profile you want to apply to the selected photo and close the Profile browser.**

That's all there is to applying a profile. Eventually, you'll find that there are just a few you use most often, but it is nice to have options. You can also include profiles in presets that you create, which I cover in Chapter 9.

Controlling color casts

White-balance adjustments — where you attempt to make objects that appeared white when you saw them in person appear white in the finished photo — are subjective. How you process your photos is how you express your vision of the scene that you captured. The color of the light has a big impact on how others react to the image. The choice you make depends, of course, on your vision.

Lightroom Classic offers three methods for adjusting the white balance:

>> **White Balance Selector tool:** This neutralizing tool is in the White Balance section of the Basic panel. You can activate it by pressing W or by clicking the eyedropper-shaped icon. Your goal is to find and select a highlight that is close to being *neutral;* that is, all three RGB values should be pretty close to each other. The Selector tool has a special Loupe — the gridlike object behind the cursor shown in Figure 8-10 — that shows you the pixels and their RGB values under the tool while you move the eyedropper to find the right spot to click. RGB values in the 80s work best, but lower values can work too. Lightroom Classic attempts to neutralize the color cast by adjusting the R, G, and B channels at that location to equal values. When the White Balance Selector tool is active, the Toolbar (under the photo) contains the following options:

- *Auto Dismiss:* By default, the White Balance Selector tool goes away after you click a spot. However, at times, you might want to try sampling multiple locations before manually dismissing the tool. Uncheck this box to stop Auto Dismiss.

- *Show Loupe:* The Loupe is a helpful tool, but you can also see the RGB values appear under the Histogram. Uncheck to turn off.

- *Scale:* Adjusts the size of the grid in the Loupe.

- *Done:* Exits the White Balance Tool. Pressing Esc also works.

White Balance Selector

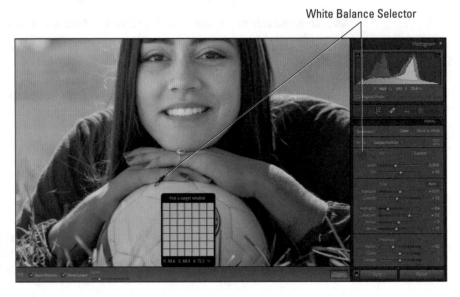

FIGURE 8-10:
The White Balance Selector tool.

>> **White-balance preset:** When working with raw images, you can set the white balance based on the lighting at the time of capture using the appropriate preset or choose Auto to let Lightroom Classic work its magic. The absolute white-balance value has already been set in rendered files (JPG, TIF, or PSD), so your preset options in Lightroom Classic are limited to leaving it as is (As Shot) or letting Lightroom Classic try to adjust automatically (Auto). Custom is displayed if the Selector tool or the Temp and Tint sliders are used to make a manual adjustment.

>> **Temperature and Tint sliders:** Make manual adjustments to the color temperature and its tint. As the colors on the sliders indicate, dragging the Temp slider to the left introduces more blue (cooling the image), and dragging the Temp slider to the right introduces more yellow (warming the image). Similarly, as indicated on the Tint slider, dragging the slider to the left introduces a greenish tint, and dragging it to the right introduces a magenta tint.

Your starting point is always going to be the As Shot setting. If your starting point using the As Shot setting looks good to you, don't feel compelled to continue adjusting. When it doesn't feel right, you need to make some decisions. My preference is to reach for the White Balance Selector tool and attempt to achieve a neutral result, and then, based on the scene, adjust the Temp and Tint sliders until it looks how I think it should. When I'm working on one photo that's part of a series shot under the same lighting conditions, I'll use the Sync button to apply the same setting to those photos as well. After you settle on a white-balance setting that you like, you can move on to making tonal adjustments.

Adjusting tonal range to bring out the best

The tone adjustments in the Basic panel provide you creative freedom to make the most of the settings you used in the camera to capture the image data. I talk about the relationship between the tonal adjustments and the Histogram earlier in this chapter, and now you're going to use all the tools at your disposal. The Tone section of the Basic panel (refer to Figure 8-8) contains the following adjustments:

>> **Auto:** The Auto setting got a complete overhaul recently and works quite well for many photos. Adobe uses Artificial Intelligence and machine learning to do a better job of optimizing the tonal settings based on the photo itself. It can make for a great starting point.

>> **Exposure:** The slider's scale is based on f-stops. Adjustments will affect the entire tonal range, but the biggest impact is on the brightest tones. Adjust as needed to improve overall image brightness. If some highlight clipping occurs, it might be possible to correct with the Highlight slider.

>> **Highlights:** Use this adjustment to recover detail in extreme highlights by reducing highlight values until they are no longer clipped.

>> **Shadows:** Helps to open detail in the light shadow areas with minimal impact on the darkest values (to help keep blacks black).

>> **Whites:** The brightest highlights. Use this slider to determine what areas of the image clip to all white (no detail).

>> **Blacks:** The darkest shadows. Use this slider to determine what areas of the image (if any) to clip to all black (no detail).

>> **Contrast:** Increases or decreases contrast in the image.

How you approach these adjustments largely depends on how well the image was exposed in-camera. Are you compensating for over- or underexposure or just optimizing a proper exposure? Does the scene contain bright highlights as well as dark shadows? This is where you need to make an evaluation based on what you see in the content area (in conjunction with the Histogram) to decide how to get from where you are to where you want to be. Here's a basic workflow you can use:

1. **Evaluate the image.**

   Note problem areas, such as clipped highlights, clipped shadows, and muddy midtones. Think about how you intended the photo to look.

2. **Click Auto in the Tone section.**

   Notice that all the sliders in the Tone section may have changed, as well as Vibrance and Saturation. Re-evaluate the photo and consider tweaking the sliders (as needed) to fine-tune the result.

3. **(Optional) Press J to turn on the clipping indicators.**

   An easy way to see exactly whether any area of the photo is being clipped.

4. **Adjust the Exposure slider.**

   Your goal is to fine-tune the overall image brightness. You can also hold the Option key (Alt for Windows) while you drag the slider to get a view of any image areas that might be clipping.

5. **Adjust the Blacks slider.**

   You always have much less detail in the shadow areas than in the highlights. In many cases, you can create a more-pleasing image by clipping the darkest shadow areas to black. As you can with the Exposure slider, you can hold the Option key (Alt for Windows) while dragging the slider to see just the areas of that are clipping to black.

6. **Adjust the Whites slider.**

   Tweak if needed to set the white point. The Option (Alt for Windows) key works to show clipping here too.

7. **Adjust the Highlights slider.**

   Not every image will need to have the highlights pulled back, but for those that do, the Highlights slider is a fantastic tool. Adjust as needed.

8. **Adjust the Shadows slider to brighten the darker areas of the photo.**

   Many images can benefit from a little bump to open up the shadows.

TIP

A quick way to return any slider to its original state is to double-click its label. Likewise, you can double-click the Tone label above the sliders to reset all sliders in that section. This works for all sliders and sections in Lightroom Classic.

I left out the Contrast slider from that process because I tend to leave it as a "finishing touch" at the end of my developing process, and I prefer the control offered by the Tone Curve panel. There's no one right way to approach this, so if you prefer using the Contrasts slider, do so.

Making images pop

Not every image will need the adjustments in the Presence section, but they make a big impact on the ones that do. However, precisely *because* they can have such a big impact, you need to be careful not to overdo it. With that warning out of the way, take another look at Figure 8-8, casting your eyes to the five sliders in the Presence section of the Basic panel:

>> **Texture:** As you can tell by its name, this adjustment targets the medium-sized texture (detail) in a photo. When moved in a positive direction, this adjustment enhances the texture in a photo (great for landscapes). If moved in a negative direction, this adjustment can be used to smooth out texture (think skin) for a softening effect. Be sure to zoom to 1:1 to better gauge the effect of using this adjustment.

>> **Clarity:** This contrast adjustment is designed to give the image a little oomph. When it was in development, Adobe considered naming it "punch" because that seemed an apt description of its effect. This adjustment is also best applied while zoomed to 1:1 to better gauge its effect on the detail in the image. Use in moderation.

>> **Dehaze:** Another form of contrast adjustment that has been formulated to reduce the impact of atmospheric haze and bring out detail in your landscape photographs. Alternatively, you can move it in a negative direction to add haze to your photo.

>> **Vibrance:** A sophisticated saturation adjustment that mostly affects the less-saturated colors while protecting skin tones and preventing clipping in the most-saturated colors. A great all-around color booster.

>> **Saturation:** Use this slider to adjust the saturation of all colors equally in both directions. Decrease saturation by dragging to the left, and increase saturation by dragging to the right (although increased saturation is not great for skin tones).

TIP

A great starting point for Presence on some photos is contained in the preinstalled Develop preset called Punch. Expand the Presets panel and look under the Classic - General presets group. Just click it one time to apply it to the selected photo and then adjust to taste. All it does is set Clarity to +30 and Vibrance to +25.

Customizing panel order

Before moving on to other panels in Develop, I want to point out a little customization trick hidden under the hood. Adobe gives you the ability to customize the order of the panels on the right side of the Develop module (currently the only place this works). Simply right-click any of the panel headers below the Histogram panel and choose Customize Develop Panel to open an interactive dialog where you can reorder those panels to suit your workflow.

Within the Customize Develop Panel dialog, you simply drag and drop the panels into your desired order. You can even uncheck the box next to a panel and hide that panel completely. I'm so used to the way things are that I'm sticking with the Default order, but feel free to check it out and see if you find it useful. If you change the order, click the Save button, which will prompt you to restart the program to see your changes take effect. You can always return things to normal by invoking the Customize Develop Panel dialog and clicking the Default Order button (and restarting the program).

TIP

While you are looking at the contextual menu that appears when right-clicking a panel header, select Solo Mode to force Lightroom Classic to close any open panel whenever you expand a different panel. This keeps only one adjustment panel open at a time and saves you from having to scroll up and down all the time to find a given slider.

Chapter **9**

Solving Problems and Saving Time

S ometimes the road to making your photos look amazing involves fixing a few problems along the way. Lightroom Classic has a specialized set of tools designed to help you correct a range of issues you might encounter. This chapter covers them, and wraps up with a look at a few panels on the left side of the Develop module that can help you save the adjustments you make as presets, preserve editing states as snapshots, and even go back in time to undo changes.

Fixing Common Problems

Just below the Histogram panel is a collection of editing tools referred to as the Tool Strip, as shown in Figure 9-1. These are often referred to as local correction tools, because they give you the ability to work on isolated areas of the photo rather than just the entire photo (global edits). The Tool Strip contains:

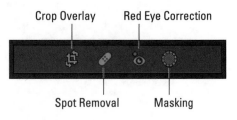

FIGURE 9-1:
The Tool Strip.

>> **Crop Overlay:** Allows for cropping to a specific aspect ratio; it also functions as a straightening tool.

>> **Spot Removal:** Functions similarly to the Clone and Heal tools in Photoshop, which primarily allow for the basic removal of sensor spots and skin blemishes by borrowing pixels from another part of the image.

>> **Red Eye Correction:** Handy for those times when you just had to use on-camera flash for people or pets.

>> **Masking:** Formerly known as the Graduated Filter, Radial Filter, and Adjustment Brush, these tools have been revamped into what is now known as Masking. All the original tools are still there (though their names changed a little), but they've gained new functionality, a new interface, and companion tools for making selections based on subject, the sky, color, luminance, and depth.

Need some practical tips on how to use all these tools? Read on.

Stronger compositions through cropping

Cropping in-camera might be the goal, but it isn't always the reality. However, even if you do get it "right" in-camera, there might still be occasions where you need to produce an image with an aspect ratio different from the aspect ratio of the original photo. The only way to change the aspect ratio is to crop. The Crop Overlay tool provides both a means for practical corrections as well as creative composition adjustments.

It's worth mentioning that the histogram always reflects the area of the photo inside the crop rectangle. In some cases, you might want to make cropping your first adjustment. This way, the histogram reflects just the data you are keeping and, therefore, be more accurate when making tonal adjustments.

TIP

You can jump into the Crop tool by clicking its icon in the Tool Strip, but I prefer using the keyboard shortcut R because it works in any module. This is especially handy after applying a crop to a batch of photos via Quick Develop in the Library module — press R to jump into Crop to finesse each photo.

As soon as you press R, the Crop Overlay appears over the photo and the following cropping options appear in the Tool Strip, as shown in Figure 9-2:

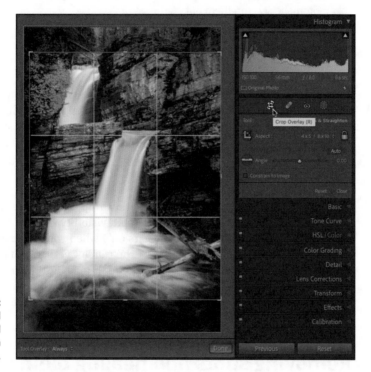

FIGURE 9-2:
The Crop tool being used to change an aspect ratio.

>> **Crop Frame Tool:** Click the icon next to Aspect to draw a cropping rectangle as an alternative to readjusting the resizing handles.

>> **Aspect Ratio drop-down menu:** Access a list of preinstalled aspect ratios or create a custom aspect ratio.

>> **Aspect Ratio Lock:** When closed, the crop rectangle can be resized, but the aspect ratio will not change. When open, you can resize and change aspect ratio as needed. Press A to toggle between open and closed.

>> **Straighten Tool:** Allows for quick straightening. Select the tool (the icon next to Angle) and then click and drag along any straight line in the photo that should be either vertical or horizontal. When you release the mouse, the photo rotates accordingly.

>> **Auto button:** If your photo has a crooked horizon, give the Auto button a click to see if Lightroom Classic can straighten it automatically for you.

>> **Angle slider:** Click and drag to rotate a photo. Click the slider handle once and use the left/right arrow keys to nudge the rotation, or click into the number field and use the Up/Down arrow keys for finer control.

>> **Constrain to Image:** If you've performed a perspective distortion correction that left empty pixels along the edges of your photo, you can check this box to automatically crop them out.

>> **Reset:** Returns the image to its uncropped state.

>> **Close:** Click to exit the Crop Overlay. (I prefer to simply press D.)

REMEMBER

Notice the crop rectangle, its resize handles, and a guide overlay inside the content area. You can resize and reshape the crop rectangle as desired, but you have to move the actual photo to reposition it behind the overlay. In other words, you can grab any resize handle to change the crop rectangle, but you need to click and drag the photo to move it to a new position. If you click and drag outside the crop rectangle, you can rotate the photo.

Note that the Toolbar contains a Tool Overlay drop-down menu that controls the visibility of the crop guide overlay. By default, visibility is set to Always, but when set to Auto the crop guide overlay appears only when you resize or reposition the crop rectangle. If you choose Tools ⇨ Crop Guide Overlay, you can then choose from any of the overlay options to assist you in making the strongest composition. Pay special attention to the keyboard shortcut for cycling through the various overlays (O) for ease of use. The Done button in the Toolbar is another option for committing the crop and exiting the tool.

Removing spots and healing blemishes

Undoubtedly, you will encounter photos that contain something you want to remove, the most common things being spots caused by dust on your sensor or blemishes in a subject's skin. Lightroom Classic comes to your aid in this regard with the Spot Removal tool, as shown in Figure 9-3. You can access the Spot Removal tool by clicking its icon in the Tool Strip or by pressing Q. When activated, you see the following Brush options:

>> **Clone/Heal:** This setting determines the behavior of the brush. The Clone brush simply takes pixels from one area and pastes them into another. The Heal brush borrows pixels from a different area but goes a step further by sampling the color and texture of the area you are "healing" and attempting to blend the two. Heal usually works best.

>> **Size:** Adjusts the size of the brush. Use the [key to decrease the size and the] key to increase the size.

>> **Feather:** Use this to soften the edge of your brush to better blend the repair with the background. The higher the number the softer the edge.

>> **Opacity:** Controls the strength of the brush. The lower the number, the more the original spot will show through the adjustment. Helpful when you only want to deemphasize an area instead of removing it.

>> **On/Off button:** That little light-switch-like button in the bottom left corner of the panel can be used to toggle the results of the tool on and off for comparison purposes.

>> **Reset:** Clears all spot-removal points.

>> **Close:** Click to exit the tool.

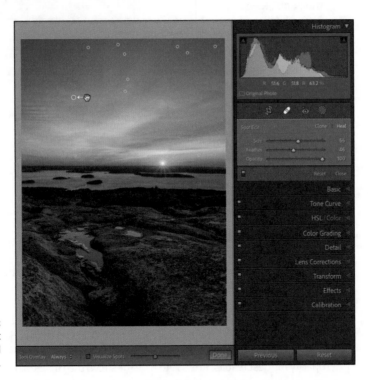

FIGURE 9-3:
The Spot Removal tool panel.

To see how this tool works, follow along as I clean up some sensor spots on a photo, as shown in Figure 9-4:

1. **Select the photo in Grid view and press Q to jump to the Spot Removal tool in Develop — if you're not there already.**

2. **Choose either Heal or Clone.**

   Heal is the most common choice because it does the best job of blending the new pixels with the surrounding area.

3. **Size the brush as needed with the [and] keys.**

4. **Set the Opacity slider to 100.**

5. **Check the Visualize Spots check box in the Toolbar to help you find the pesky spots (refer to Figure 9-4).**

   This black and white mode is designed to make spots easy to, um, spot. You can adjust the associated slider to the right to make spots more visible. Press the spacebar and click on the photo to zoom in.

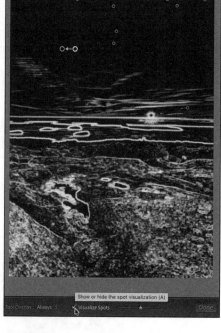

FIGURE 9-4:
Removing sensor spots with Visualize Spots enabled.

6. **Single-click a spot to have Lightroom Classic apply a correction.**

   The moment you click, a circle will appear over the spot you clicked, with a line connecting it to another circle over the location where it chose for sampling the correction. Press the forward slash (/) key to force it to find a better source if needed.

7. **Adjust source and target circles as needed for best results.**

   After you apply the brush to the area, you can click and drag either circle to reposition as needed. Use the sliders to adjust the brush size, feather, and opacity for best results. Press H to hide (or show) the circles. Simply single-click any existing circle to readjust that correction.

8. **Repeat as needed until all spots are gone.**

9. **Press Q to accept the change and exit the tool.**

You can go back later and readjust if needed because this is a completely nondestructive adjustment. You can delete an active circle by pressing the Delete key (Backspace for Windows).

This is the most common type of use for the Spot Removal brush, but in a pinch, it can be used to remove larger distractions too. In truth, Photoshop provides a far better suite of tools for retouching and removing distractions larger than a sensor spot. That said, if you want to see what can be done in Lightroom Classic, simply paint with the brush over the area you want to remove (rather than single-click), and it will automatically attempt to find a sample in the photo to use for removing the area you brushed (and just like with spots, you can adjust the sample area for better results).

It works the same way as it did for spots; it just uses a larger area of the photo. For example, you could successfully use it to remove a piece of trash from the middle of a grassy field because there is likely to be a lot of open grass in the field for it to sample, but you probably wouldn't have the same success when trying to remove your ex from that vacation photo you took years ago (but you could in Photoshop).

Correcting red-eye problems

Although the dreaded red-eye is always best avoided at the moment of capture, it's still great to remove it with minimum hassle when it's encountered. There isn't much to see with this tool until you apply it to an eye. Once applied, it is in Edit mode and you have the following options:

>> **Pupil Size:** Adjusts the size of the affected area inside the pupil.

>> **Darken:** Darkens or lightens the affected pupil.

>> **On/Off button:** That little button in the bottom left corner of the panel can be used to toggle the results of the tool on and off.

>> **Reset:** Clears all red-eye correction spots.

>> **Close:** Exits from the Red Eye Correction tool.

Applying the correction is pretty straightforward. Here's what you do to fix the red-eyed cutie in Figure 9-5:

1. Select the photo in Grid view and press D to jump to Develop.

2. Click the Red Eye Correction tool icon in the Tool Strip.

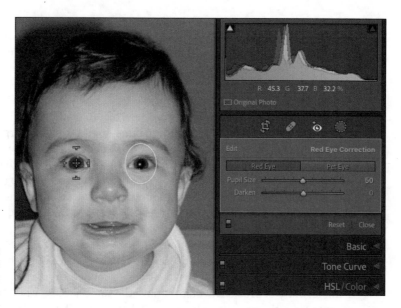

FIGURE 9-5:
The Red Eye
Correction
tool.

3. **Click the first eye, then adjust the size of the tool to exceed the size of the eye.**

   You can control the tool's size with the [and] keys or by simply clicking and dragging until you reach the desired size. Press and hold the spacebar to zoom in for a closer look if needed.

   After you release the mouse, Lightroom Classic moves to Edit mode, analyzing the area and finding the "red" that needs to be removed. You're just telling Lightroom Classic where to look.

4. **In Edit mode, adjust the Pupil Size and Darken sliders as needed for best results.**

   You just have to eyeball this one (sorry!).

5. **Repeat for the other eye.**

6. **Click the Close button or the Done button to exit.**

Correcting pet eye problems

Pets have eyes too! Sometimes Fido gets in the shot, and the flash from your camera reflects off the back of his eyes in a way that makes it appear as though he has lasers blasting from his pupils. That's known as *pet eye*, and the Red Eye Correction tool has a Pet Eye mode for just that occasion.

After you click the Pet Eye button (within the Red Eye Correction tool), the operation is essentially the same as I outline for people. The exceptions are that you can't control the Darken amount, and you have an option to add a fake catch-light (that little highlight reflecting the light in someone's eyes), as shown in Figure 9-6. You'll know right away if the fake catchlight helps or not, so give it a shot. There was already a natural catchlight present here, so I left the box unchecked. If you do add one, you can click and drag it to reposition within the darkened area.

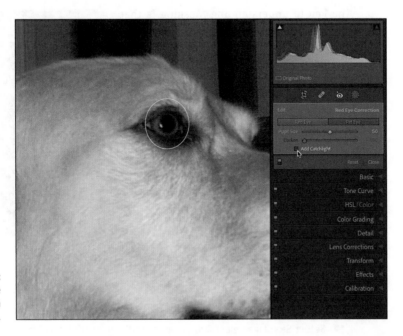

REMEMBER

In a typical workflow, you want to always perform all your global (entire photo) adjustments first, which aside from the adjustments in the Basic panel may also include some or all of the other adjustment panels below it, before you start using the Masking tools. However, because we're already looking at the contents of the Tool Strip, I'm going to cover these tools now.

Get oriented to Masking

The revamped Masking tool represents one of the biggest and most power-ful changes to Lightroom Classic in years. If you've used an older version of Lightroom Classic you may find this new interface disorienting, but once you get aquainted with what it has to offer, I think you're going to be amazed at what you can accomplish.

If you've ever shot with a graduated neutral density filter to properly expose a photo containing a bright sky and darker land, you'll appreciate what Lightroom

Classic's Masking is trying to do. However, unlike the actual filter that goes in front of your lens, Masking allows you to adjust exposure, contrast, saturation, clarity, sharpness, and more, after the photo has been taken! You might find yourself using the real filter less and less. However, Masking goes way beyond just the Linear Gradient tool by providing seven other ways to select a specific area of the photo that you want to adjust without affecting other areas.

The key to understanding Masking is that the first step involves choosing the type of mask you want to add. From there you apply the mask to the photo, refine the mask to cover the area you want to adjust, and then dial-in the settings needed to achieve the desired result. It may sound complicated, but it makes more sense when you start to put it to work. To open the Masking panel, click the Masking icon in the Tool Strip or use one of the keyboard shortcuts shown to open the panel and activate a specific Masking tool (refer to Figure 9-7). The Mask types are as follows:

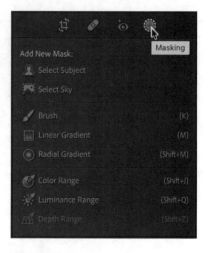

FIGURE 9-7:
The Masking panel.

>> **Select Subject:** Using the power of Adobe Sensei (Adobe's AI and machine learning technology), you can select the subject of your photo with a single click.

>> **Select Sky:** Like Select Subject except this tool can detect and select the sky in a photo.

>> **Brush:** Provides the ability to "paint" with multiple adjustment settings. Think of it as a Dodge and Burn tool on steroids! A good example is the application of additional sharpening to the eyes in a portrait without sharpening the surrounding skin, but that just scratches the surface of what this tool can do.

>> **Linear Gradient:** Enables the application of multiple adjustment settings in a user-controlled gradual fade across any area of the photo. For example, you can correct an overcast sky by applying a gradual exposure compensation and saturation boost to just the sky and having it fade naturally at the horizon.

>> **Radial Gradient:** Enables the application of multiple adjustments in a user-controlled oval-shaped fade in any area of the photo. For example, you can brighten a person's face by drawing an oval Radial gradient around it, and then increasing exposure within the inner area of the oval.

>> **Color Range:** Create a selection based on a range of colors within the photo.

>> **Luminance Range:** Create a selection based on a range of brightness values within the photo.

>> **Depth Range:** Use the depth map embedded in photos taken by some mobile devices to create a selection based on distance from the camera.

Each of these types of masks can be used alone or in any combination of other types of masks. For example, to edit a portrait you might start with Select Subject to select the person, and then use the Brush to subtract or add to that original mask to include just the areas of the photo you want to adjust. Additionally, each of these mask types can be inverted, so perhaps you would start with Select Sky to leverage the power of Adobe Sensei to make the initial selection, and then invert that mask to select the foreground instead to make an adjustment. Let's go through the process of applying a Linear Gradient mask to start to see how these work in practice and get familiar with other parts of the interface that will appear when any mask type is applied.

Applying a mask

Once you activate the type of mask you want to use, the interface changes to reveal a panel containing all the masks you can apply, a panel containing all the settings you can use to adjust the masked area, and a panel specific to the type of mask being used. Refer to Figure 9-8 to see these panels in the context of applying a Linear Gradient to a 50% gray background to better see the affected area. For this example, we're using the Linear Gradient to show the interface changes common to all mask types. To apply the initial mask, with the Masking panel open, click the Linear Gradient tool to activate it (or press M as shown in the panel). Once enabled, the interface changes as follows:

>> **Masks:** The floating Masks panel contains all masks applied to the photo, as well as the tools for controlling the color overlay, a button for creating new masks, and functionality for renaming masks (click the three-dot menu next to mask) and controlling their visibility. You can reposition the Masks panel anywhere within the content area or dock it below the Tool Strip by dragging and dropping it into position. Click the question mark icon at the top right of the panel (highly recommended) to access additional Masking help and a list of all Masking shortcuts.

>> **Tool-specific panel:** The contents of this area depends on the type of mask that is active. In this case, it provides a check box to invert the Linear Gradient.

>> **Effect:** Contains all the settings you can use, alone or in tandem, to achieve your desired results. The drop-down menu contains existing and custom Masking presets, which allow you to save specific settings for reuse (these are shared among all Masking tools). The disclosure triangle to the right of the

Effect drop-down menu controls which Effect mode you're in (when the triangle points down you access all sliders individually, but when clicked to point left, all sliders collapse into a single Amount slider, allowing you to fine-tune the dialed-in settings as one). Note that you can quickly reset all sliders by double-clicking the word Effect, and that there is a Reset Sliders Automatically check box that resets all sliders each time a new mask is applied (checked by default).

>> **On/Off:** Click the On/Off toggle button at the bottom to disable the results of the adjustment. Good for a quick comparison to how things looked before. Click the Delete All Masks button to clear all masks at once.

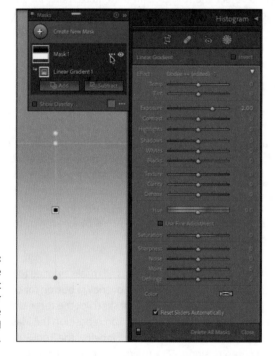

FIGURE 9-8:
Note the panels that appear after a mask type is applied to a photo.

The actual Linear Gradient is represented by the three lines shown in Figure 9-8. The space between the lines is where the gradual adjustment takes place. The way to apply it is to click into the photo where you want the fading of the effect to begin and drag toward the area you don't want affected by the settings. In the 50% gray test image, I initially clicked where the bottom line appears and dragged upward (with +2 Exposure dialed in). The result is that the area below where I clicked got the maximum effect of the settings, the space between the guide lines was gradually faded, and the area above the mask was unchanged.

TIP

When placing a Linear Gradient, you can click and drag in any direction. I encourage you to grab a photo and just play with this tool until you get a good feel for how it works. After you apply the mask, you can increase and decrease the fade area by clicking and dragging either outside guideline or move the entire mask by clicking and dragging the Edit pin — the icon with the black center. You can even rotate the filter by clicking and dragging the center line. Hold the Shift key when you first apply the filter to prevent any rotation and to achieve a perfectly horizontal or vertical line. You can apply multiple masks (of any type) and readjust at any time simply by selecting the desired mask in the Masks panel or its corresponding pin on the photo. Press Delete (Backspace for Windows) to delete a selected pin and the associated mask.

TIP

If you place your cursor over a pin, the affected area is masked to show you where your adjustment will be applied. This is especially helpful with subtle adjustments. The mask vanishes when you move away from the pin. Press Shift+O while the mask is on to cycle through white, black, red, and green highlight colors (which may help you see it better based on the colors in the photo you are adjusting). This works the same with the other mask types. You can also press O to show (or hide) the mask.

Putting the tool to use

The best way to explain this tool is with an example. Looking at the Before view of the photo (top) in Figure 9-9 shows without the Linear Gradient, and the After view (bottom) shows with it. My goal was to add more contrast to the sky without affecting the foreground. Here's how:

1. **Select a photo in Grid view and press D to jump to Develop.**

2. **Press M or click the Linear Gradient icon in the Masking panel.**

   You can even press M from Grid view to jump right to the Masking interface.

3. **Set Show Edit Pins to Auto and Overlay Mode to Color Overlay in the Toolbar.**

4. **Click and drag toward the area you don't want affected by the mask.**

   This is a crucial step. In this example, I don't want to affect the foreground with my adjustments, so I click right below the horizon line and drag downward. Everything above the point I click gets the maximum effect of the adjustment. The effect is gradually faded in the space between where I start dragging and where I stop. The area below where I stop is completely unaffected.

5. **Adjust mask position and size as needed.**

   Don't worry if you didn't click and drag in just the right spot the first time. You can resize, rotate, and reposition the mask as needed.

6. **Adjust Effect settings as needed.**

As soon as you start moving an adjustment slider, the color overlay vanishes automatically. In this example, I used Exposure, Dehaze, Contrast, and Clarity to make the sky and mountains more dramatic. Using a combination of settings in Masking is part of what makes it so powerful.

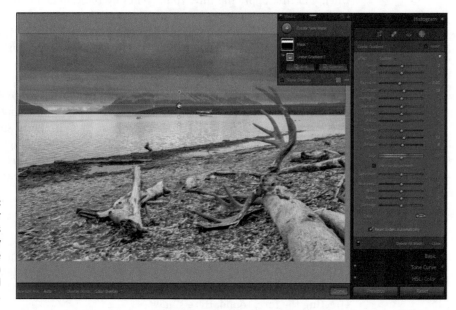

FIGURE 9-9: The Linear Gradient is affecting only the area above the horizon in a gradual transition.

Adding to or subtracting from a mask

But that's not all! Sometimes you can apply a mask and have it affect only the desired region, but other times you may find that you want to fine-tune your mask to avoid affecting certain things (like the trees and moose antlers in Figure 9-9 that protrude above the horizon), and that's where the ability to add or subtract comes into play.

Note that you can use any of the other mask types to add or subtract from a mask, which is essentially enabling one type of mask to edit another. For this photo I'll use a Color Range mask to subtract from my Linear Gradient to exclude the moose antlers and trees from being affected by the adjustment. The basic process of adding or subtracting from a mask is the same regardless of the mask type.

1. **Select the mask you want to add/subtract in the Masks panel.**

2. **Click the Add button to add to the mask or the Subtract button to subtract from the mask, and then choose the mask type you want to use to perform that task from the pop-up menu that appears.**

For my photo I chose subtract from mask with Color Range to subtract a specific range of color from within the existing mask. This adds the new mask type to the Masks panel, with a plus or minus sign to indicate add or subtract (refer to Figure 9-10).

3. **Configure the parameters of the new mask type to refine the existing mask as desired.**

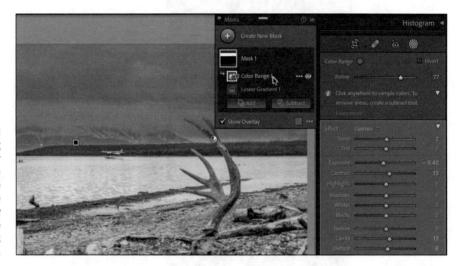

FIGURE 9-10: Subtracting from a Linear Gradient with a Color Range mask. The red overlay shows where the mask will affect.

How you configure the parameters of the new mask depends on the type of mask you select. Let's take a closer look at the panels specific to Color Range, Luminance Range, and Depth Range together because they each have unique controls in a similar interface. Before diving into these mask types I want to stress that they can each be used completely on their own as well as in combination with another mask.

Selecting Color Range changes the cursor to the Color Range Selector tool and displays the associated Refine slider in the Color Range panel that appears, as shown at the top of Figure 9-11. Click the Color Range Selector on the color in your photo you want to use to limit the range of the mask. Hold the Shift key while clicking to add up to five sample points, or click-drag at first to include a wider range of hues. Adjust the Refine slider to the left to limit the range or to the right to increase the range. Press O to enable the mask overlay to see how the mask is constrained.

Selecting Luminance Range changes the cursor to the Luminance Range Selector tool and displays the associated Range and Falloff sliders, as shown in the center of Figure 9-11. Click the Luminance Range Selector tool on the area in your photo that represents the brightness values you want to use to limit the range of the mask. Once clicked, the Range slider changes to reflect the range of tones selected. Adjust the range to include or exclude tonal values; then adjust the Falloff sliders on either end of the range to further refine the smoothness of the area affected by the mask. Check the Show Luminance Map box to see a grayscale representation of the brightness values in the photo as a visual aid for selecting the desired tones.

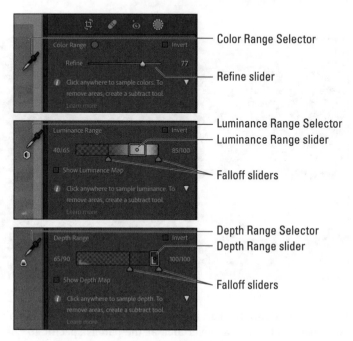

Color Range Selector

Refine slider

Luminance Range Selector
Luminance Range slider

Falloff sliders

Depth Range Selector
Depth Range slider

Falloff sliders

FIGURE 9-11:
From top to bottom: Color Range, Luminance Range, and Depth Range options.

The Depth Range mask will only be available when a photo with a compatible depth map is selected. If this option is grayed out, then Lightroom Classic doesn't support the depth map embedded in the selected photo or there isn't one. (At the time of this writing, this feature works only with photos from iPhones with dual lenses shooting in HEIC format.) Once selected, it changes the cursor to the Depth Range Selector tool and displays the associated Range and Falloff sliders, as shown at the bottom of Figure 9-11. Click the Depth Range Selector tool on the area in your photo you want to use to limit the range of the mask based on how far that is from the camera. Once clicked, the Range slider will change to reflect the depth selected. Adjust the range to include or exclude regions closer or further from the camera; then adjust the Falloff sliders on either end of the range to further refine the area affected by the mask. Check the Show Depth Map box to see a grayscale representation of the depth map embedded in the photo as a visual aid for selecting the desired regions. I've made an HEIC photo with a depth map available for exploring the Depth option if you'd like to try it out: www. lightroomers.com/L4D/Depth.zip.

You may be wondering about Select Sky and why didn't I use that to create the initial mask in the photo of the Alaskan lake? The sole reason was that I wanted that gradual fade toward the horizon that only the Linear Gradient can provide. However, you will undoubtedly encounter photos where having a circular filter works better than the Linear Gradient. That's where the Linear Gradient's very close relative, the Radial Gradient, comes in handy. The only real difference between the two filters is its shape, so I'm going to skip a rehash of the sliders and options in the panel and just highlight where it is different.

Radial Gradient

As I mention at the end of the previous section, the Radial Gradient shares the same panel and options as the Linear Gradient with exceptions related to controlling the fade from the edge and whether you are applying the settings to the inside or outside of the oval. Figure 9-12 shows all the same sliders as before, but at the top is a section with a Feather slider and Invert check box.

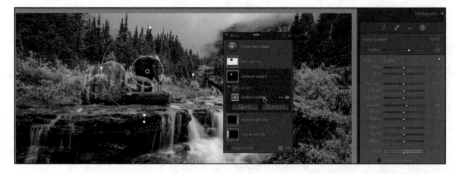

FIGURE 9-12:
The Radial
Gradient.

You can access the Radial Gradient by clicking its icon in the Masking panel or by pressing Shift+M from the Library or Develop. After you enable the Radial Gradient, click the photo and drag outward to create the oval that defines the area you are adjusting. You can use the O key shortcut to see the mask overlaying the affected area (if not already showing). If the mask is on the inside of the circle and you want to adjust the outside of the circle, check the Invert box to swap regions (or vice versa). You can click the center pin and move the Radial Filter as needed to the desired position, and you can click and drag the outside edge to resize or even rotate the filter. If needed, hold the Shift key while dragging out a filter to constrain to a circle.

I use this type of mask for things like adding a custom off-center vignette, adding small "pools of light" to draw the viewer's eye around a photo, adding sharpening to a subject's eyes (very subtle), and so on. Right-click a pin to see a contextual menu of other useful options. It is incredibly versatile and can be used in conjunction with any of the other mask types, or on its own.

Brush

If you thought the Linear and Radial Gradients were cool, your jaw will hit the floor when you get to know the Brush. It works in essentially the same way, except that you use a brush to paint on the effects with a great deal of control as opposed to drawing out an oval or linear gradient. Just like the other two local adjustment tools, the Brush allows you to paint with any combination of exposure, contrast, saturation, clarity, sharpness, and so on. This allows for an amazing level of local adjustment possibilities!

To activate the Brush, you click its icon in the Masking panel or select your photo and press K from the Library or Develop. When the Brush is active, you see its settings appear below the Tool Strip. The settings are the same as with the gradient masks with the following exceptions, due to its being a brush:

>> **Brush:** Controls the brush settings. You can't adjust any of these settings after the effect is applied, so you want to get this right before you start. Here are the options:

- *A/B:* You can configure two different brush settings to make switching between favored settings easier.

- *Erase:* Allows you to "paint" with an eraser to clean up stray strokes. You can click the Erase button to activate or you can hold down Option (Alt for Windows) while painting. **Note:** The Brush cursor switches from a + to a – when Erase is enabled.

- *Size:* Brush size can also be adjusted by pressing the [and] keys.

- *Feather:* Adjusts the softness of the edge of the brush. Can also be adjusted by holding down Shift in conjunction with the [and] keys.

- *Flow:* A low flow amount allows you to build up the effect slowly with each stroke. A high flow amount applies more of the effect with each stroke.

- *Density:* Limits the strength of the effect.

- Auto Mask: When this box is checked, Lightroom Classic attempts to detect the edges of the object you're painting to prevent the effect from spilling over the edge and affecting other areas. The clearer the edge, the better Auto Mask works.

When you first apply a brush stroke to your photo, Lightroom Classic marks the first spot of contact with an Edit "pin," as shown in Figure 9-13. You can click and release as often as needed to continue brushing the effect to other areas of your photo. All your painting continues to be associated with that original Edit pin until you deactivate the Brush or decide to create a new mask. At any point, you can activate an Edit pin by clicking it once to adjust the settings applied by the associated strokes. The settings panel highlights when you're in Edit mode to show you what settings can still be adjusted. Click the Done button in the Toolbar or press K to commit the edit and exit the tool.

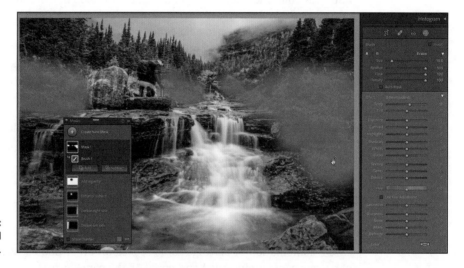

FIGURE 9-13: Brush and Edit pin.

Select Subject and Select Sky

Yes, I saved the best for last. More and more we are seeing Adobe Sensei–powered technologies make their way into various Adobe software, and why not? Subject detection and selection is a perfect job for a machine-learning algorithm to be used to do the heavy lifting and allow us to finesse the final results. Unlike the other Masking tools, there are no special controls within these options. If you have a photo with a prominent subject (like the photo on the cover of this book) and you want to select that subject, simply click the Select Subject button and let Lightroom Classic do all the work. The more clearly defined the main subject is, the better the results will be. The same is true for Select Sky, if there is a recognizable sky in your photo, then click the Select Sky button to select it in one move. I've been consistently impressed with the results of each of these options, and thanks to the ability to improve masks by adding or subtracting with other mask types, we've gained an incredible amount of control for selectively editing areas of our photos that we'd previously only be able to do in Photoshop.

TIP

Head over to lightroomkillertips.com/intersect-mask to learn how to use the powerful Intersect feature, then search the tutorials to see more examples of all these local adjustment and Masking tools in action.

Presets, Snapshots, and History

Understanding how the Presets, Snapshots, and History panels function greatly improves your understanding of how all the Develop module settings are applied.

REMEMBER

Lightroom Classic is a *metadata editor,* which means that every adjustment you make is recorded as a set of instructions to be applied during some form of output. You see a live preview of the changes you make, but it's just that, a preview. None of the changes actually "happen" until you do something, such as export a copy or print.

The Presets, Snapshots, and History panels allow you to interact with the set of instructions Lightroom Classic comes up with in some cool ways. The next few sections fill you in on the details.

Saving time with presets

The Presets panel, located on the left side of the Develop module, is where you can save a combination of settings to be reused on other photos. Various groupings of presets come preinstalled and populate the panel at first. Any new presets you create (see the next section) are going to be stored under the User Presets section by default, or you can create new folders to store them.

Creating your own presets

Because a preset is simply a combination of settings pulled from the active photo, the first thing you need to do is apply some adjustments to said photo. After you take care of that business, here's how you save those adjustments as a new preset:

1. **Click the + icon at the top of the Presets panel and choose Create Preset.**

   Doing so launches the New Develop Preset dialog, shown in Figure 9-14.

2. **Enter a name for your new preset in the Preset Name field.**

3. **(Optional) Click the Group drop-down menu to choose where to place the preset.**

This step is optional because all presets are placed in the User Presets folder by default. You only need to change the location if you want them somewhere else. That said, at the time of this writing this is the *easiest* way to create a new preset group.

4. **Check the box next to each setting you want to include in the preset.**

The Check All and Check None buttons at the bottom of the dialog can speed the selection process.

5. **Click Create.**

The new preset appears in the Presets panel within the group you select.

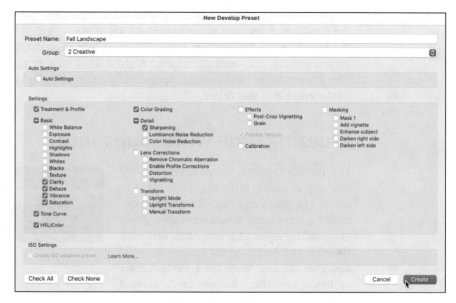

FIGURE 9-14: The New Develop Preset dialog.

Move your cursor over any preset to see a preview of its effect in the Navigator panel and the main content area. If you find the live preview in the content area to be distracting, you can go to the Performance tab of the Preferences and uncheck Enable Hover Preview of Presets in Loupe to disable it. Additionally, if you find some presets are missing from the panel, go to the Presets tab and check Show Partially Compatible Develop Presets to keep them from being hidden.

TIP

If you realize you forgot to add a particular setting or made a new adjustment and want to add it to the preset, just right-click the preset and choose Update with Current Settings from the contextual menu that appears. This launches the Update Develop Preset dialog (which is the spitting image of the New Develop Preset dialog). Check and uncheck desired settings and click Update.

Managing your presets

While the preinstalled presets are useful learning tools, you may find that they can clutter up the panel after you start creating your own custom preset groups. You can hide any preset group you no longer want to see by clicking the + icon at the top of the Presets panel and choosing Manage Presets. When the Manage Presets dialog appears, simply uncheck any group you no longer want to see in the panel (you can always come back and show them again).

Once you've started creating your own custom groups, you'll be able to drag and drop custom presets between them to keep them organized. For any frequently used presets (that goes for preinstalled presets too) consider marking them as a favorite by right-clicking and choosing Add to Favorites, which puts them in that special Favorites grouping that appears at the top of the list. (You may not see the group until you add some favorites.) To delete a custom preset, right-click the preset in the Presets panel and choose Delete. (You can't delete the preinstalled presets, only hide the group.) Right-click a custom preset folder (or the User Presets folder) and choose Import to import presets you've downloaded from the Internet into that folder.

Freezing time with snapshots

The Snapshots panel, shown in Figure 9-15, is a way to collect different states (or versions) of a photo and store them so you can revisit a state later. Whatever state a photo is in can be saved as a snapshot. Just click the + icon at the top of the Snapshots panel and give the new snapshot a name. Create as many snapshots as you need. Moving your cursor over the snapshots shows a live preview in the Navigator panel.

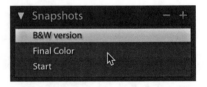

FIGURE 9-15:
The Snapshots panel.

TIP

If you make additional tweaks after saving a snapshot and like that version better, right-click the snapshot and choose Update with Current Settings from the contextual menu that appears. You can even set a snapshot as the "before" state for comparison purposes from that same contextual menu. To remove a snapshot, just select it and click the – (minus sign) icon at the top of the panel.

Going back in time with the History panel

It's never too late for a do-over in Lightroom Classic. The History panel, below Snapshots, records every adjustment and tweak you make in the Develop module.

You can open a photo any time and step to any earlier point in its Develop history by clicking an earlier History step. You can even save a History state as a snapshot by right-clicking and choosing Create Snapshot from the contextual menu that appears. You can use that same menu to set a specific history step to the "before" state for comparison purposes as you work. (You may not always want to compare against the import state after you've been working for a while.)

One thing to keep in mind, though, is if you click an earlier history step the photo will revert to that moment in time. If you make any adjustment to the photo from that point, all the previous history steps above where you clicked will be wiped away (because you are now taking the photo in a different direction from that point in time). This is where saving a snapshot can be helpful if you want to preserve an editing state and then take the editing in a new direction.

Chapter **10**

Taking Your Photos to the Next Level

I address the most common adjustments you make to most of your images in Chapters 8 and 9. In this chapter, I explore the rest of what the Develop module has to offer (that is, all the adjustments below the Basic panel). These are the settings you can use to really set your photos apart. Often the difference between an okay photo and a fantastic one is subtle — so subtle that the untrained eye may not even perceive what that difference is, but you know it when you see it. Typically, this difference is related to the attention to detail and finishing touches applied by a person skilled at their craft. The tools in this chapter focus on the techniques you can use to give each photo that "something special" that elevates it above a well-exposed capture.

Working with Contrast and Color

Being able to manipulate contrast and color digitally is very powerful and a lot of fun. Like anything else, the more you do it, the better you get at it. More important, the more you do it, the more you refine your eye and your own style. The adjustments you make in this area have a dramatic effect on how people react to your work. You can easily lose a little perspective on your own work after you've looked at it, tweaked it, and changed it. To help with that problem, take advantage of the tools Lightroom Classic offers — from creating snapshots of your progress to preserving certain settings as presets, from creating virtual copies to creating multiple versions — to bring some objectivity back into the creative process. Never forget that everything you do in Lightroom Classic can be undone! Take some time to step back and look at the history to see how far you've come, and possibly change course if things aren't going the way you'd envisioned.

REMEMBER

Keep in mind, though, that the basic tonal adjustments you've made already aren't set in stone. If you decide to work with the Tone Curve, convert to B&W, or apply a preset, for example, go back and tweak your earlier settings for better results. All these adjustments are performed on the same set of image data, which is why the Histogram panel is attached to the top of the right panel. Refer to it often, and toggle your clipping indicators on and off from time to time (by pressing J) to make sure that contrast boost didn't blow out a highlight or that a creative vignette didn't clip some important detail to black. No setting is made in isolation.

Mastering the Tone Curve

The Tone Curve panel, shown in Figure 10-1, provides a set of tools for adjusting the amount of contrast in your photos, as well as providing another means for fine-tuning brightness values. Heck, using the individual R, G, and B curves, you can even affect color! There's a lot of power packed into this little panel. *Contrast* gives photos a depth and a richness that most people find pleasing. Images lacking contrast are often referred to as *flat*. Contrast is increased or decreased by adjusting the brightness of the tones within your photo. A typical contrast adjustment might involve decreasing

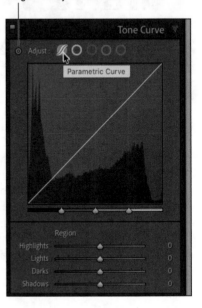

Targeted Adjustment tool

FIGURE 10-1:
The Tone Curve panel.

the brightness of the darkest tones (making them darker) while simultaneously increasing the brightness of the lighter tones (making them brighter), which increases contrast between these bright and dark regions and results in a subtle S shape in the curve. The more exaggerated you make the bends (or curves) in that S appear, the greater amount of contrast you see in your photo.

In the top half of the Tone Curve panel, you see a square window that contains the histogram of the active photo in the background and a diagonal line running from the lower left corner to the upper right corner. That diagonal line is the *curve*. By bending that line, you're in effect increasing or decreasing the brightness of all the pixels at a given point in the histogram. In Figure 10-1, the curve represents Lightroom Classic's default *linear* curve (even though the line is flat, the default profile does include a slight contrast boost).

Along the top are a series of circular icons, which control the type of tone curve being displayed. By default it is set to the parametric curve, represented by the first icon. The second icon switches to the point curve, and the three colored icons allow you to apply a curve to the red, green, and blue channels respectively. More on those later.

REMEMBER

Any curve adjustments you make are reflected in the *real* histogram — the one perched in the Histogram panel, sitting there on top of the Tone Curve panel. The histogram inside the Tone Curve panel, however, remains unchanged no matter how many adjustments you perform — as a reminder of the *before* curve state. The greater the curve adjustment you make, the more difference you see between these two histograms.

Enough of the preliminaries. Time to look at how you make things happen and bend that line. As is consistent with every other part of Lightroom Classic, you can achieve the same result in a few ways. Here are the ways you can make contrast adjustments with the Tone Curve panel:

>> Click and drag points on the curve itself using any or all of the five different curves.

>> Adjust the sliders below the curve.

>> Click and drag the photo with the Targeted Adjustment tool.

>> Apply a Point Curve preset.

Some of these methods may sound a bit techy — especially the Targeted Adjustment tool — but don't let that worry you. I go over each method in detail in the next few sections.

Interacting with the curve

Starting with the *parametric curve* (because we're changing a set of parameters), you make adjustments by manually manipulating the curve. That line represents all the tones, from black to white, that could exist in your photo. The Tone Curve histogram is a graph showing you the number of pixels in your photo at each tonal level. By clicking a point on that line, you can move that point up or down to increase or decrease the brightness of all the pixels at that tonal level. As an alternative, you can hover the cursor over a point in the window and use the up- and down-arrow keys to make the adjustment in + or − 5 increments (hold the Shift key for + or − 20 increments).

When you make adjustments, you may notice that there are hard stops in place, represented by the highlighted region, that limit how far you can go at any given point on the curve, as shown in Figure 10-2. This limit exists only in the parametric curve. In the upcoming section, "Manipulating the point curve," I explore how to gain access to the *point curve* that doesn't have these built-in limits.

TIP

Because being able to go back is always good, you can access a helpful Reset contextual menu by right-clicking anywhere inside the window. Double-clicking the word Region resets all sliders, and double-clicking the label of any single slider resets just that one.

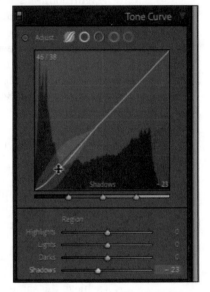

FIGURE 10-2:
The built-in limits of the parametric curve.

Sliding the sliders

Not too much to this one: The Highlights, Lights, Darks, and Shadows sliders correspond to the four regions that make up the complete tonal range of your image. Click and drag a slider to increase or decrease the brightness of the pixels in the corresponding region. Alternatively, you can place your cursor over the number field to the right of the sliders, and a small scrubby slider appears that you can click and drag to make an adjustment.

Using the Targeted Adjustment Tool

Pronounced *tat* for short, this is the tool for people who'd rather just work right in the photo instead of looking at sliders, numbers, or curves. After a little practice, you may just find it feels more natural and intuitive.

Click the TAT icon (shown in Figure 10-1) to activate it and then move your cursor over the photo. Notice that the cursor changes to a *crosshair* (this is the working end of the TAT tool) with the TAT icon trailing behind it (this is just a reminder that the tool is active). To make an adjustment, click a spot in the photo that represents the tonal region you want to adjust and then drag up to make that tonal range brighter or down to make it darker. As you click and drag, you see the adjustments reflected in the Tone Curve panel. The TAT is associated with the type of curve selected from the buttons across the top of the panel, and it works the same way for each curve.

Manipulating the point curve

The parametric curve is great for those new to using curves, but for the most control, you'll want to click that icon to the right of the parametric curve icon to switch to point curve mode, as shown in Figure 10-3. Notice that the Region sliders go away, and a Point Curve drop-down menu appears.

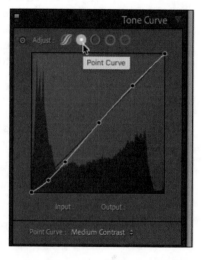

When using the point curve, the adjustment you create affects all three (RGB) channels equally. It works the same way as the curve in parametric mode, but you no longer have any limitations on how severe your curve can become. This is awesome for people who want total control or to apply creative effects not otherwise possible. Some additional things to keep in mind with the point curve:

FIGURE 10-3:
Switching to point curve mode.

>> Clicking the curve adds a point (up to a maximum of 16 total).

>> You can delete a point by right-clicking it and choosing Delete from the contextual menu.

>> You can right-click the area around the curve and choose Reset Channel from the contextual menu to reset back to linear.

>> Hold the Option key (Alt for Windows) while dragging a point for finer control.

>> Hold the Shift key while dragging a point to constrain movement to only up/down.

>> Use can save a custom point curve by clicking the Point Curve drop-down menu and choosing Save from the menu.

>> Using the individual red, green, and blue channel icons, you can adjust each channel independently.

When using the individual color channel curves, you'll see a color gradient appear in the background of the panel corresponding to the color you've chosen. Dragging upward will shift the affected tones toward the corresponding color, whereas dragging down will shift the tones toward its opposing color displayed in the panel. The individual color channel curves are for advanced color correction and creative effects due to how significantly they can shift colors in a photo. Experiment with each one to get a feel for how it works, then right-click within the area around the curve to reset as needed.

Applying a preset

If you're working with raw images, there is likely some amount of contrast built into the profile being applied (see Chapter 8 for more on profiles). A quick way to modify contrast is to choose one of the contrast presets found in the Point Curve drop-down menu, and if you like it, you're done! Keep in mind that you aren't required by law to change the contrast if you're already happy with the default state, but here are the preset options you can select in the Point Curve drop-down menu:

>> **Linear:** Takes the curve out of the curve, which means no additional contrast adjustment has been made beyond what is in the applied profile. Applied by default.

>> **Medium Contrast:** Adds a slight *S* curve, which means slightly darker shadows and slightly brighter highlights.

>> **Strong Contrast:** A larger *S* curve than medium contrast, which means darker shadows and brighter highlights.

As I mention in the previous section, if you save a custom point curve, those will also be available via this drop-down menu and can be applied as desired.

Enhancing and changing colors

Who doesn't like the HSL/Color panel? In fact, this is one of those panels where you might find yourself getting a little carried away simply because it *is* so much fun. My advice to you: Gather some practice images and get all that wild colorizing out of your system. That way, when you really need to use this panel, you can be a little more subtle.

Unless you've selected a true *monochrome* image (a photo that really has only one channel), the photos you work with in Lightroom Classic are RGB (Red, Green, Blue) images, which means you always have the information contained in each of the three RGB channels to work with, even when you look at a photo you've converted to B&W in Lightroom Classic.

REMEMBER

When the Treatment setting in the Basic panel is set to Color, this panel is named HSL/Color, and when Treatment is set to Black & White this panel is named B&W. Because B&W conversion is a topic unto itself, I cover it in detail in the next section.

The HSL/Color panel is two panels in one. The HSL and Color options are essentially variations on the same set of controls, which allow you to adjust the hue, saturation, and luminance values in your photo. I want to call your attention to a unique aspect of this panel — the HSL/Color labels in the panel's header are also the buttons used to switch between each option. The label you select remains highlighted to indicate which option is active.

Figure 10-4 shows the Color face of the HSL/Color panel — the Reds section, to be more precise. Along the top of the panel is a row of color circles that represents each of the colors you can adjust. Click any circle to activate the controls for that color, or click the multi-colored button (far right) to see all the controls at once. Each color has three possible adjustments:

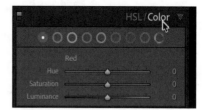

FIGURE 10-4:
The HSL/Color panel set to Color.

>> **Hue:** This adjustment shifts the color between all its possible hues.

>> **Saturation:** Use this slider to change the intensity of the hue.

>> **Luminance:** This slider changes the brightness level of the hue.

The HSL options, shown in Figure 10-5, group the adjustments by hue, saturation, and luminance rather than by color. You can see the labels for each grouping across the top of the panel. Click each label to activate the controls for that group, or click All to see the controls for all three groups at once.

I think you'll find that using the HSL face of the panel is a more intuitive way to work, mainly because of the way the Targeted Adjustment tool (TAT) has been integrated for each group of adjustments. The Targeted Adjustment tool

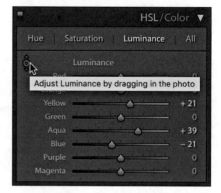

FIGURE 10-5:
The HSL section of the panel set to Luminance.

functions just like it did in the Tone Curve panel, except it controls the adjustment of sliders in your chosen group: Hue, Saturation, or Luminance. I most commonly use this tool to adjust luminance and/or saturation of individual colors using the TAT. I think it is too easy to stray into odd colors when you start tweaking the hue.

Creating black-and-white images

In the absence of color, an image becomes a study in light and shadow, texture and detail in a very different way than would be the case with color photos. Because of this, black and white (B&W) photos can often achieve a visual impact that color photos can't. When you're converting a color photo to black and white, the process starts with a conversion to B&W, but the process doesn't end there. To see all that's involved, start by looking at the B&W panel and then follow along as I address how you can call on a few other Lightroom Classic panels to enhance the final result. To initiate a B&W conversion and transform the HSL/Color panel to B&W, try one of the following methods:

>> Press V.

>> Click the Black & White button in the Treatment section of the Basic panel.

>> Click a preset that converts to B&W.

>> Choose a B&W profile from the Profile Browser.

Note: There are several B&W presets and profiles that come preinstalled with Lightroom Classic. I highly recommend exploring those to see what is possible, and potentially use one as a starting point. To see how this whole B&W conversion process works, follow along as I recount the steps I take to move a photo from its Color state to a B&W state:

1. **Select the photo in the Filmstrip and open the Profile Browser in the Basic panel.**

   Click the B&W button to only show B&W profiles in the Browser.

2. **Move your cursor over each profile to find one you like as a starting point and click it to apply.**

   I ended up with B&W 10 as the starting point for the photo in Figure 10-6. Remember, depending on the profile you select, you might be able to further modify the look using the associated Amount slider (near the top of Browser) for that profile. Close the Profile Browser when you're done.

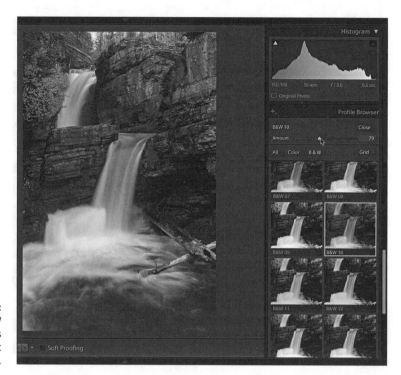

FIGURE 10-6:
The B&W profiles are a great starting point.

3. **Adjust white-balance settings in the Basic panel as needed.**

   Keep in mind that, even though you see a B&W image, all the color data in the original image is still at your disposal. Adjusting the Temp and Tint sliders can bring out additional detail and texture.

4. **Readjust basic tonal settings in the Basic panel as needed.**

   As with white balance, now that you're working with a range of B&W values, you may find that an adjustment to exposure or to the black clipping level is required to achieve your desired result.

5. **Expand the B&W panel, as shown in Figure 10-7.**

   TIP

   This is your opportunity to pick up where Lightroom Classic left off and adjust the mix of color data to bring out the tonal qualities of the image you're after. Try clicking the Auto button to see how that looks. Double-click the Black & White Mix label to reset all sliders back to 0 if needed.

6. **(Optional) Click the Targeted Adjustment tool (TAT) inside the B&W Mix panel.**

   Although you can certainly adjust individual color sliders in the panel, you'll find that working right inside the photo with the TAT is a much more intuitive and satisfying process.

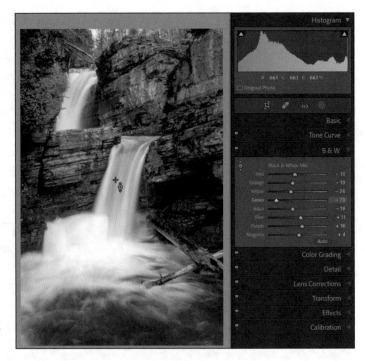

FIGURE 10-7:
The B&W
Mix controls.

7. **If you decide to use the TAT, click a tone in the photo and drag down to darken or drag up to brighten.**

TIP

This is where your creativity and vision come together! While you click and drag the TAT, the corresponding B&W Mix sliders move within the panel. You can always undo an adjustment by pressing ⌘+Z (Ctrl+Z for Windows) or by stepping back to an earlier history state. This exploration process is also a good time to make use of the Snapshots panel if you want to preserve a particular state. (For more on the Snapshots panel, see Chapter 9.)

8. **If you chose the TAT route, click the Done button in the Toolbar to quit the TAT after you complete your mix adjustments.**

Figure 10-7 shows you the kinds of transformations you can achieve with the B&W panel.

Just because you've completed the B&W mix doesn't mean the photo is finished. Depending on the photo and the result in your mind's eye, you may go on to do any (or all) of the following to finish the job:

>> Use the Adjustment Brush in the Tool Strip to make Dodge and Burn local adjustments.

>> Use the Tone Curve panel to increase contrast.

>> Adjust Clarity, Texture, and/or Dehaze.

>> Use the Color Grading panel to add color to the highlights and shadows.

>> Use the Effects panel to darken or lighten the edges or add grain.

The best way to know when you're done is done is to roll up your sleeves and experiment. The wonderful thing about Lightroom Classic is that none of these adjustments alters the pixels in your original images. You can always go back. Using the Snapshots panel to preserve key states in the development process or even virtual copies to branch out into multiple versions gives you a lot of room to move.

Adding color to shadows and highlights

A common use of the Color Grading panel — the panel stuck right under the HSL/Color (or B&W) panel (and formerly known as Split Toning) — is to add a hint of a color tint to B&W images. Of course you can and should try using it with color photos too! Color Grading allows you to add a color tint to the highlights, midtones, and shadows (or any combination of the three), with Hue, Saturation, and Luminance sliders for each tonal region.

The panel opens displaying a color wheel for each tonal region, which is called 3-way view (see Figure 10-8). Across the top are icons that allow for switching from 3-way to view a larger color wheel for just one tonal region at a time, as shown in Figure 10-9 for the Shadows. Within a color wheel, you can click and drag to dial-in a specific hue and saturation value for the desired tint. The tint is applied to that tonal region in real time, so what you see is what you get. When viewing a single tonal range you can click the disclosure triangle to reveal the Hue, Saturation, and Luminance sliders, which can also be manipulated to fine-tune the look you want.

Hue and Saturation control the color of the tint, whereas the Luminance slider allows you to control the brightness of the corresponding tonal range. Because you can apply a tint only to pixels that are not pure white, it can be helpful to use the Luminance slider to darken the highlights to better see the applied tint to that region. When in 3-way view, the Luminance slider appears below each color wheel. The eye icon below each color wheel allows you to hide the effect of the corresponding color wheel when clicked.

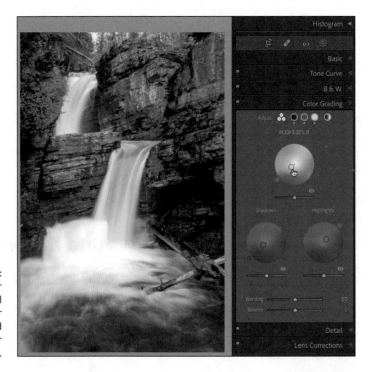

FIGURE 10-8:
The Color Grading panel allows for creative and practical color adjustments.

In the bottom of the panel you'll find the Blending and Balance sliders. Blending controls how much mixing of tints happens between the tonal ranges, so if set to 0 there would be no mixing of tints, whereas if set to 100 there would be maximum mixing of the applied tints. The Balance slider can shift the tonal ranges that are considered highlights or shadows. If Balance were set to 100, it would force the tint applied to the highlights across almost all pixels in the entire image, and a setting of -100 would force the shadow tint across almost all pixels. I suggest applying a strong tint to the shadows and an opposite tint to the highlights, then experiment with different Blending and Balance settings to see how they work.

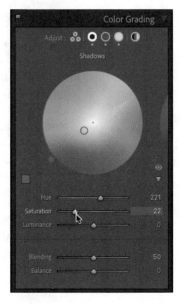

FIGURE 10-9:
The Color Grading panel showing just the controls for adding color to the Shadows.

TIP

To learn even more about Color Grading, check out my tutorial on Lightroom Killer Tips: `https://lightroomkillertips.com/introducing-color-grading`.

The Devil's in the Details

Working your way down the right side of the Lightroom Classic interface, your next stop is the Detail panel, which is your place for getting up close and personal with your photos. I think you'll agree with me that sometimes, you need to zoom to the 1:1 view to see what's happening in your photo. In fact, the only way you can really see the adjustments made in the Detail panel is when you're in at least 1:1 zoom level (or greater). To make that easier, the folks at Adobe added a nice little 1:1 Preview window to the Detail panel. (See Figure 10-10.) You can click and drag inside the Preview window to view different areas of the photo or click the squarish crosshair to the left of the window to focus on a different area of the photo. If you want to zoom closer, you can right-click inside the window to choose either the 1:1 or 2:1 zoom level from the contextual menu that appears.

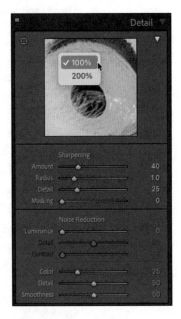

FIGURE 10-10:
The Detail panel.

Applying capture sharpening

Sharpening can't correct an out-of-focus image, but it can increase the perception of detail in a properly focused image. Lightroom Classic has come a long way in regard to sharpening. You can find output sharpening to use in both Print and Web modules, as well as in the Export dialog. In addition, you can even selectively apply sharpness using Masking for more creative and localized sharpening applications. When put together in a sharpening workflow, you can apply the sharpening in the Detail panel as it was originally intended, which is simply to compensate for the inherent softness in raw captures. This is referred to as *capture sharpening.*

Sharpening is a very powerful adjustment, and as with most powerful things, you should never use more than the minimum required to get the job done. Increasing sharpness can bring details to life, which can translate into a greater visual impact. Increasing sharpness too much can make a photo appear crunchy and overprocessed and cause viewers to have a negative reaction to the image. You want your sharpness setting to be *just right* — if anything, you might want to err on the softer side.

One of the key traits that humans find pleasing to the eye is the separation of edges around certain details (sharpening). The human eye is drawn to this edge detail, and sharpening can be used to bring a viewer in closer. Lightroom Classic's sharpening controls are all about edge detection and enhancement. The controls are as follows:

>> **Amount:** This is simply the amount of sharpening being applied. An increase in the amount translates to an increase in sharpening.

>> **Radius:** This determines how far that sharpening amount extends from the edges being sharpened. The higher the radius, the farther the reach from the edges.

>> **Detail:** This determines how much of the finer detail between the prominent edges has sharpening applied to it. The higher the setting, the more the finer detail edges are sharpened.

>> **Masking:** Provides a means to protect areas of the image from having sharpening applied. No mask means all areas have sharpening applied to them. A high Masking value means only the most defined edges are sharpened.

By default, all raw photos have a moderate amount of sharpening applied. However, you may want to move beyond the defaults, depending on the subject matter of your photos. One of the best ways to understand how this panel was intended to be used is to examine the settings contained in the two sharpening presets against the default sharpening settings. Table 10-1 compares the default values against the values found in the presets Sharpen – Scenic and Sharpen – Faces (found in the Presets panel on the left side of the Lightroom Classic interface under the Classic – General group).

TABLE 10-1

Comparison of Preset Sharpening Settings

Settings	Default	Scenic	Faces
Amount	40	40	35
Radius	1.0	0.8	1.4
Detail	25	35	15
Masking	0	0	60

Here's what the Adobe folks were thinking when they came up with a Scenic preset and a Faces preset. In a typical scenic photo, you see a lot of details. In fact, overall detail is a favored trait. You *want* to see details. Detail draws in the eye. Now think about a portrait. Detail is certainly important, but only in certain places. Sharpness of the eyes is very important. Showing every pore and wrinkle in sharp relief is not important.

Looking at the settings of the Scenic preset, you see the amount is set to 40, compared to 35 in Faces. Not a huge difference, but it's not surprising that scenic landscapes would get a greater amount of sharpening. I come back to Radius at the end, but for now, I want to move on to the Detail setting. The Scenic Detail setting is 10 points higher than the default, whereas the Portraits setting is 10 points lower than the default. This too makes sense because you definitely want to bring out the finer detail in a landscape, but not in a person's skin. Now, as you compare the Masking setting of 0 for Scenic versus 60 for Faces, you can see that sharpening is being applied to all areas of the landscape image, but only on the most defined edges of the portrait. This high Masking value also explains why the radius was slightly bumped up in the portrait image to thicken the edges of the most defined features, knowing that the finer detail would be left unsharpened.

So ask yourself the following question: Is your photo more like a portrait, where only the most defined edges should be sharpened, or is your photo more like a landscape, where even the finest detail needs a boost? With that determination in mind, I suggest applying the appropriate preset even if you just use it as a new starting point over the default.

To see how all this works in tandem with the Detail panel, follow along as I walk through one example. Grab a portrait photo of your own, because it will be easier to see the effect of the Detail panel settings on your screen than in the limited reproduction ability of the book.

1. **Click the eye (or an equally important detail) to zoom into 1:1 view.**

   You can see the effects of the sharpening only when you're zoomed to 1:1 or are looking at the 1:1 Preview in the Detail panel.

2. **In the Presets panel on the left side of the Lightroom Classic interface, apply the Sharpen – Faces preset.**

   In many cases, you can stop right there, but for the sake of explaining the process, I want you to see if you can finesse this starting point. If you don't see the Classic – General preset group, refer to the "Managing your presets" section in Chapter 9 to make it visible.

3. **Increase the Amount setting and then dial the setting back until you see nice edges without any jagged pixels or white haloes along edges.**

   Hold the Option key (Alt for Windows) while dragging the slider to see your photo in B&W. Sharpening is applied only to the luminance (brightness data), not to the color data, so seeing the photo in B&W provides another way to see what exactly is happening to the photo.

TIP

4. **Leave the Radius at its default.**

By making the decision about what preset to apply, you're already in the ballpark. If anything, you may want to dial back Radius, but your energy is better spent on the other three adjustments.

5. **Hold the Option key (Alt for Windows) and increase the Detail slider until you can see unwanted detail appear, and then dial the slider back until only your key edges are visible.**

TIP

By using the Option (Alt) modifier with this adjustment right from the start, you can really focus on just the detail. I typically dial up Detail until I can see pores on the skin and then dial it back until those pores are diminished. Keep in mind that by applying the Faces preset, you already have a high Masking amount being applied, which limits the areas being sharpened.

6. **Increase the Masking amount as necessary to compensate for increases made to the Detail setting.**

The Option (Alt) modifier works with this slider too! In this case, you see the mask itself. Areas of white in the mask are the areas where sharpening will be applied. Black areas will have no sharpening.

7. **Check other areas of the photo at 1:1 to evaluate the level of sharpening applied.**

At the end of that process, the settings I preferred were not very far from the Portraits preset. Would anyone notice that difference in a normal viewing environment? Not likely. When you're processing tens, hundreds, or thousands of photos, you don't want to spend this kind of time finessing the capture sharpening on a photo-by-photo basis. Get a good feel for what the sliders can do, create your own presets (or use the existing ones) that suit your needs/tastes, and apply those presets in batches to your photos.

Dealing with noise

The bottom section of the Detail panel deals with noise reduction — no, not that acoustic paneling stuff. In terms of digital photography, *noise* is simply random electrical signals recorded by the camera's sensor that can degrade the quality of the photo. In the absence of light, these random signals are more visible because the sensor records less actual data, which is why noise issues are common in underexposed and high-ISO photos.

Lightroom Classic's noise-reduction options are simple (refer to Figure 10-10 to see the entire Detail panel), but they can be effective when it comes to reducing minor noise issues. You have one set of sliders for dealing with luminance noise reduction, and another set of sliders for reducing the effects of color noise. After you figure out how to differentiate between the two, it's simply a matter of adjusting the respective set of sliders just enough (and no more) to solve the problem. Here's my handy guide to telling luminance noise from color noise apart:

>> **Luminance noise tends to look like the more familiar *grain* you see in film.** You have fluctuations in brightness levels, whereas color remains essentially consistent — common in areas of blue sky.

>> **Color noise can be recognized by the presence of multicolored pixels (like Christmas tree lights).** Typically present in the shadow areas.

With luminance noise, the most likely place you'll encounter that headache is in blue skies. Figure 10-11 shows a Before and After (at 3:1 zoom) example of a blue sky with the typical grainy signs of luminance noise. To counteract the noise level in the Before image, I adjusted the Luminance slider until the tones in the sky smoothed out (note, try increasing the Masking slider above to avoid sharpening noise and you may find you don't need to apply any noise reduction). Use the Detail (helps preserve areas of minute detail when set to higher value) and Contrast (sets amount of edge detection used to identify noise) sliders to fine-tune results.

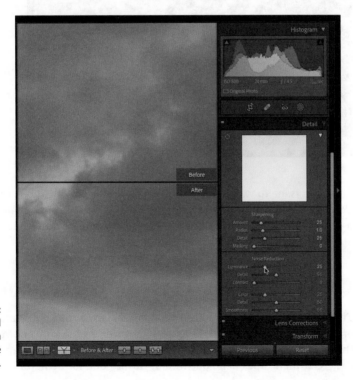

FIGURE 10-11:
A Before and After view of a luminance noise correction.

Figure 10-12 shows a Before and After (at 3:1 zoom) example of a color noise reduction on an ISO 800 photo. The default setting of Color = 25 is usually good enough for most lower-ISO photos. If color noise is still visible, continue to increase the Color slider until you've neutralized as many of the random multi-colored pixels as you can. Use the Detail (same as with luminance above) and Smoothness (helps reduce color mottling artifacts at higher ISOs) sliders to fine-tune its application.

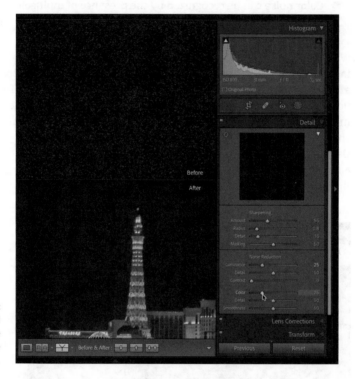

FIGURE 10-12: A Before and After example of a color noise correction.

The main issue to watch for with any type of noise reduction is the loss of detail. Too much noise reduction can turn your photo into a mush of pixels resembling a watercolor painting. Having a little noise and more detail rather than less noise and pixel mush is usually better.

Correcting lens distortions and vignetting

The Lens Corrections panel has two tabs, labeled Profile and Manual. I review the options in the Profile tab first because that's often the only one you'll need. With the introduction of lens profiles several versions back, correcting lens distortions (where straight lines bend outward or inward due to the nature of the lens used) became as easy as checking a box — the Enable Profile Corrections box, to be specific. Figure 10-13 shows Before and After views for a correction of the common barrel distortion (lines bend outward) found in wide-angle lenses. When you check that box, Lightroom Classic automatically applies the correct lens profile by reading the photo's metadata to determine the camera and lens combo used, which will correct lens distortion and lens vignetting (darkening of the edges). Lightroom Classic has a list of supported lenses, which grows with every update.

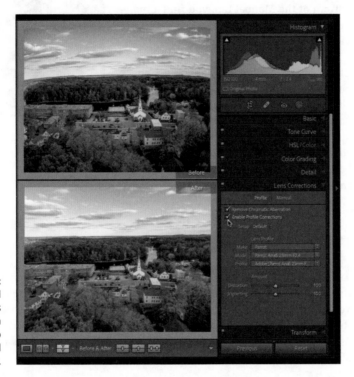

FIGURE 10-13:
Before and After views of applying a lens profile to correct barrel distortion.

If your lens isn't automatically found, you can select the make and model of your lens, which opens a list of all profiles for that lens that you can choose from. Check here for the complete list of supported lenses and resources for creating custom lens profiles if your lens isn't supported: https://helpx.adobe.com/camera-raw/kb/supported-lenses.html.

After you apply a profile, you can use the Distortion and Vignetting sliders in the Amount section at the bottom to turn down the adjustment (and bring back some distortion or vignetting). You'll most commonly leave these at the default settings, but sometimes it is nice to bring back some natural lens vignetting instead of adding it in the Effects panel.

If the barrel or pincushion distortion was not completely corrected, there is an additional Distortion slider on the Manual tab that can be used to fine-tune the correction (see Figure 10-14). Move the Distortion slider to the right to further correct barrel distortion and to the left to correct any remaining pincushion distortion. At the bottom of the Manual tab, you find a manual control for further fine-tuning the vignetting correction, if needed.

The Remove Chromatic Aberration check box at the top of the panel is an easy one-click correction aimed at what is called *lateral chromatic aberration,* which can appear as a colored fringe in the corners of some images. All you need to do is check the box to remove it. For ideas on dealing with the more challenging axial chromatic aberration, see the next section.

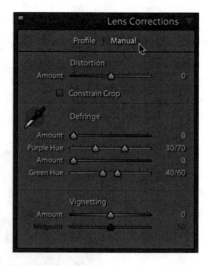

FIGURE 10-14:
The Manual tab of the Lens Corrections panel.

Reducing chromatic aberration

Axial chromatic aberration, when present, most commonly appears throughout the photo in the form of a reddish or greenish fringe along high contrast edges. You can also sometimes encounter purplish fringing around specular highlights (bright highlights, like sun glinting off metal), which is called *sensor blooming.* All these forms of fringing can be reduced using the tools in the Defringe section of the Manual tab within the Lens Corrections panel, as shown in Figure 10-14.

Within the Defringe section of the panel, you find the following tools:

>> **Fringe Color Selector:** Can be used to select the range of hues contained within the fringe area and set the Defringe Amount and Hue sliders with a single click on the fringe. Works best when zoomed to 1:1.

>> **Amount:** The purplish color of the top Amount slider is the giveaway that this controls the amount of correction applied for removing reddish-purple fringe.

>> **Purple Hue:** These sliders control the range of reddish-purple hues that will be affected by the Amount slider above. The range can be shifted and expanded as needed to make the desired correction.

- **Amount:** The greenish color of this Amount slider is the giveaway that this controls the amount of correction for removing greenish-blue fringe.

- **Green Hue:** These sliders control the range of greenish-blue hues that will be affected by the Amount slider above. The range can be shifted and expanded as needed to make the desired correction.

The basic idea is that if you see reddish-purple fringing appearing in your photo, you can increase the corresponding Amount slider until the fringe is removed and adjust the Purple Hue slider to hone in on the exact hue of the fringe in question. Likewise, if you see a greenish fringe appearing along high-contrast edges, use the corresponding green Amount slider and Green Hue sliders to remove that fringe from your photo. Figure 10-15 shows Before and After views of just this type of correction. You may find it helpful to zoom to even greater than 1:1 to better see and correct the fringe.

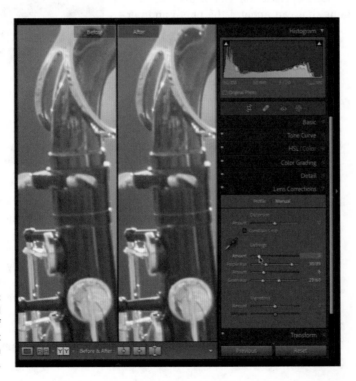

FIGURE 10-15: Before and After views of a chromatic aberration correction.

TIP

If you find that your Defringe correction accidentally removes color from objects that should be that color, you can use the Adjustment Brush configured with a negative amount of Defringe to paint over that region and remove the Defringe correction to restore the color.

Transforming perspective distortions

Perspective distortions are caused by how you hold the camera relative to the subject. A common example of this is when you tilt the camera backward to take in the top of a tall building. Because the camera is no longer perpendicular to the building, you've introduced a perspective distortion that makes it appear as though the building is leaning backward. You may also encounter the dreaded crooked horizon caused by not holding the camera level. Many versions ago, Adobe added the Upright tools, as shown in Figure 10-16, to the Develop module. Upright consists of a set of functions that can analyze the photo and perform the needed correction.

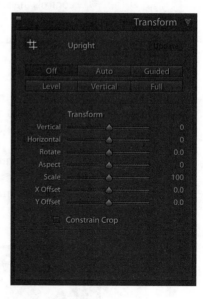

FIGURE 10-16:
Transform panel options.

» **Guided Upright Tool:** Located in the upper left corner of the panel. See Guided description below.

» **Off:** Turns off all Upright adjustments.

» **Auto:** Automatically performs a leveling adjustment combined with a vertical and horizontal perspective distortion correction. Usually provided a more natural-looking correction.

» **Guided:** If none of the one-click fixes provided by the other Upright buttons do the trick, choose this Guided button or click right on the Guided Upright Tool to manually draw out two (or more) guides along edges of objects (like buildings) that should be perfectly horizontal or perfectly vertical, and a corresponding correction is applied. The guides can be manually tweaked, nudged, and adjusted if not placed correctly the first time. A magnified loupe appears alongside the cursor to help you pinpoint guide placement.

» **Level:** Great for fixing crooked horizons.

» **Vertical:** Performs the same leveling adjustment as the Level button, combined with vertical perspective correction.

» **Full:** If your photo suffers from horizontal and vertical perspective distortion, along with a crooked horizon and possibly a need to be rotated horizontally, the Full button is worth a click. Save this one for the most severe distortion problems.

As powerful and accurate as the Upright functions can be, they sometimes need a little nudging to make the result look natural. You can further refine the adjustments made by the Upright functions using the manual controls within the Transform section (if needed):

>> **Vertical:** Correct or tweak vertical distortion problems.

>> **Horizontal:** Correct or tweak horizontal distortion problems.

>> **Rotate:** Can be used to fine-tune a leveling correction. Similar to the Angle slider in the Crop tool.

>> **Aspect:** You can drag to the left to squish or drag to the right to stretch the photo to make objects in the photo appear more normal after a perspective distortion correction. See Figure 10-17 for an example.

>> **Scale:** Makes the photo larger (or smaller) within the existing canvas, which can be useful if there are empty pixels left in the photo after a perspective correction and you want to keep the photo at its original pixel dimensions.

>> **X Offset:** Can be used to reposition the photo on the canvas along the x-axis (horizontally).

>> **Y Offset:** Can be used to reposition the photo on the canvas along the y-axis (vertically). The X and Y Offset controls are useful for tweaking the position of the photo on the canvas after a distortion correction to ensure that the important part of the photo remains visible.

>> **Constrain Crop:** Check this box to let Lightroom Classic automatically crop the image to hide empty areas of pixels after a distortion correction. This reduces the overall pixel dimensions of the photo.

For example, if you look at the Before view of the photo in Figure 10-17, you can see that the building appears to be slightly leaning backward, which was caused by the fact that I pointed my camera upward to capture the photo. After trying the Auto, Full, and Guided upright options, I felt that the Auto adjustment did the best job of correcting the perspective distortion. However, it did result in the building appearing to be stretched taller than it should be, so I moved the Aspect slider in a negative direction to squish the building down slightly to make it appear less stretched.

REMEMBER

All these adjustments are nondestructive and can be easily reset, so feel free to click every button and move every slider to see how it works.

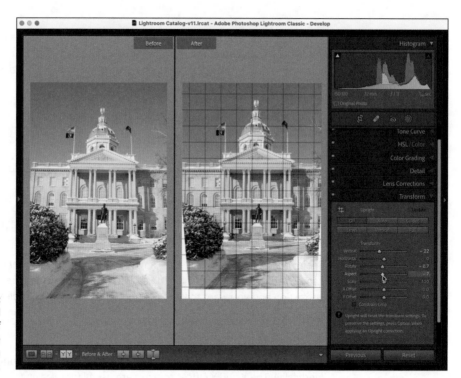

FIGURE 10-17:
Before and After views of a perspective distortion correction.

Creative Effects

If you've ever wanted to add simulated film grain or creatively add a vignette into your digitally pure photographs, the Effects panel is the place to go. Originally intended to be a correction tool (before Adobe introduced the Lens Corrections panel), the Post-Crop Vignetting section is more often used these days for the creative effects it can produce. A *bad* vignette happens when you have unwanted darkening around the edge of a photo, usually caused by the reduction of light entering the lens (such as interference from stacked filters). Proving the adage "When life gives you lemons, make lemonade," some folks decided they kind of liked that darkening around the image because it almost acted as a matte or a framing device. Similarly, due to photography's roots in film, digital photography often attempts to emulate certain film stocks. Although film stock colors can be mimicked with a Profile, the Effects panel is where you go to add simulated film grain. The Effects panel, shown in Figure 10-18, has two sections:

>> **Post-Crop Vignetting:** Reach for this tool when you want to add a vignette for creative effect. Not only do you have multiple sliders to refine the effect, but it works equally on the cropped and uncropped versions as well (meaning that the effect automatically conforms to the edges of the photo after it has been cropped).

>> **Grain:** Reach for this tool when you want to add filmlike grain for creative effect.

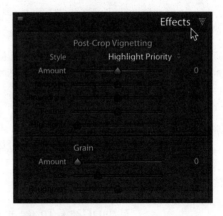

FIGURE 10-18:
The Effects panel.

Creative vignette applications

The Post-Crop vignette controls were added years ago after the explosion in popularity of adding a vignette as a creative effect. The goal here isn't to remove a vignette but to apply one! Applying a vignette is a simple way to create a framing effect that draws the eye into the photo. Like any creative effect, you can easily overdo it, but I really enjoy the effect all the same. Another great thing about the Post-Crop vignette is that it reapplies the vignette settings to the cropped version of the photo should you use the Crop tool after having already applied a creative vignette. You can play around with five separate sliders in the Post-Crop section:

>> **Style:** This drop-down menu contains three options — Highlight Priority, Color Priority, and Paint Overlay — that control how the vignette blends with the colors in the photo. Highlight priority is the default and usually the best option. Color Priority is similar to Highlight, but it tries to avoid shifts in hue around the affected area (use this if you see color shifts in the vignette). Paint Overlay simply applies a black or white (depending on the Amount slider setting) overlay along the photo's edge.

>> **Amount:** As you might expect, this slider controls the amount of the added vignette. Move to the left to darken and to the right to brighten.

>> **Midpoint:** This slider increases or decreases the area at the center unaffected by the vignette. Moving the slider to the left reduces the midpoint and by extension maximizes the range the vignette can extend into the center of the photo. Moving the slider to the right has the opposite effect.

>> **Roundness:** Increasing the Roundness value results in a more circular vignette, whereas decreasing roundness produces a more elliptical result.

>> **Feather:** This slider controls the amount of fade applied to the edge of the vignette into the midpoint. A feather setting of 0 results in a hard-edged solid border, whereas a feather setting of 100 results in the most gradual transition from the midpoint to the edge of the photo.

>> **Highlights:** This slider is used to apply a different level of processing to the brighter areas of the photo affected by the vignette when Highlight or Color Priority styles are used.

There's no right or wrong way to apply a vignette; it's completely a matter of personal taste. To see an example, check out Figure 10-19, where I attempt to mimic an old-postcard look by adding a white frame (positive Amount) around the photo along with a grainy texture.

Creative grain applications

The addition of grain is also an entirely personal choice, and as such, you may never venture this far down the panel. That said, file this information away because it may come in handy down the road. You can adjust the following three sliders (refer to Figure 10-19):

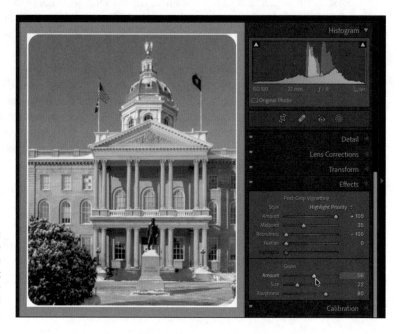

FIGURE 10-19:
An example of a creative vignette that adds a white border around the photo.

>> **Amount:** Use this to control the overall strength of the grain effect.

>> **Size:** The larger the grain, the softer and less pronounced the edges of the grain will be.

>> **Roughness:** Think of this as the way to control frequency of the grain (from coarse to fine).

TIP

Check out the preinstalled Grain and Vignetting preset groups to see some example settings you can use as starting points. I used the preset Grain – Medium as the starting point for the effect shown in Figure 10-19.

Modifying the Calibration Settings

The Calibration panel (see Figure 10-20), possibly the least-visited panel, provides the ability to change the process version used on your photo and the legacy controls for changing the baseline rendering of colors in raw photos. Wait, what's this process version all about? The process version is the underlying algorithm used to render the raw data in your photographs. Over the years, Adobe has improved on that algorithm to do a better job of reducing noise, sharpening details, and basically making the most of the data captured by your camera. Here's what this panel has to offer:

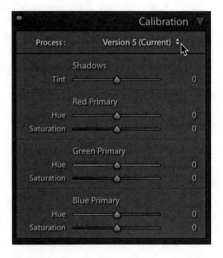

FIGURE 10-20:
The Calibration panel.

>> **Process:** Shows the process version applied to your photo and gives you the means to switch to a different process version.

>> **Shadows:** Allows for the correction of a tint in the shadow areas.

>> **Red, Green, and Blue primaries:** Lets you adjust the hue and/or saturation of each of the primary colors in your photos.

The only reason you'd ever need to visit this panel is to change the process version. The Shadows, Red Primary, Green Primary, and Blue Primary sliders have been made obsolete by all the new Profile options made available with the latest version of Lightroom Classic, and are vestigial controls left behind for any long-time Lightroom Classic user who may have used them to modify photos years ago.

At the time of this writing, Process Version 5 is the latest and greatest. However, it is likely that the Process Version (PV) will be updated again in the future, and at that time the new PV will become the default PV to enable access to whatever new features/improvements are dependent upon the updated PV. As a result, existing photos using the older PV will need to be updated to the latest PV if you want to use the new features that are tied to the new PV.

The updating process has gotten much more seamless, so much so that you may not even notice it happened. For example, if I grab an old photo set to PV 3 and bring it to Develop, all I need to do is move the new Texture slider (or any feature dependent on the latest PV) and Lightroom Classic quietly updates the PV for me. Occasionally updating the PV can come with a slight visual change to the photo as Lightroom Classic translates the edits to the new PV, but this is rare. For more on updating Process Version, check out this tutorial I wrote at Photofocus: `https://photofocus.com/software/lightroom-faq-updating-process-version`.

If you select a photo in Develop that is set to an older PV, a lightning-bolt icon appears at the bottom right of the Histogram panel to indicate that it is an older PV. You can click that icon to manually update the PV, or you can change the PV in the Calibration panel.

4

Sharing Your Work with the World

3. **Configure settings as required to meet your output needs.**

4. **(Optional) Save settings as a preset for reuse.**

In some cases you may not need, or want, to create a preset for every export.

The following sections provide a closer look at each step in the workflow. I follow up that discussion with a real-world example for saving an export preset.

Step 1: Selecting the images you want to export

The photos you select for export are determined by your needs at the time. You can export images from within any Lightroom Classic module, but the Library module gives you the greatest access to your entire portfolio, and exporting from there usually makes the most sense. So if you're not there already, press G to jump to the Library's Grid view. From here, you have access to all your folders and collections, as well as the Library Filter bar, meaning that you can go ahead and track down the images you want. (Go ahead; take your time.)

After you locate the images you want to export, you can select them by any of the following methods:

» Pressing ⌘+A (Ctrl+A for Windows) to select all photos within a folder or other grouping of photos.

» Clicking the first image in a series, holding the Shift key, and clicking the last image in the series to select all images in between.

» Holding the ⌘ key (Ctrl key for Windows) and clicking each image individually to make a noncontiguous selection.

Step 2: Initiating the Export command

After you select the images, you can initiate an export from any module (except where noted) through the following means:

» **Choose File ⇨ Export.** Launches the Export dialog.

» **Choose File ⇨ Export with Previous.** Skips the Export dialog and simply exports selected files by using the settings from the last export.

» **Choose File ⇨ Export with Preset ⇨ Select Preset.** Allows you to select a preset and export without additional configuration of the Export dialog.

» **Press ⌘+Shift+E (Ctrl+Shift+E for Windows).** Keyboard shortcut that launches the Export dialog.

>> **Press ⌘+Option+Shift+E (Ctrl+Alt+Shift+E for Windows).** Keyboard shortcut for Export with Previous.

>> **Right-click a selected photo and choose one of the previously mentioned export options from the contextual menu that appears.**

>> **Click the Export button at the bottom of the left panel in the Library module.** Only visible in the Library module, but comes in handy.

TIP

I encourage you to use the keyboard shortcuts in your export workflow as soon and as often as possible. They'll be second nature before you know it, and they're great timesavers.

Step 3: Configuring settings to meet your output needs

Okay, okay, I admit it. The broad overview of the Export dialog's panels I provide earlier in the chapter is fine, but we're going to need to drill deeper to understand how each panel works. So get ready for the gory details.

The first choice you're going to make is if you plan to export to your hard drive, to a CD/DVD burner (if you even still have one!), an email, or some export plug-in you've installed. Your most common choice will be Hard Drive. From there, you configure all the panels relating to the choice you made. Although additional panels will appear with different export plug-ins, they are too specific and varied to be covered here; I focus only on the panels that come with the hard drive because that covers the most options.

THE EXPORT LOCATION PANEL

The Export Location panel, shown in Figure 11-2, is used to configure where you want to save a batch of copies on your hard drive. Even if you ultimately burn these copies to DVD or hand them off to another application, Lightroom Classic first needs to save the copies to your hard drive.

Where you choose to save the files is driven by two factors: how you manage your files and what you determine your output needs to be. The Export To drop-down menu provides a few options for designating a location:

>> **Specific Folder:** When you select this option, you can point Lightroom Classic to any folder on your disk. Just make sure it has enough free space to hold all the new copies. Click the Choose button and navigate to the folder you want to use.

>> **Same Folder As Original Photo:** This option does exactly what it describes, which is to put your exported copies back into the same folder as the original.

>> **Choose Folder Later:** This option is useful when you're creating presets and don't want to hard-code a specific location into the preset. When you use a preset, Lightroom Classic prompts you to provide a location.

>> **User Locations:** At the bottom of the drop-down menu will be a list of common user locations like Desktop, Documents, Home, Movies, and Pictures folders to make it easy to select.

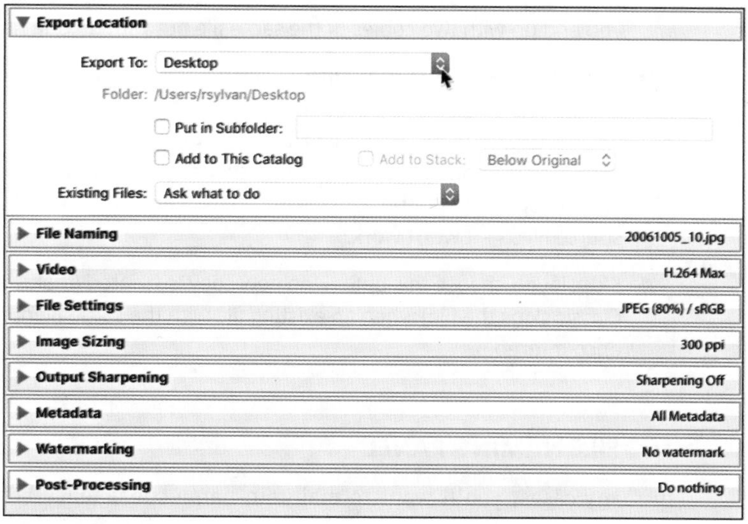

▼ Export Location		
Export To:	Desktop	
Folder:	/Users/rsylvan/Desktop	
	☐ Put in Subfolder:	
	☐ Add to This Catalog ☐ Add to Stack: Below Original ◇	
Existing Files:	Ask what to do	
▶ File Naming		20061005_10.jpg
▶ Video		H.264 Max
▶ File Settings		JPEG (80%) / sRGB
▶ Image Sizing		300 ppi
▶ Output Sharpening		Sharpening Off
▶ Metadata		All Metadata
▶ Watermarking		No watermark
▶ Post-Processing		Do nothing

FIGURE 11-2:
The Export Location panel expanded.

After you choose the location for the export, you have a few additional options to consider:

>> **Put in Subfolder:** This option allows you to create a subfolder within the designated export location. Check the box and enter a name for the subfolder in the corresponding text field.

>> **Add to This Catalog:** Think of this as an Automatic Import option. After your copies are exported, they appear inside Lightroom Classic without your having to go through the Import dialog.

>> **Add to Stack:** Stacking is a function that allows you to arrange groups of photos under a single thumbnail for organizational purposes. This option is available only when you're exporting copies back to the same exact folder as the originals (and not putting them in a subfolder). When checked, the exported photos appear *stacked* with the source photos when you view that folder in Lightroom Classic.

Because you may export photos into a folder that already contains other photos, you must tell Lightroom Classic how to handle situations where your exported copies have the same name and are the same file type as the existing photos. You have four options under the Existing Files drop-down menu:

>> **Ask What to Do:** This option is the safest option and the one I recommend using. If such a situation occurs, Lightroom Classic prompts you for further instructions and then you choose one of the other three options. I like having the reminder.

>> **Choose a New Name for the Exported File:** In this case, Lightroom Classic simply appends a new sequence number to the end of the exported file, so you end up with two copies of the same file but with unique names.

>> **Overwrite WITHOUT WARNING:** Does what it says (and it even uses all caps in the drop-down menu). Only choose this option if you are really sure it is what you want to do. Note that Lightroom Classic does not allow you to overwrite the source photos, so don't choose this option thinking you can export copies with Lightroom Classic adjustments and save over the existing source files — it won't work.

>> **Skip:** If you choose this option, no new copy is created (that is, Lightroom Classic skips the file) when an existing file with the same filename is encountered.

THE FILE NAMING PANEL

In many cases, you'll want to maintain name consistency between your source files and your exported copies. By simply choosing the Filename template, you can achieve just that. Other times, you may want to use custom names that are completely different or perhaps some variation of the original name, as shown in Figure 11-3. In any case, because you're always creating copies, you must tell Lightroom Classic how you want them named, and just as when you use the Import command or rename files in the Library module, Lightroom Classic uses filename templates to do it.

Click the Template drop-down list and choose one of the installed templates, or you can click Edit and create a custom filename template using the good old Filename Template Editor. See Chapter 4 for more information about creating filename templates.

THE VIDEO PANEL

If you have a video file selected for export, you need to check the Include Video Files check box to access the (limited) format options for video, as shown in Figure 11-4.

>> **DPX:** A lossless format suited for sending to professional video editing tools (like Adobe Premiere). Includes the option to set the quality to 24p, 25p, or 30p. Choose this only if you know it is required.

>> **H.264:** Good for exporting compressed video files for viewing and sharing. A description of each quality setting appears under it when selected. I recommend this option for most people.

>> **Original, unedited file:** Produces an exact copy of the original.

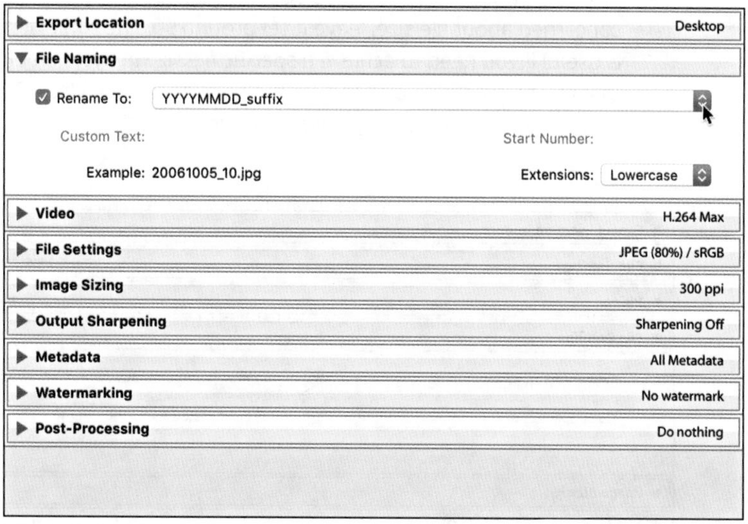

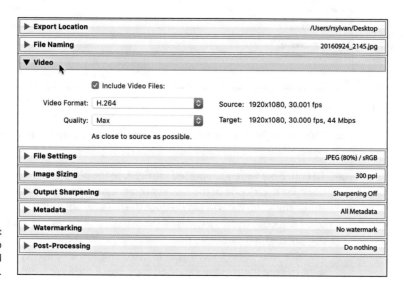

FIGURE 11-3: The File Naming panel.

FIGURE 11-4: The video panel expanded.

THE FILE SETTINGS PANEL

Choose your file format based on your output needs (such as choosing JPEG for photos going on a website). Some formats require additional settings. Here's a list of the formats and their options:

>> **JPEG:** When you choose the JPEG (or JPG) format, you also need to choose the level of compression to be applied to each JPEG file. You make this selection by using the Quality slider, as shown in Figure 11-5. The higher the quality value, the less compression — and the larger the file size. JPEG compression is always a tradeoff between file size and image quality. If you're not too concerned about file size, leave it set around 90. The Limit File Size To option is useful if you need to achieve a specific file size in bytes, but keep in mind that you may need to also reduce the pixel dimensions (see "The Image Sizing panel" later in this chapter) when exporting large files.

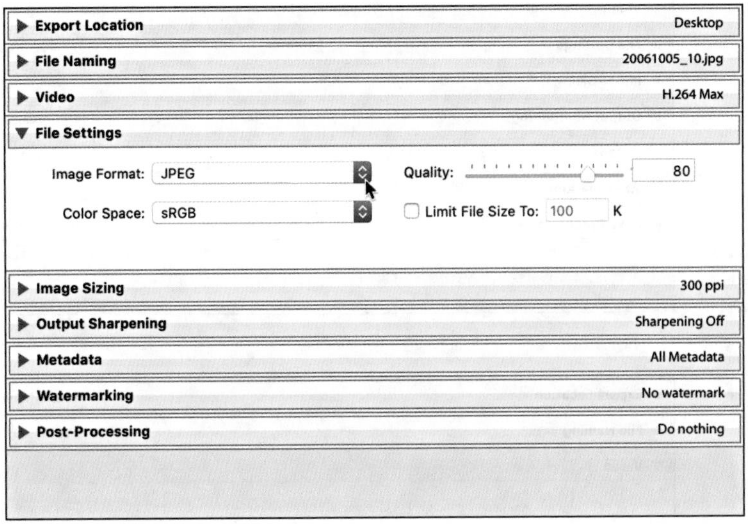

▶ **Export Location**	Desktop
▶ **File Naming**	20061005_10.jpg
▶ **Video**	H.264 Max
▼ **File Settings**	

Image Format: JPEG · · · · · · · · · · · · · · · Quality: ─────────── 80

Color Space: sRGB ☐ Limit File Size To: 100 K

▶ **Image Sizing**	300 ppi
▶ **Output Sharpening**	Sharpening Off
▶ **Metadata**	All Metadata
▶ **Watermarking**	No watermark
▶ **Post-Processing**	Do nothing

FIGURE 11-5:
The File Settings panel expanded to show JPEG format and Quality slider.

>> **PSD:** PSD is Photoshop's native file format. You can choose between 8- and 16-bit.

>> **TIFF:** TIFF is a widely supported format. Use the panel's Compression drop-down list to pick one of the lossless compression options. "None" is pretty straightforward; ZIP and LZW reduce the file size, but the length of time to open and close the file increases. (Note that not all image editors can open compressed TIFF files. Also note that only the ZIP compression option is available with 16-bit files.) If your photo contains transparent pixels and you want to keep them in the exported copy, check the Save Transparency box.

>> **PNG:** Good for web graphics, but can also work well as an alternative to JPG.

>> **DNG:** This is Adobe's open format for raw (unprocessed by the camera) photos. See Chapter 7 for more on DNG. Note that the Use Lossy Compression option is occasionally useful for situations in which you want to keep the exported copy as a DNG file while also reducing its pixel dimensions by using the options in the Image Sizing panel.

>> **Original:** Selecting Original from the drop-down list results in the creation of an exact copy of your source image. (Raw and DNG photos include Lightroom Classic edits in the photo's XMP metadata.) No additional file settings are available with this option.

Two additional options, which appear only when you choose JPEG, TIFF, and PSD formats, warrant a separate discussion. (Raw files are always 16–bit and don't have a color space.)

>> **Color Space:** A photo's color space is what determines the range of possible colors it can contain. You need to decide what color space you want these copies converted into during the export process. Your choice of color space is determined by the reason you are exporting these copies to begin with and where they will be used. You can find a more in-depth discussion of color spaces in Chapter 3, but here's a look at your choices:

   ● *sRGB*: This color space contains the narrowest range of colors and is the standard for exporting photos destined for the web. It's also used by some print services.

   ● *AdobeRGB (1998):* Contains a wider range of colors than sRGB and is most often used when additional editing or printing is the next destination for your files.

   ● *ProPhoto RGB:* Contains the widest range of colors and should only be used with 16-bit files. (I discuss bit depth in the next boldfaced bullet.) This is the best option when you want to retain all the color information that was in your source files. Not recommended when delivering copies destined for the web or anyone not used to working with ProPhoto color space.

   ● *Other:* Whereas the previous three options are the most common, there may also be advanced situations where you need to convert your files to a custom color space for printing purposes. Consult your print service to see whether it provides or requires custom profiles, and it will help you get them installed. By choosing Other, you'll be taken to the Choose Profiles dialog, where you can select a color profile.

>> **Bit Depth:** *Bit depth* determines the amount of data a file contains. The higher the bit depth, the more data is contained in the file (which also means its file

size is going to be larger too). If you're working with raw files, you're working with 16-bit files. If you're working with JPEG files, you're working with 8-bit files. During export, you have the option of saving PSD and TIFF files as 16-bit. If you choose JPEG, bit depth is grayed out, but know that JPEGs are all 8-bit by default. Saving files in 16-bit only makes sense when both the source files were originally 16-bit and when the output needs require this original data (such as when you plan to archive the exported copies to DVD or edit them in some other image editor). In all other situations, 8-bit is the more common choice.

THE IMAGE SIZING PANEL

Sometimes, you need to save your exported copies in a different size from the source photos, such as when you want to email them or put them in a web page. To do so, you use options in the Image Sizing panel (see Figure 11-6). Lightroom Classic can make the exported images smaller or larger than the original images — a process known as *resampling*. The six options for resizing your exports are

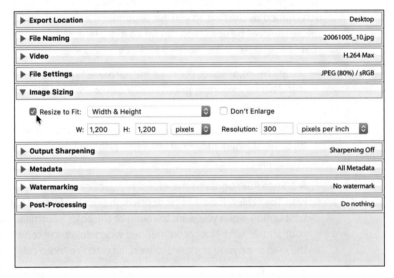

FIGURE 11-6: The Image Sizing panel.

>> **Width & Height:** The values entered for width and height define the maximum amount each side can be resized to fit while maintaining original aspect ratio.

>> **Dimensions:** This option resizes exported images to fit within the entered dimensions while maintaining aspect ratio. When this option is selected, height and width are no longer associated with the values fields. You just

enter the maximum dimensions you want the images resized to fit, and Lightroom Classic does the rest regardless of orientation.

>> **Megapixels:** If you need to resize to a specific total number of pixels (width times height), this is your option.

>> **Long Edge** and **Shortest Edge:** These options function in the same manner. You set the maximum value for the edge in question, and Lightroom Classic resizes all images to fit.

>> **Percentage:** This option is useful when you want to create exported copies that are a certain percentage smaller than the original.

Check the Don't Enlarge box to prevent an image from being resampled larger than its original pixel dimensions. (This option is grayed out when Resize to Fit is unchecked.)

If your output needs require your photos to print at a specific size and at a specific number of pixels per inch (PPI), you can set its *resolution* value — the metadata tag used by software to determine how big the printed file appears. For example, the value of 300 PPI is commonly requested by print services, in which case you would enter **300** and choose pixels per inch. 300 PPI is always a safe choice, but if your photos are destined for the web only, this value is meaningless and can be ignored.

THE OUTPUT SHARPENING PANEL

I love having the ability to add sharpening tailored for the specific output destination as part of the export process. The Output Sharpening panel, shown in Figure 11-7, is where you choose and configure your output sharpening settings. The possible output settings are defined as

>> **Screen:** Use this option when your photo's final viewing destination will be on a computer screen (that is, on a web page).

>> **Matte Paper:** Use this option when you're sending your photos to be printed on a type of photo paper that has a matte (non-shiny) finish.

>> **Glossy Paper:** Use this option when you're sending your photos to be printed on a type of photo paper that has a glossy (shiny) finish.

After you identify the output you are sharpening for, you can set the amount of sharpening to apply; your choices here range from Low (almost none) to High (often too much), with Standard in the middle (just right).

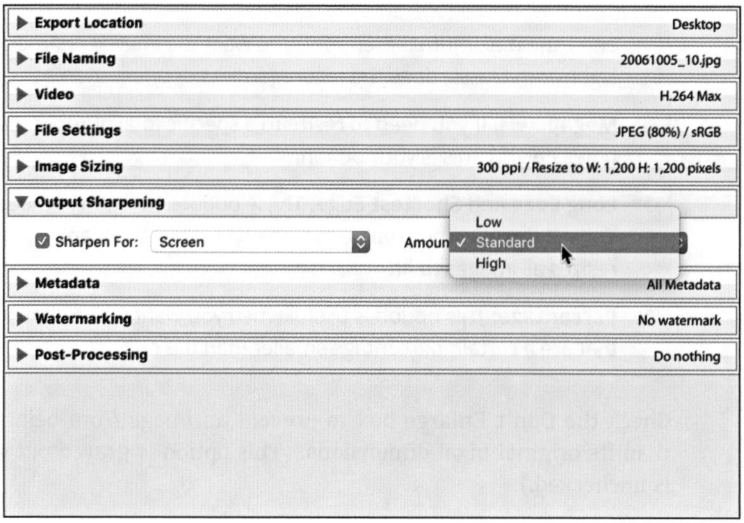

FIGURE 11-7:
The Output
Sharpening
panel.

THE METADATA PANEL

The Metadata panel, shown in Figure 11-8, allows you some level of control over what metadata is included in the exported copies. Clicking the Include drop-down menu offers the following options:

>> **Copyright Only:** Only the metadata entered into the Copyright field of the Metadata panel is applied to copies.

>> **Copyright & Contact Info Only:** This is the same as the previous option with the inclusion of any contact information you applied via the Metadata panel (or a metadata template).

>> **All Except Camera Raw Info:** Camera Raw Info means the actual slider values dialed into Lightroom Classic, written as part of the metadata (the adjustments themselves are applied to the pixels regardless of any of these settings). So this option builds on the previous option and then includes all other metadata except the slider values (Camera Raw Info).

>> **All Except Camera & Camera Raw Info:** This does everything that the previous option does but leaves out the camera-generated EXIF metadata and the Camera Raw Info.

>> **All Metadata:** Nothing is left out. All EXIF metadata created by the camera, plus everything added in Lightroom Classic, is applied to copies.

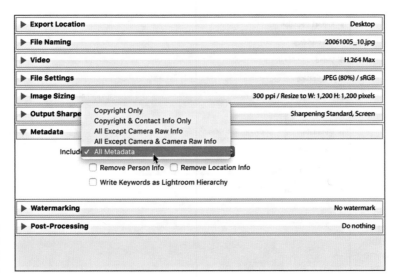

FIGURE 11-8:
The Metadata
panel
expanded.

The Metadata panel has three additional check boxes:

>> **Remove Person Info:** If you used People view to tag photos with the names of the people shown, you can check this box to avoid writing that information into the metadata of the exported copies.

>> **Remove Location Info:** If your photos have GPS information in them, you can check this box to avoid writing that information into the metadata of exported copies.

>> **Write Keywords as Lightroom Hierarchy:** Keywords are the descriptive terms you assign to your photos in the Library module. When you enable this option, and use keywords with parent/child relationships (meaning that the keywords are in a hierarchical structure), the exported copies retain that same keyword structure. This feature is useful for photos that will be imported into another Lightroom Classic catalog or managed with Adobe Bridge. Chapter 6 explains Lightroom Classic's use of keywords.

THE WATERMARKING PANEL

You can apply one of three types of watermarks to exported copies. Check the Watermark box (see Figure 11-9) to enable the drop-down choices. The most basic is the Simple Copyright Watermark, which pulls the information from the Copyright field of each file's metadata and renders it as a watermark in the lower left corner of each exported copy. This type of watermark has no configuration options.

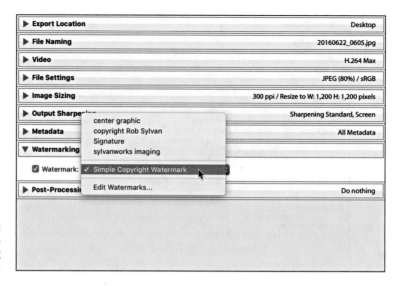

center graphic
copyright Rob Sylvan
Signature
sylvanworks imaging
✓ Simple Copyright Watermark

Edit Watermarks...

FIGURE 11-9:
The
Watermarking
options.

For greater control, choose Edit Watermarks to enter the Watermark Editor, where you can create either a text-based or graphical watermark with more control and save it as a preset for easy reuse. See Chapter 15 for a closer look at the Watermark Editor.

THE POST-PROCESSING PANEL

This is an optional panel, but it can provide a nice productivity boost to your output when you know your photos are going to be opened in some other application after they have been created (such as for additional image editing or viewing in your file browser). The Post-Processing panel (with the After Export drop-down list expanded) is shown in Figure 11-10. With the help of the options in this panel, you can tell Lightroom Classic to hand off your exported images to another application — in effect, having Lightroom Classic perform what is commonly referred to as an "export action" on your photos. The After Export drop-down list includes the following preinstalled options:

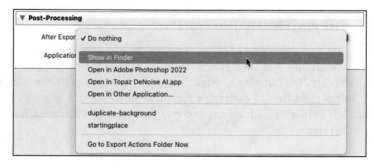

FIGURE 11-10:
Post-
Processing
panel
expanded to
show After
Export options.

▼ Post-Processing

After Expor | ✓ Do nothing
Application | Show in Finder
Open in Adobe Photoshop 2022
Open in Topaz DeNoise AI.app
Open in Other Application...

duplicate-background
startingplace

Go to Export Actions Folder Now

>> **Show in Finder (Show in Explorer for Windows):** Automatically opens the folder containing the exported images in your file browser.

>> **Open in Photoshop:** If you have Photoshop installed, you have the option to open the exported images in Photoshop after they're saved to the export location.

>> **Open in Additional Editor:** If you configured an additional external editor (covered later in this chapter, in "Configuring Your External Editors") you see it listed here as an option.

>> **Open in Other Application:** Selecting this option gives you the opportunity to designate another application (such as an email client, an alternative image editor, or an FTP client) that will be invoked at the end of the export. Lightroom Classic attempts to open the exported photos in that application; just keep in mind that not every application can accept images this way. Click the Choose button and navigate to the application you want to send your photos to.

At the bottom of the After Export drop-down list is the Go to Export Actions Folder Now command. Selecting this option opens Finder (or Windows Explorer for Windows) with Lightroom Classic's Export Actions folder selected. You can place either an executable file or an alias (shortcut for Windows) to an executable file in the Export Actions folder to include it as an option in the After Export drop-down list the next time you start Lightroom Classic. This is another way to set things up so you can send your photos to a specific program or a Photoshop droplet with one quick command.

TECHNICAL STUFF

"What's a droplet?" you say. A *droplet* is a Photoshop action that you manage to turn (with Photoshop's help) into a tiny executable file. After you create a droplet, you can literally drag and drop photos on top of it to run the photos through the action automatically — a really powerful way to run a batch of images through a favorite action, such as applying a specific Photoshop filter, converting to an alternative color space, or applying a custom watermark. By including the droplet as an export action, Lightroom Classic automatically runs the exported copies through the droplet after they are created.

Saving settings as a preset for reuse

Presets are such an awesome timesaver! Just think about it — you get to save scads of commonly used settings and then access them any time you want to directly from the Export with Preset menu (choose File ⇨ Export with Preset). Sweet!

Refer to Figure 11-1 to see the Presets panel — it's there on the left side. You get four preinstalled presets to start you off, right under the Lightroom Classic Presets heading — presets that can't be ditched or updated, by the way. They are

>> **Burn Full-Sized JPEGs:** Sets JPG as the file format with the least compression and no resizing and then adds burning the exported images to a disc as an After Export step.

>> **Export to DNG:** Sets DNG as the file format, which essentially means you're set to convert to DNG on export. Note that using this preset makes sense only when your source files are raw format.

>> **For Email:** Sets JPG as the file format with JPG compression set to 60 and resizes all images to fit within 500 x 500 pixels. This option tells Lightroom Classic to pass exported copies to your default mail client when you export them.

>> **For Email (Hard Drive):** Sets JPG as the file format with JPG compression set to 50 and resizes all images to fit within 640 x 640 pixels. Note that this preset doesn't actually pass files to your email client; it just configures the export to an email-friendly size and saves the files to a location of your choosing on your hard drive.

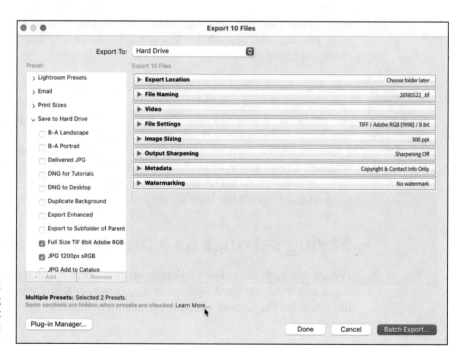

FIGURE 11-11: Selecting multiple export presets for a batch export.

I'm the first to admit that the preinstalled presets aren't incredibly sophisticated, but they can make good starting points and can help you see the possibilities. For example, I do like to email photos to friends and family, so I took the For Email preset as a starting point and customized it to my liking. Here's how I did that:

1. **Click the For Email preset to load its settings into the Export dialog.**

    When selecting a preset, click the preset's name to load its settings. The check box to the left of the preset name is for batch exports, which is covered next.

2. **Expand the File Settings panel.**

    I prefer a higher Quality setting, so I set mine to 70.

3. **Expand the Image Sizing panel.**

    I prefer a larger pixel dimension, so I set mine to 1000 pixels.

4. **Expand the Output Sharpening panel.**

    I checked the Sharpen For box and selected Screen at a Standard amount.

5. **Leave the settings in the remaining panels as they are.**

    This is up to you, of course, but the remaining settings work great for me, so I didn't need to change them.

6. **Click the Add button at the bottom left of the Presets panel.**

    This opens the New Preset dialog.

7. **Enter a descriptive name in the Preset Name field.**

8. **(Optional) Create a new folder in the process of saving your preset.**

    TIP

    You can click the Folder drop-down list and choose an existing preset folder or create a new one. I find that keeping presets organized in folders makes it easier to find the one I'm looking for.

9. **Click the Create button to complete the process and add the preset to the Preset panel.**

WARNING

You can delete custom presets and folders by highlighting them and clicking the Remove button. Note, however, that removing a folder deletes any presets inside it!

You can update custom presets with new settings by adjusting the settings as you want, right-clicking the preset, and then choosing Update with Current Settings. To close the Export dialog without creating copies, click Done.

Creating a Batch Export

As I mention previously, if you want to load the settings of a single preset into the Export dialog, just click the preset's name. The check box to the left of each preset is for when you want to apply the settings of more than one preset to the photos being exported. Why might you want to do that? What if you needed to deliver copies to someone who requested a full size TIF and a JPG that was resized down for social media sharing? Or maybe you need to export the same photo in a range of sizes? You could perform the export in separate instances, but with the batch export function you can create multiple versions of the copies in one fell swoop!

The first step in the process is to create the presets to match the desired export purposes. In my example (refer to Figure 11-11) I have checked the box next to the preset for the full size TIF and the box next to the resized JPG. As soon as you check the first box, the panels on the Export dialog are set to read-only (meaning you can't change the settings further for this export). Once you've checked the boxes for each preset you want to apply to this batch, click the Batch Export button to advance. If your presets included the Choose folder later option (from the Export Location panel), then you'll be presented with a dialog for choosing the folders for where these copies will be saved; otherwise, it uses the export location included in the preset. From there, click Export to begin the process of creating the copies based on the selected settings.

Configuring Your External Editors

Sending a photo to an external editor is basically a specialized type of export, so let's take a closer look at what's involved. I go over the External Editor settings back in Chapter 3 — along with all the other preference settings — but I want to remind you of them because this is where you actually use them. Because Lightroom Classic is an Adobe product, it does play favorites with Photoshop. Lightroom Classic reserves the primary (default) external editor slot for Photoshop and will automatically recognize it if installed. Although you can't manually configure the default editor, you can choose any other image-editing application as the secondary editor (and save the settings as a custom preset). Here's how to set up your primary external editor settings, as shown in Figure 11-12:

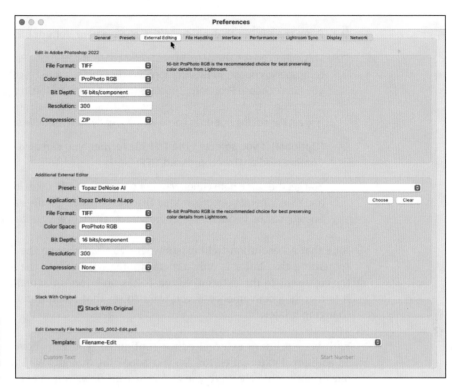

FIGURE 11-12:
External
Editing
preference
settings.

1. **Choose Lightroom Classic ⇨ Preferences (Edit ⇨ Preferences for Windows) from the main menu.**

The Preferences window appears.

2. **In the Preferences window, click the External Editing tab.**

3. **Choose your default file type from the File Format drop-down list.**

PSD and TIFF file formats are, for all intents and purposes, equal to the task of supporting anything you can imagine doing in Photoshop. TIFF is a more widely supported format outside the Adobe family, whereas PSD is Photoshop's native file format. I tend to lean toward TIFF, but you really can't go wrong either way.

4. **Choose your default color space from the Color Space drop-down list.**

Your choices here are ProPhoto RGB, Adobe RGB, Display P3, and sRGB. If you've configured your camera to save photos in raw format and want to maintain as much of the original color as possible throughout the editing process, choose ProPhoto RGB. If you've configured your camera to save photos in JPG format, you've already made a color space choice in your camera settings, so you may as well choose that same color space here to be consistent.

5. **From the Bit Depth drop-down list, choose your default bit depth.**

This option goes hand in hand with color space. If you chose ProPhoto as your color space, choose 16 Bits/Component. (ProPhoto is a 16-bit color space.) If you didn't choose ProPhoto, choose 8 Bits/Component. The important difference is that a 16-bit file contains much more data than an 8-bit file, which is great for editing but does come with a greatly increased file size.

6. **(Optional) If you selected the TIFF file format, you can also choose either Compressed or Uncompressed TIFF.**

You get the same data either way, but compressed TIFF takes longer to open and save, whereas uncompressed TIFF files have a larger file size. I favor uncompressed because I prefer the speed benefit over the size cost.

Note that a Resolution field exists where you can change the default 240 PPI to something else, but it is only a metadata tag written into the Resolution field of the copy sent to the external editor. It has no effect on actual pixel dimensions. It is merely a convenience if you want to set that resolution tag now instead of changing it later.

With your primary external editor configured, you can move on to setting up an additional external editor. Do you need one, though? Well, whether you need one or not is entirely up to you and your workflow. You may not have Photoshop installed, or perhaps you prefer another image editor for certain tasks. Lightroom Classic just provides you the option. Here's how to set up an additional external editor:

1. **Click the Choose button in the Additional External Editor section of the External Editing preferences dialog (refer to Figure 11-12).**

2. **In the dialog that appears, navigate to the application file you want to use, and then select it and click Choose.**

TIP

On a Mac, look in the Applications folder. On a PC, you find the application files in the Program Files folder. In both cases, Lightroom Classic should open the correct folder by default, but if it doesn't you'll have to navigate to the right place. After you've selected the application and clicked Choose, you're brought back to the External Editing dialog with your application choice displayed.

3. **Configure File Format, Color Space, and Bit Depth as desired.**

The choices you make here depend on the image editor you choose (not every application supports 16-bit files, for example), but be consistent with the settings you choose for your primary editor.

4. **Choose Save Current Settings as New Preset from the Preset drop-down menu.**

Doing so launches the New Preset dialog. This step is optional but recommended. By saving your Additional Editor settings as a preset, you can actually configure more than one additional editor, which gives you more options for how you want to edit your photos. You could even save different configuration settings for the same application.

5. **Give the preset a descriptive name and click Create.**

The preset names appear in the External Editor menu when you choose to send a photo out for additional work, so give it a name that tells you the name of the application and possibly hints at the settings. Doing so makes life easier for you when you want to use the preset.

After you create that preset, you can go back to Step 1 and repeat the process to configure additional applications. At any point in the future, you can return to this dialog and add new editors. Note, some third-party image editors will create presets here when installed.

6. **Click OK to close the Preferences dialog.**

When Lightroom Classic creates a copy of your source photo to send to an external editor, it needs to give that copy a new name — technically, just a variation on the source photo's name. The naming convention you want Lightroom Classic to use when it creates these copies is the last option in the External Editing preference dialog. By default, Lightroom Classic appends –Edit to the end of the filename. (You can see an example of this to the right of the Edit Externally File Naming heading.) If that works for you, you don't need to do anything else. If you want to customize how edited files are named, you can choose Edit from the Template drop-down menu and configure a naming convention of your choice in the same Filename Template Editor I cover in Chapter 4.

If you choose to work with the PSD format, open Photoshop's preferences and turn on Maximize Compatibility. Choose Photoshop ➪ Preferences ➪ File Handling (Edit ➪ Preferences ➪ File Handling for Windows) from the main menu and set Maximize PSD and PSB File Compatibility to Always. Doing so enables Lightroom Classic to import your layered PSD files without any problems.

Basic Editing in an External Editor

The most common reason to send a photo from Lightroom Classic to an external editor is when you simply need to do something with a photo that Lightroom Classic cannot do (or doesn't do as well as some other editor). This typically comes after you make all the Lightroom Classic adjustments your photo requires and before you're ready to move to some form of output (book, print, slideshow, web, file export). Here's how to send photos to an external editor from Grid view in the Library module:

1. **Select your photo(s) in either the Filmstrip or Grid view.**

   Technically, you can access the External Editor menu from just about anywhere you can see a photo inside Lightroom Classic, but the most likely place will be either Grid view in the Library module or the Filmstrip in any module. (Refer to Chapter 1 for an overview of Lightroom Classic's interface components.)

REMEMBER

   You can send more than one image to your external editor. Just be aware that the more files you send, the more computer resources are required to process that much data.

2. **Right-click the photo and choose your external editor from the contextual pop-up menu that appears by choosing Edit in ⇨ Edit in (*your editor*).**

   Figure 11-13 shows the menu options if you have the latest version of Photoshop as your primary editor. In this example, I sent my selected photo to Photoshop, but the process works the same for all editors. You can see the additional editor presets I made earlier in the chapter are listed there as well. After you select your editor, Lightroom Classic does a few things, such as

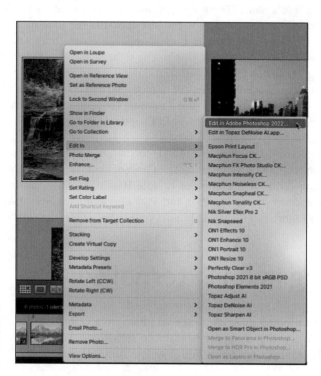

FIGURE 11-13:
The Edit in
External Editor
contextual
menu.

- Rendering a copy of the selected photo based on your external editor default settings.

- Opening that photo in your external editor.

Note that what's really happening here is a file hand-off between Lightroom Classic and your external editor. If you're working with raw files in Lightroom Classic, a rendered copy of the raw file must be created before it can be sent to your external editor. However, if you're sending a rendered file (PSD, TIF, PNG, or JPG) to your external editor, you have the following choices, as shown in Figure 11-14:

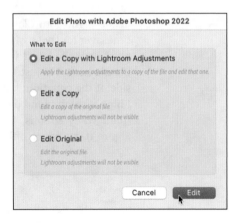

FIGURE 11-14:
The Edit Photo with External Editor options.

- **Edit a Copy with Lightroom Adjustments:** This is the only option that enables you to incorporate your Lightroom Classic adjustments into the copy you edit in the external editor. If you selected a layered PSD or TIF file and you choose this option, the layers will be flattened in the copy so that the adjustments can be applied.

- **Edit a Copy:** This option simply creates an exact copy of the selected photo and opens it in your editor. If the original photo was a PSD or TIF file and it contained layers, those layers are also in this new copy. No adjustments are applied.

- **Edit Original:** Your original image is opened in the editor as it was the last time you saved and closed it in an external editor.

3. **Perform desired edits in the external editor.**

4. **Save and then close the photo in the external editor.**

Don't choose Save As in this step because you'd be making a new copy of that file that Lightroom Classic doesn't know anything about. By saving and then closing the file, you're telling Lightroom Classic you're done working on it. Lightroom Classic updates its preview of the edited photo to reflect the changes.

Advanced Editing Options with Photoshop

Photoshop has some advanced external-editing options that leverage powerful functionality built into Photoshop. This integration creates a direct path from inside Lightroom Classic right into the chosen Photoshop option, so it's a real timesaver for those who were using these options previously. For this to work, you must have the latest version of Photoshop installed. Because this is a Lightroom Classic book, I'll just highlight what you need to know on the Lightroom Classic side of the equation; but if you want to learn more about Photoshop specifically, I highly recommend picking up a copy of Peter Bauer's *Photoshop CC For Dummies* (John Wiley & Sons, Inc.). You can choose from four menu options, shown in Figure 11-15, which only appear if you have Photoshop installed:

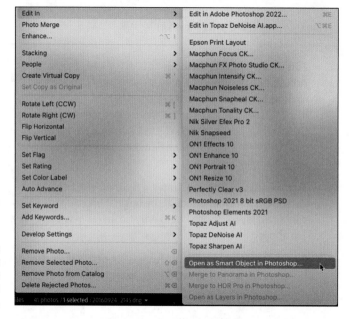

FIGURE 11-15:
Edit in
Photoshop
menu
commands.

>> **Open as Smart Object in Photoshop:** A *smart object* is a special kind of Photoshop layer that embeds a copy of the photo you select in Lightroom Classic inside the layer. The benefit of this option is that you retain the ability to go back and edit the embedded source file at any time while working in Photoshop.

Going the smart object route is most useful when your source photo happens to be a raw file, because then a copy of the raw file itself is embedded within the smart object. If you want to make further adjustments to the raw file, you can open it from the smart object into Photoshop's raw editor plug-in, called Adobe Camera Raw, make your adjustments, and then put the edited photo back inside the smart object to continue your Photoshop editing. This can be a very powerful editing combination.

>> **Merge to Panorama in Photoshop:** A *panorama* is a photo that encompasses a very wide field of view (sometimes as much as a full 360 degrees). Although some cameras are available that can capture a single panoramic photo, it is far more common these days for a photographer to create a panorama from a series of photos which, although taken from the same point, manage to cover a wide range of the scene. Photoshop has a powerful feature called *Photomerge* that can take a series of these photographs and seamlessly combine them into a single merged photo. This Lightroom Classic function allows you to select your series of photos in Lightroom Classic and send them directly to Photomerge inside Photoshop.

>> **Merge to HDR in Photoshop:** HDR stands for *High Dynamic Range*, which means a photo that contains detail all the way from the brightest highlights to the darkest shadows. Our eyes (and brain) are quite good at this by design; just imagine standing in your house looking out at a bright sunny day. You can see detail in the shadows of the room you are in as well as the white puffy clouds in the sky outside the window. Now try to take a photo of that same view that captures the shadow detail of the interior as well as the highlight detail of the clouds — you can't! Your camera just can't capture detail across that wide of a range of brightness levels, at least not in a single photo.

You can take a series of photos of the same scene, changing the exposure with each photo, to capture a different range of brightness values (from dark shadows to bright highlights) and then combine them all into a single photo that contains the full high dynamic range of brightness levels. To do so, you use the Merge to HDR command. If you have such a series of photos, you can select them in Lightroom Classic and then use this menu command to send them directly to Photoshop's Merge to HDR, which then does the work of combining the photos into a single image.

>> **Open as Layers in Photoshop:** This option is not as fancy as the other three, but it may be the one you use most often. What it does is allow you to select multiple photos in Lightroom Classic and send them all to a single new document in Photoshop, with each photo being placed on its own separate layer. This is extremely handy when you have two or more photos that you'd like to combine into a single composite photo, such as taking multiple photos of the same group of people and creating a composite that shows a final version where everyone's eyes are open and mouths are shut.

The workflow with these advanced options is essentially the same as the basic editing, in that you still

1. **Select the photos you want to send to Photoshop from within Lightroom Classic.**

2. **Choose the type of editing option you want to use from the Photo ⇨ Edit In menu.**

3. **Perform the work inside Photoshop.**

4. **Save and close the file in Photoshop and return to Lightroom Classic.**

REMEMBER

If you have only a single photo selected, the only Photoshop option enabled is Open as Smart Object in Photoshop, because the other three options require multiple photos to be selected.

The options here for creating HDR and panoramic photos with Photoshop are useful, but be sure to check out the section in Chapter 7 on using Lightroom Classic's built-in Photo Merge functions for creating HDR, Panos, and even HDR Panos.

» **Establishing a book workflow**

» **Customizing book layouts**

» **Uploading your book**

Chapter **12**

Designing a Book

Photo books are a great way to showcase your work, make excellent gifts, and can even be made available for sale. The Book module in Lightroom Classic gives you the tools to design a book from scratch using the photos you've already selected and edited in your workflow. Adobe has partnered exclusively with Blurb.com to provide seamless upload and purchase right from within Lightroom Classic. You can choose from a variety of book sizes, paper types, and page templates to create eye-popping photo books with ease.

Exploring the Book Module

I'd like to take a moment to reinforce that each Lightroom Classic module is structured essentially the same way, which means the interface behaves the same no matter where you are! You can show and hide, and collapse and expand, panels as needed to maximize your work area, and only display the controls you need (refer to Chapter 1 for a refresher on the entire interface).

The module-to-module consistency is an asset to improving your efficiency as you move through your workflow, but as you see as you read about the various modules, each has its own set of panels, tools, and menus devoted to the task at hand. This chapter helps you get oriented to the Book module workspace.

Getting to know the panels and tools

As is typical for all Lightroom Classic modules, the organizational and preview panels are on the left side of the content area, whereas the right side holds the configuration panels. The Filmstrip is across the bottom and the Module Picker is across the top. Specific to each module are the tools provided for completing the task. Here's a brief introduction to the Book interface (minus the repeating elements I cover throughout book), from left to right as shown in Figure 12-1:

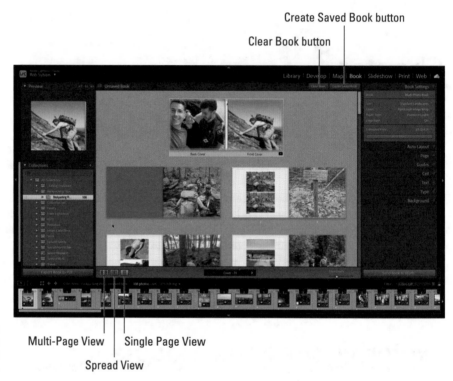

Create Saved Book button

Clear Book button

Multi-Page View | Single Page View

Spread View

>> **Preview:** Displays a preview of the currently selected page of the book.

>> **Collections:** Provides access to all the collections you've created, as well as the controls to add new ones that retain all the Book settings. Refer to Chapter 6 for a Collections refresher, if needed.

>> **Filmstrip:** Displays thumbnails of the active source of photos. The Filmstrip can be used to drag and drop photos onto photo cells within a page of the book.

>> **Content area:** Displays an updating and fully interactive preview of your Book layout.

- » **Toolbar:** Provides controls for accessing different views of the book and navigating between pages.

- » **Book Settings:** Choose book type, book size, cover type, paper type, and estimated cost of printing book through Blurb.

- » **Auto Layout:** Quickly lay out an entire book with a few clicks.

- » **Page:** Choose from a variety of page templates, add page numbering, and add new pages to your book.

- » **Guides:** Enable or disable various visual guides to help lay out your book.

- » **Cell:** Control cell padding and photo borders.

- » **Text:** Controls for photo text and page text.

- » **Type:** Format the font used when text appears within the book.

- » **Background:** Customize the page backgrounds in your book.

Becoming familiar with the menu options

The Lightroom Classic (Mac only), File, Edit, View, Window, and Help menus remain largely consistent throughout Lightroom Classic. Unique to the Book module is the Book menu, which contains commands for creating a saved book, navigating between pages, updating metadata-based captions, and accessing your Book Preferences, as shown in Figure 12-2. The Book Preferences dialog allows you to configure your default options for photo zoom (whether a photo is set to fill a photo cell or simply fit within the cell, maintaining its current aspect ratio), whether you start a new book by automatically filling the layout or not, and the text-box options. There are no wrong answers here, but once you start creating books you might want to customize these settings to fit your needs.

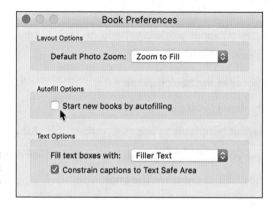

FIGURE 12-2:
The Book preferences dialog.

TIP

I recommend leaving the Constrain captions to the Text Safe Area box checked in the Book Preferences to ensure that you don't accidentally move a caption outside the printable margins of a page.

The Create Saved Book command (notice the button above the content area with the same name) allows you to create a special type of collection containing all the photos in the Filmstrip as well as the settings you've dialed into the Book module. This special collection appears in the Collections panel, and double-clicking its icon returns you to the Book module with all settings loaded. (I explore this in the "Employing a book workflow" section later in this chapter.)

Setting Up a Book

There are any number of reasons for creating a photo book. Some questions you may want to think about before you begin are

>> Who is your intended audience and what story are you telling?

>> What photo order will make the most sense and have the most impact (including the front and back covers)?

>> Is there any supporting information (such as captions) that will make this book stronger or more targeted to this audience?

>> What is your budget for this book project?

With that in mind and knowing that new questions will emerge, you can enter your book-making workflow on the right footing.

Employing a book workflow

Lightroom Classic is all about workflows, and designing a book is no different. Here's a high-level overview of the process:

1. **Bring your photos to the Book module.**

2. **Configure your book settings.**

3. **Select page layout templates to use as a starting point for auto layout.**

4. **(Optional) Save your settings and photos as a saved Book collection.**

5. **Customize the order of photos in the book.**

6. **Customize the design of each page.**

7. **Edit the front and back covers.**

8. **Output the book.**

In the next few sections, I take a closer look at each of the steps in the book-making process.

Step 1: Bring your photos to the Book module

The Library module is the most likely place you'll begin to gather your photos before moving to the Book module because it provides the greatest access to your portfolio and contains tools for finding, organizing, and grouping. Whether you select a folder or a collection, or create a grouping based on keywords or metadata, you need to identify and select the photos you want to include in the book (refer to Chapter 5 for a refresher on viewing and finding photos).

TIP

One of the best ways to begin the process is to use a collection because it can contain photos from every corner of your imported portfolio. The other benefits of using a collection are

>> You can manually control the order the images appear in the Book before you begin the layout.

>> You can create an infinite number of collections and sort them independently.

TIP

You can only do a manual sort when you're working within a single folder or a single collection. If you want to manually sort images that are across a range of folders (or collections), you need to put them into a single collection and then sort. Lightroom Classic refers to this sort order as *Custom Order*. After you're in a single folder or a collection, grab the image, not the border, and drag and drop in the order you want, as shown in Figure 12-3. You can do this from the Grid view of the Library module, the Filmstrip in any module, or in the Grid view of the Secondary Display when enabled. The order in which your photos appear in the Filmstrip is the order in which they will be added to the book using Auto Layout (coming up).

FIGURE 12-3:
Manually sorting images within a collection from the Filmstrip.

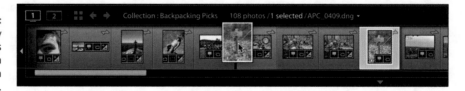

After you've collected your photos for the book, it's time to bring them into the Book module. Notice that the image grouping you created in the Library module is still displayed in the Filmstrip. If needed, you can further refine your image grouping with the Filtering options provided in the Filmstrip (above thumbnails). For example, you could filter your grouping to only images with a rating of three stars or greater by clicking the third star above the thumbnails. The other filtering options (flags, color labels, and so on) work the same way (refer to Chapter 6 for a refresher on filtering).

Step 2: Configure your book settings

You'll want to start in the Book Settings panel to choose the type of book (Blurb Photo Book, Blurb Magazine, Blurb Trade book, PDF, or JPG) from the Book drop-down menu, as shown in Figure 12-4. The choice you make for the book will determine the size of your book as well as what other options are available to customize.

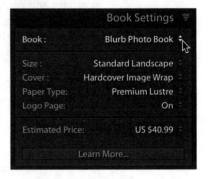

FIGURE 12-4:
The Book Settings panel.

Although you can choose PDF or JPG from the Book menu, which would result in your being able to export the book as a PDF or series of JPG files, respectively, I'm going to focus on creating a Photo Book because that is the most common choice. Be sure to visit Blurb.com to learn more about each of the book types and paper choices, and how to create a free Blurb account to expedite the purchasing process when your book is complete.

Once you've selected your book type, you'll need to make choices on the following aspects of your book:

>> **Size:** You must choose from one of the available sizes for the type of book you choose.

>> **Cover:** Choose from the available types of covers for the book type.

>> **Paper Type:** Each book has a selection of paper options to choose from. Visit Blurb.com to learn more about each paper type, and consider ordering a Swatch Kit while you are there to receive paper samples in the mail to evaluate.

>> **Logo Page:** Only photo books offer the option to add a page with the Blurb logo at the back of the book to receive a discount on the book price. Choosing to have it on results in a 25-percent discount off the base price of the book. I recommend leaving it on for your first book.

These settings form the basis of the book you will create. If you change the book size later, Lightroom Classic will have to change the format and re-layout your book, so it is good to finalize this before you begin.

Step 3: Select page layout templates to use as a starting point for auto layout

By default, when you enter the Book module for the first time, it automatically lays out your book based on the preset selected in the Auto Layout panel. Earlier, I mention the Book Preferences under the Book menu (refer to Figure 12-2), and one of the options there is to start new books by autofilling, which is checked by default. I recommend unchecking that option so that you have time to choose your own layout preset first, and then you can trigger the Auto Layout command manually from the Auto Layout panel.

If your book was laid out automatically and you want to start over, just click the Clear Layout button to start over. To customize your own Auto Layout preset, click the Preset drop-down menu and choose Edit Auto Layout Preset to open the Auto Layout Preset Editor, as shown in Figure 12-5. Here you can choose from all of the various page templates to configure what you want used on the left and right pages of your book. You can further customize individual pages any way you want later on, but setting up Auto Layout with a desired preset gets you off to a fast start. Once you've configured your desired layout options, click the Preset drop-down a second time and choose Save Current Settings as a New Preset to preserve that for the future. Click Done to exit the editor and then click the Auto Layout button in the panel to put it into action. Note that Auto Layout is limited to 240 pages when printing through Blurb (PDF-only books don't have a page limit).

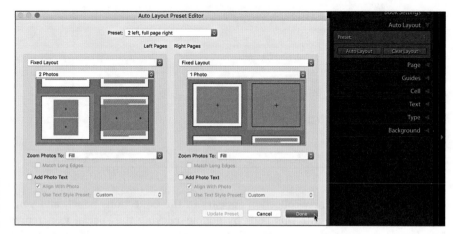

FIGURE 12-5:
The Auto Layout Preset Editor.

Step 4: Save your photos and settings as a special collection

When you create a saved Book collection in the Book module, Lightroom Classic saves all photos in the Filmstrip and your Book settings to a special collection with the icon of a Book. Here's how it works (process is the same in Slideshow, Print, and Web modules):

1. **Click the Create Saved Book button above the content area.**

This opens the Create Book dialog, as shown in Figure 12-6.

2. **Give the book a meaningful name and configure as desired.**

These special saved creations can be put inside regular collections or collection sets. These are the only form of collections that can exist inside another collection. Because they are collections, you can also use this opportunity to fill them with virtual copies (not typically done), set one as the target collection (makes it easy to add more photos later), or sync them with the cloud-based Lightroom. If you save the book before including all photos in the layout, you'll see an option to Include only used photos in this dialog. If checked, then any photos not yet included in your layout will be left out of the saved Book (I'd leave it unchecked).

3. **Click the Create button to complete the process.**

This creates a new collection from the photos used in the book and the book settings. This will continuously update as you work, so you only need to do this once. (The button vanishes after you create a saved book collection.)

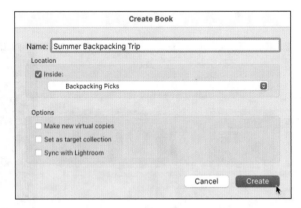

FIGURE 12-6:
The Create Book dialog.

The new collection appears in the Collections panel, and you can quickly jump back into this book by double-clicking the special icon representing the saved creation. Each module has its own icon representing that module.

Step 5: Customize the order of the photos in the book

Now that Auto Layout has run, you are ready to start customizing the order of the photos. Even if you took the time to arrange the photos in a desired order before entering the book module, you may find that when looking at the actual layouts of individual pages that some photos work better next to each other than others. Perhaps the story flows better with a few tweaks to the order, maybe the colors in two photos clash when placed side by side, or perhaps you decide to add new pages and new photos after creating the initial layout. Whatever the reason, the fix is very easy. You can drag and drop photos from one cell to another to swap them on a layout, or you can drag and drop photos from the Filmstrip into any photo cell you want.

Note that a number will appear at the top of each thumbnail in the Filmstrip to indicate how many times that photo appears in the book. A photo with no number at the top doesn't appear in the book, so be sure to keep an eye on the Filmstrip as you continue to edit your book.

BOOK VIEW OPTIONS

You can view your book in a few ways as you work through it. Located on the left side of the Toolbar (refer to Figure 12-1) are three buttons for switching between views (the same options and their keyboard shortcuts are visible under the View menu too). From left to right, they are

>> **Multi-Page View:** Best for viewing all the pages at once, and useful for drag and dropping pages into a new order. Click a page to select it; then click the yellow border to move the page to a new location in the book. The Thumbnails slider at the other end of the Toolbar changes the size of the page thumbnails.

>> **Spread View:** Great for viewing a two-page spread close up. This is a great view when you want to move photos between pages or just see how pages look side by side in the book.

>> **Single Page View:** The best view for customizing a single page or just wanting to see one page up close. Useful when adding text to a page.

You can zoom in even closer using the buttons on the top of the Preview panel, or you can choose View ⇨ Zoomed Page View. Press the I key to show/hide the Info overlay that appears in the upper left of the content area.

Step 6: Customize the design of each page

This is where the real work begins. Auto Layout gives you a good place to start, but you've got the tools to take your book to the next level by varying the page layouts, adding text, changing the background, and more. Generally speaking, the panels on the right side are arranged in a logical top-down order, but in the Book module you're likely to skip around and choose a panel based on the task at hand. In the following sections, I take a deeper dive into what you can do in each of the remaining panels.

PAGE PANEL

The first option to consider in the Page panel is whether to include page numbers in your book. Check the Page Numbers box to include them in your book and access the options for where they will be placed. These options are all WYSIWYG (what you see is what you get), so experiment with various location and display options to see what works best.

You can also add new pages based on one of the page templates or add a new blank page that you can customize yourself by using the relevant buttons at the bottom of the panel. Clicking the Page Picker, shown in Figure 12-7, reveals all of the pre-installed templates as well as any custom pages you have created. To change the template used on a given page, simply select that page and choose a new template via the Page Picker in the Page panel or the Page Picker that appears at the bottom of the selected page.

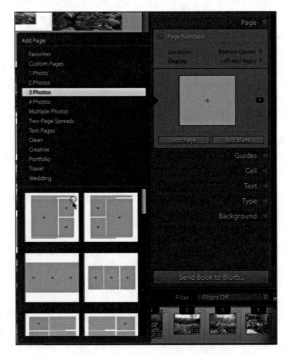

FIGURE 12-7: The Page panel showing the contents of the Page Picker.

As you explore all of the preinstalled templates, you may find a few that you want to mark as Favorites for easy access in future book projects. To mark a template as a Favorite, simply move your cursor over the desired template in the Page Picker and click the small round button that appears in the upper right corner of the template thumbnail. Doing so will add that template to the Favorites section at the top of the Page Picker dialog. Clicking that same small button a second time will remove that template from Favorites.

You can also customize a preinstalled template or customize a blank page from scratch by adding new cells, removing existing cells, arranging the cells on the page, and resizing the cells as you want. Here's how to start with a blank page, add a new photo cell, resize the cell, reposition the cell, and save it as a custom page for reuse:

1. **Select a page in the book where you want to add the new page, and click Add Blank.**

   It can be helpful to work in Single Page view for this. I also recommend showing all of the guides as you begin a custom page and starting with Grid Snap set to Grid.

2. **Right-click an empty area of the page and choose Add Cell ⇨ Photo from the contextual menu, as shown in Figure 12-8.**

   This places a photo cell on the page. This cell will be active, and the resize handles are visible for easy resizing. Reposition the cell by clicking and dragging the center yellow handle. Resize the cell by using any of the resize handles along the outside edge of the cell. Use the guides to assist in placing the cell precisely where you want it to go. You can use that same contextual menu to add more cells or remove cells. Continue customizing the page until it meets your needs.

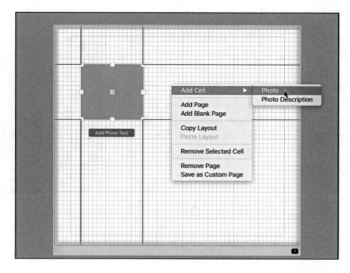

FIGURE 12-8: Adding a new cell to customize a page.

3. **Right-click anywhere on the page and choose Save as Custom Page from the contextual menu.**

   This saves your page for reuse and stores it under the Custom Pages section of the Page Picker. Note that you can also mark custom pages as Favorites.

GUIDES PANEL

Having visual guides when creating a page layout can be incredibly helpful (and sometimes annoying). Expand the Guides panel, as shown in Figure 12-9, to see visual aids at your disposal. You can show (or hide) them all at once by checking (or unchecking) the box next to Show Guides. I recommend starting with them all checked; then turn them off one by one to see which you find helpful as you work. Hover your cursor over each one to see a tooltip with a short description of what each one does.

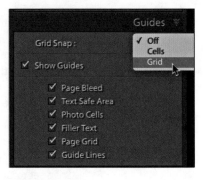

FIGURE 12-9:
The Guides panel.

At the top of the panel is the Grid Snap drop-down menu. There are three options to choose from: Off, Cells, and Grid. These are useful when you are placing or moving a photo or text cell around on a page. If you want help aligning a cell to the page grid (check Page Grid under Guides to see it), choose Grid from the Grid Snap drop-down menu. If it is more helpful to have a cell snap to another cell in the layout, choose Cells instead. Turn it off if it gets in your way.

CELL PANEL

You need to select a cell to enable the options in the Cell panel, shown in Figure 12-10. Padding controls how much space (padding) appears around a photo or text within the boundaries of the cell. Be sure to click the disclosure triangle next to Padding to set the controls for each side independently (if desired). Quite often padding is set to 0 for all sides.

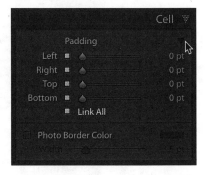

FIGURE 12-10:
The Cell panel.

If you'd like to have a border around the photo cell, you can check the Photo Border Color box to enable it and then use the Width slider to adjust how far it extends from the edge of the cell outward. Click the associated color swatch to set the border color.

TEXT PANEL

There are two types of text cells you can add to a page (or cover):

» **Photo Text:** Associated with each individual photo on a page. Because Photo Text is connected with the photo that appears within the Photo Cell, you can configure Lightroom Classic to populate the text field with metadata from the photo itself (such as its Title or Caption field) by using text templates (covered in Chapter 13) or simply type directly into the field. The cell can be anchored above, over, or below the photo with the buttons in the panel. The offset slider allows you to position the text relative to where it is anchored.

» **Page Text:** Associated with the entire page. Type directly in the field to add text. The cell can be anchored at the top or bottom of the page, and the offset slider allows you to tweak positioning relative to its anchor.

You can add or remove Photo Text by selecting a photo cell and checking or unchecking the Photo Text box in the Text panel (see Figure 12-11). Page Text can be added or removed by selecting the page and checking or unchecking the Page Text box.

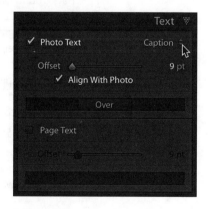

FIGURE 12-11:
The Text panel.

TYPE PANEL

You can use the controls in the Type panel, shown in Figure 12-12, to format the text you enter into either a Photo or Page Text cell. Start by selecting the text within the cell you want to format and then configure the attributes of the text you want to change. You'll mostly be focused on choosing a font and its color, but you can expand the disclosure triangle next to the character color swatch to reveal additional text options. Hover your cursor over each option in the panel to reveal a short description in a tooltip. Once you configure a set of attributes that you want to preserve for reuse, click the Text Style Preset drop-down menu at the top of the panel to save current settings as a new preset.

Note that you cannot preview the fonts within the Book module in any way other than applying the font to the text in your book. You may want to preview fonts ahead of time in another application (such as Photoshop) or your operating system's font viewer for ease of selection. The fonts available in the Book module are simply the fonts installed on your system.

BACKGROUND PANEL

When it comes to the background of the pages of your book (has no effect on the cover), you have a few options to consider (aside from leaving it a blank white page):

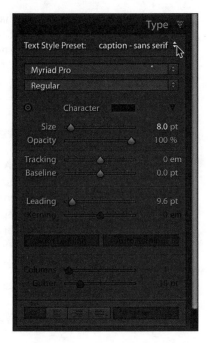

FIGURE 12-12:
The Type panel.

>> **Add a Graphic:** You can add a graphic to the background of the pages of your book in two ways. You can click the Background Graphic Picker, as shown in Figure 12-13, and choose one of the preinstalled graphics found under the Photos, Travel, or Weddings categories inside the picker. You can change the color of one of the preinstalled graphics via the color picker next to the Graphic check box. Or you can select any photo in the Filmstrip and drag it to the place that says Drag Photo Here (right-click that area and choose Remove Photo to clear the photo). After choosing either type of graphic, you can adjust its opacity via the slider.

>> **Change Color:** Whether you add a graphic or not, you can also change the color by simply checking the Background Color box and then clicking the associated swatch to access the color picker and choose the desired color.

If you want the background to be applied to all pages in the book, check the Apply Background Globally check box at the top of the panel before making your selection. If you want to apply the background only to selected pages, select the pages first and then choose the graphic you want to add (leaving Apply Background Globally unchecked).

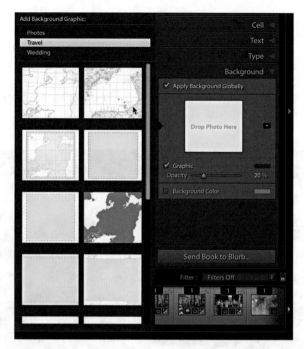

FIGURE 12-13:
The
Background
panel
showing the
preinstalled
graphics.

Step 7: Edit the cover

There's no reason to edit the cover last except that by this time in the process, you will have spent a lot of time looking at the photos used in this project, and you may have new ideas for what you want to do with the cover. Feel free to do this right at the start of the book-making process because you can always update it as you go. Assuming that you ran Auto Layout at the start, it will have populated the cover photo cells right out of the gate. You can replace those photos by using drag and drop, just as you do on the inside pages.

Depending on the type of book you chose at the start, you may have one or a few choices for your book cover. For example, a Blurb Magazine has only a softcover option. Keep in mind that it is only possible to add text to the spine of a hardcover book. You can add text for a title, subtitle, author, and other relevant information by using any combination of Photo Text and Page Text, and the same controls you used for formatting text on the inside pages.

Adding text to the spine of a hardcover book can be fidgety, as shown in Figure 12-14. I find it helpful to zoom to 1:1 view (by using the button on the Preview panel) and then hover the cursor over the spine until I see the text cell highlight. Then I simply single-click the cell and start typing. Make sure that the font size is small enough for the text to fit on the spine by using the controls in the Type panel.

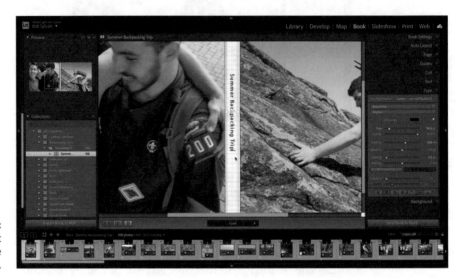

FIGURE 12-14: Entering text on the spine of a book.

Step 8: Output the book

Congratulations! You've completed all your layout tweaks and you're ready to print. A good practice before clicking the Send Book to Blurb button is to click the Export Book to PDF button (located at the bottom of the left panel group). After you click the button, Lightroom Classic prompts you to enter a filename for your book and choose where you want it to be saved. After you specify your choices, click Save. After the PDF is complete, open it up in any PDF reader software and verify that the layouts look the way you want, text appears where it should, and everything is as you designed it. (Note that the cover exports as a separate PDF file due to its different dimensions than the pages of the book.) Check Blurb's help docs if you get any errors during the output process.

When you are ready to complete the process and have the book printed, click the Send Book to Blurb button (located at the bottom of the right panel group). This is where having already created an account (when you visited Blurb.com earlier to learn about book and paper types) comes in handy. You're asked to sign into your Blurb account (though you can create a new account now by clicking the Not a Member link on the Purchase Book dialog). You'll also see the cost of the book and a summary of the book options you chose in Book Settings, as shown in Figure 12-15. From here the book is rendered and uploaded to the Blurb servers in the background.

Some things to keep in mind

I want to close out this chapter with some tips to keep in mind as you begin making your own books. The first thing people ask about is if there is a way to soft-proof a book in Lightroom Classic before uploading to Blurb, and the answer is no. Blurb does provide a profile for people using other software to create books, but you can't use that profile in Lightroom Classic.

When the book is uploaded to Blurb all the file conversions, color space conversions, and output sharpening

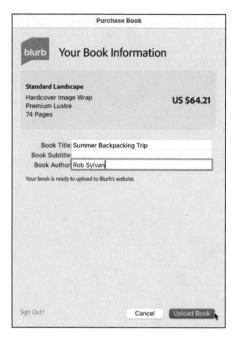

FIGURE 12-15:
The Purchase Book dialog.

happens behind the scenes without user input. That means we can build our books with any photos in our Lightroom Classic catalog and let the Book module handle things on the back end.

I recommend ordering the Swatch Kit I mention earlier to get a good sense of the papers and how photos look printed on each paper type. Using that information, start with a small square book on your preferred paper, with only 20 pages of photos that are a good representation of your work. Treat that as a test run, and work with Blurb's customer support team if you have any problems with the printing. If all is well, go forth with that knowledge making larger books. Keep your eye out for discounts on Blurb books; they seem to always run some sort of deal. Working in Lightroom Classic's Book module has different options than Blurb's own book-making software, so if you find that you're lacking in options, you can always export photos as JPGs out of Lightroom and bring them into any other book-making software.

Chapter **13**

Producing a Slideshow

The Slideshow module offers a flexible interface for creating simple yet professional presentations of your photos. Slideshows aren't only useful for sharing your images with clients, peers, family, and friends, but they can also be a practical tool for reviewing your own work. You have relatively few settings to configure, and the changes update in the main workspace area while you work, so you'll be displaying your images in no time at all!

You can create a slideshow from any grouping of images you can dream of pulling together. Whether the images are a folder, a collection, or an on-the-fly assemblage of images based on dates, keywords, and/or metadata, if you can group them, you can show them. You don't need to be in the Slideshow module to play a slideshow either. Press ⌘+Return (Ctrl+Enter for Windows) from within any module to run an impromptu slideshow, which uses the last configured settings from the Slideshow module to run a show with the active images.

Exploring the Slideshow Module

An important point that bears repeating: The consistency of Lightroom Classic's interface across modules is a key strength as a workflow tool. That's true as far as it goes — otherwise, I wouldn't say it — but be aware that each module performs a unique set of tasks, which means that each module requires a specialized set of panels, tools, and menus. You have to be acquainted with each set.

Getting to know the panels and tools

Before showing you around the Slideshow module, I want to remind you that you can show and hide, and collapse and expand, panels as needed to maximize your work area and display only the controls you need. Refer to Chapter 1 for a complete rundown of the interface controls.

Okay, time to dive in! The left panel contains the organizational and preview panels, whereas the right panel is where the adjusting, tweaking, and modification panels are found. Each module has its own specialized toolbar, but the images always take center stage. Here's a brief introduction to the Slideshow interface (minus any elements that appear across modules), as shown in Figure 13-1:

>> **Preview panel:** Displays a preview of each slideshow's layout while you move your cursor over the templates listed in the Template Browser.

>> **Template Browser:** This Template Browser (or template organizer) is where you find the preinstalled templates as well as all your saved templates.

>> **Export PDF and Export Video buttons:** These buttons provide an alternate output option for your slideshow. Clicking the PDF button creates a single PDF document, and clicking the Video button exports an MP4 file you can play in any video playback software. Hold down the Option (Alt for Windows) to change the Export PDF button to Export JPEG and export a series of still JPEGs of your slideshow.

>> **Options panel:** Controls the look of the photo's border and drop shadow, and how the photo appears within the layout guides.

>> **Layout panel:** The settings in this panel determine the size and location of the photos on the slide.

>> **Overlays panel:** Controls the look of the overlay elements (such as identity plate, text, and ratings) that you can add to enhance a slideshow.

>> **Backdrop panel:** This is where you configure the look of the *backdrop,* which is the part of the slide not covered by the photos.

>> **Titles panel:** Allows you to add optional intro and/or ending slides to your slideshow. This provides a nice finishing touch to any slideshow.

>> **Music panel:** Add, arrange, and remove music tracks to play with your slideshow.

>> **Playback panel:** The place where you configure slide timing, balance audio in video files with music, control pan and zoom effects across slides, and choose playback screens (if using multiple monitors) and other playback settings.

- **» Preview and Play buttons:** Clicking the Preview button plays the slideshow within the Content area, and clicking the Play button controls the start of the full-screen show.

- **» Content area:** Displays a live preview of the active image (or the *most selected* image) within the slide layout.

- **» Toolbar:** Contains the controls for navigation, designating which photos to use in the show, playback, rotating the overlay elements, and the addition of text overlays.

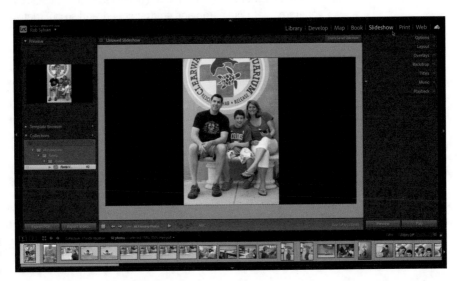

FIGURE 13-1:
The Slideshow
interface.

Becoming familiar with the menu options

The Lightroom Classic (Mac only), File, Edit, View, Window, and Help menus remain largely consistent throughout Lightroom Classic. The menu commands unique to the Slideshow module are related to creation and playback:

- **» Slideshow menu:** Here you find the commands for creating new templates and template folders; exporting a slideshow to PDF, JPEG, or video; adding text overlays; and rotating an image within the slide. The Create Saved Slideshow command allows you to save the current settings and photos as a special collection (same as the button of the same name above the content area).

- **» Play menu:** Contains commands for playing, ending, and navigating within a slideshow. The Content command provides the option to choose which photos within the active image grouping end up being displayed in the show (same task as the Use drop-down menu in the Toolbar).

Creating a Slideshow

Your photos, your intended audience, your reason for showing these images, and your own creativity drive the look of your slideshow. Some questions you want to think about before you begin are

>> Who is my intended audience and what story am I telling them?

>> What image order will make the most sense and impact?

>> Is there any supporting information (such as captions, titles, camera-generated data like f-stop and shutter speed, and so on) that will make this presentation stronger or more targeted to this audience?

>> How much time do I have?

>> Would the addition of an audio component make this slideshow stronger?

With that in mind and knowing that new questions will emerge, you can enter your slideshow workflow on the right footing.

Employing a slideshow workflow

Lightroom Classic is all about workflows. To me, *workflows* are ways to build efficiencies into the repetitive tasks required to reach a desired outcome. Creating a slideshow presentation is no different. The creation of every slideshow follows the same basic steps. Here's an overview of the process:

1. **Select your photos and switch to the Slideshow module.**

2. **Select a template for your starting point.**

3. **Customize the slideshow as desired.**

4. **(Optional) Save your settings as a new template for reuse.**

5. **(Optional) Save your settings and photos as a special slideshow collection.**

The next few sections take a closer look at each of these steps in the process.

Step 1: Bring your photos to the Slideshow module

The Library module is your organizational hub. You've already spent time putting photos into a folder structure, embedding keywords in them, and organizing them into collections. You have an array of camera-generated metadata that can also be used to refine your image groupings further. All these options are accessible from the Library module, and that's why the first step in slideshow creation starts there.

One of the best ways to begin the slideshow process is to use (or create) a collection because it can contain photos from every corner of your portfolio (as I did in Figure 13-1). The other benefits of using a collection are

>> **You can manually control the order in which the images appear in the slideshow.**

You can only do a manual sort when you're working within a single folder or a single collection. So if you want to manually sort images that are across a range of folders (or collections), you need to put them into a single collection and then sort. Lightroom Classic refers to this sort order as *Custom Order.*

>> **You can create an infinite number of collections and sort them independently.**

With your photos in hand (so to speak), bring them into the Slideshow module by clicking Slideshow in the Module Picker. Notice the image grouping you created in the Library module appears in the Filmstrip of the Slideshow module.

Step 2: Select a template for your starting point

A Lightroom Classic template is simply a way of saving unique combinations of settings for reuse. The preinstalled templates are helpful for seeing possibilities but also serve as great jumping-off points for creating your own custom slideshows. You can see a thumbnail layout of any template in the Preview panel by moving your cursor over its name. The five preinstalled templates, shown in Figure 13-2, are listed under the Lightroom Templates heading. Here are the key settings used in each:

>> **Caption and Rating:** Displays the contents of the Caption field from each image's metadata as well as its star rating (if applied).

>> **Crop to Fill:** Layout guides are maximized to fill the screen, and the Zoom to Fill Frame option is enabled (I go over this setting in the next section), which results in images appearing full screen.

>> **Exif Metadata:** Also includes an identity plate but adds several text overlays, which display creator and capture data pulled from each file's EXIF metadata — the information recorded with each photo by the camera, as in f-stop, shutter speed, and similar items.

>> **Simple:** Makes use of an identity plate (a personalized graphic or text element) and a black background.

>> **Widescreen:** The layout guides are maximized to fill the screen, but the Zoom to Fill Frame option is disabled, so images are resized to fit within the layout frame without being cropped or distorted.

Step 3: Customize the slideshow

The right-side panels are where the rubber meets the road when customizing your slideshow. The panels are arranged with an efficient workflow in mind, so start at the top and work your way down. In the beginning of this chapter, I give you a brief introduction to all the panels, but to get you up to speed on how you actually use them, I need to drill down further. In the sections that follow, I go over the key controls within each panel.

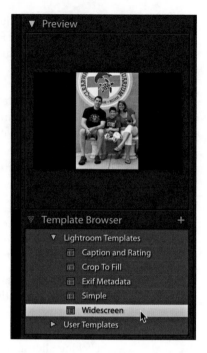

FIGURE 13-2:
The Template Browser and Preview panel displaying Widescreen template.

OPTIONS PANEL

You find three controls in this panel, as shown in Figure 13-3. All three function independently to determine the appearance of the photo on the slide. Here's what they do:

>> **Zoom to Fill Frame:** When the Zoom to Fill Frame option is enabled, the aspect ratio of your images is ignored in favor of the *frame* created by the layout guides (see the following "Layout panel" section). In other words, photos appear zoomed in and cropped if they don't have the same aspect ratio as the frame. With this option disabled, the aspect ratio of each image is respected, and the image is sized to fit within the frame accordingly. Figures 13-4 and 13-5 show the difference this setting can have on the same portrait-oriented image.

WARNING

With Zoom to Fill Frame enabled, all photos are centered in the image area and zoomed until the frame area is filled edge to edge. If a photo appears cropped, you can adjust its position within the frame by clicking and dragging the image to reposition.

>> **Stroke Border:** A stroke border can be used to set the image off the background. Check the box to enable the stroke and then click the color swatch to choose a color. The width of the stroke can range from 1 to 20 pixels. Note that the stroke appears inside the layout frame, so increasing the width of the stroke decreases the size of the photo.

Cast Shadow: The ability to add a drop shadow to each image is another way to set it off from the background. You can adjust the shadow's visibility with the Opacity setting, its distance from the photo with the Offset setting, the hardness of its edges with the Radius

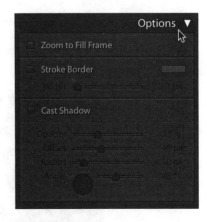

FIGURE 13-3:
The Options panel.

setting, and its direction with the Angle setting. Note that the drop shadow can appear outside the layout frame, so if the layout frame goes to the edge of the slide, a shadow may not be visible. Likewise, if your background color is set to black, you won't see the shadow.

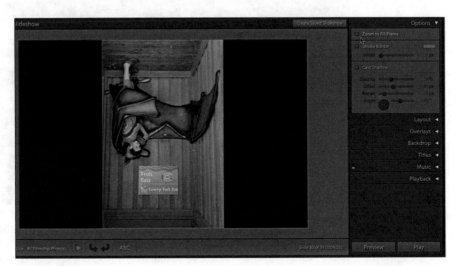

FIGURE 13-4:
Zoom to Fill Frame disabled.

LAYOUT PANEL

Use the controls in the Layout panel to determine the size and placement of the photos on the slide by adjusting the left, right, top, and bottom guides. The guides create the frame that defines the area within which the photos appear and are easier to adjust when visible. Click the Show Guides box to toggle their visibility on and off. In Figure 13-6, the guides are visible. Note that they never appear when the slideshow is playing.

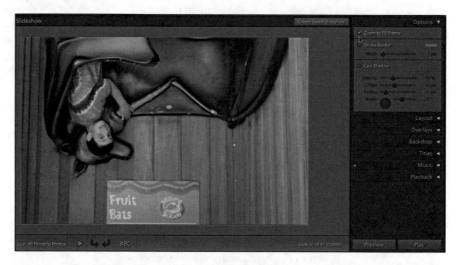

FIGURE 13-5:
Zoom to
Fill Frame
enabled.

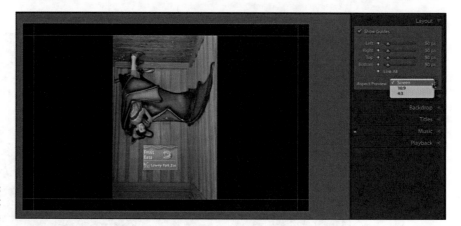

FIGURE 13-6:
The Layout
panel.

TIP

Guides can be adjusted in tandem or individually, depending upon the configuration of which link boxes (the white square buttons next to each guide) are enabled.

Here are the three ways to adjust the guides:

>> **Click and drag the guide.** When the cursor is placed over a guide in the content area, it changes to a double-sided arrow. Click the guide and drag to adjust its position.

- **Use the sliders.** Click and drag the sliders in the Layout panel to move the guides in big increments. Place the cursor over the number field, and it changes to a small, scrubby slider. Click and drag to move the guides in small increments.

- **Change the numbers.** Double-click the number field and enter a pixel amount. This number represents the distance in pixels from the edge of the slide. When the number field is active, you can use the up- and down-arrow keys to increase and decrease that number.

The Aspect Preview drop-down menu lets you see how the slideshow appears on different aspect-ratio displays. Choose Screen if the slideshow will display on the same monitor you are using now, or choose the correct aspect ratio for where the slideshow will play from the list.

OVERLAYS PANEL

Although photos should definitely take center stage in a slideshow, you still have a lot of room to add supporting cast members, such as an identity plate, rating stars, and text. You can add and modify these supporting elements in the Overlays panel, as shown in Figure 13-7. Here's a closer look at each overlay element:

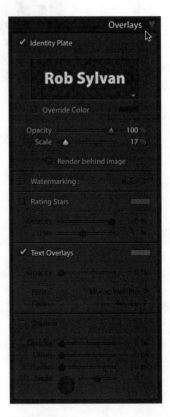

FIGURE 13-7:
The Overlays panel.

- **Identity Plate:** Identity plates can be used to brand your slideshows. Checking the Identity Plate box causes the default identity plate to appear on the slide. You can reposition the plate anywhere on the slide by clicking and dragging it into position. Note that when you drag the identity plate across the slide, you'll see anchor points along the slide or guide edges connecting to the nearest Resize handle on the identity plate, as shown in Figure 13-8. These anchor points appear with every overlay element and can be a great help in aligning elements on the slide.

  You can choose a saved identity plate or create a new one by clicking the Identity Plate drop-down arrow. (Check out Chapter 5 for more on creating identity plates.) You can override the color of your identity plate —

without affecting the saved identity plate — by checking the Override Color box and clicking the color swatch to choose a new color. You can adjust the visibility of the identity plate with the Opacity slider. This is a great way to turn your identity plate into a low-opacity watermark for exported slideshows.

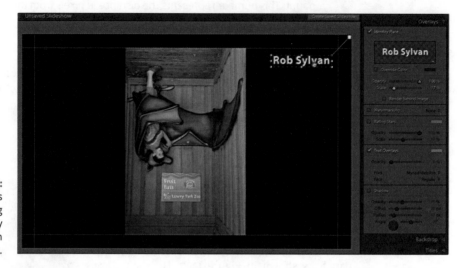

Identity plates can be resized by using either the Resize handles on the object or the Scale slider. Checking the Render behind Image box causes your identity plate to become a background element and display behind the photo, stroke, and shadow.

>> **Watermarking:** Similar to an identity plate in some ways, a watermark can be customized text or a graphic that appears on your photo. You can employ your saved watermarks from here, in the Web module, in the Print module, and when exporting copies. The process to create one is the same in all cases. See Chapter 15 for more on watermark creation.

>> **Rating Stars:** Check the Rating Stars box to display the ratings overlay element on the slide. If you haven't applied ratings, you won't see the rating element on the slide. You can apply a rating to the active image while in the Slideshow module by pressing your 1 to 5 number keys, respectively (even while the slideshow is playing).

You can change the color of the rating stars by clicking the color swatch. The Opacity and Scale sliders work the same as for the identity plate, and the element can be repositioned similarly as well.

>> **Text Overlays:** Although there can be only one identity plate and rating element per slide, you can use any number of text-overlay elements in your presentation. Figure 13-9 shows a title and a date text element in the lower left corner. A customized identity plate appears at the top.

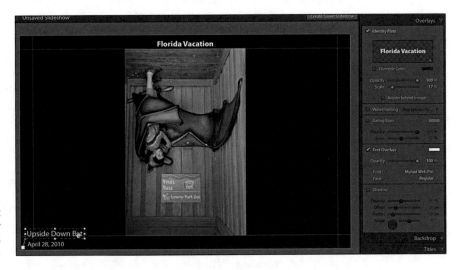

FIGURE 13-9:
Multiple text
overlay
elements
in use.

You can add a new text overlay by clicking the ABC button in the Toolbar or by pressing ⌘+T (Ctrl+T for Windows). After the overlay appears on the slide, you can configure the textual content from the Toolbar by clicking the ABC drop-down menu and selecting an existing text template, or choosing Edit from the bottom of the menu to create your own text template with the Text Template Editor. (I'll go through a step-by-step example of the Text Template Editor shortly.) If you choose the Custom Text template, an input field appears on the Toolbar. Just enter your text and press Enter.

REMEMBER

Any Text Overlay you add is going to appear on every slide. If you want the contents of the Text Overlay to change with each photo, choose a text template that displays the title, caption, or some other information that is pulled dynamically from each photo's own metadata (refer to Chapter 6).

Because multiple text overlays can be used in a slideshow, they each need to be adjusted independently. After you select a text element, the dotted border and Resize handles appear. You can adjust the text element's color, opacity, and font by using the controls in the Overlays panel. Text elements can be resized only by using the Resize handles and are repositioned in the same manner as the other overlay elements. To remove any overlay, select it and press Delete.

» **Shadow:** Before getting into how this setting works, I need to point out this is one of the few areas where there's a difference between the Mac and Windows versions of Lightroom Classic. If you're a Windows user, you won't see the Shadow section in the Overlays panel (sorry!). I hope the engineers can overcome whatever operating system obstacle stands in the way of including this for Windows in a future version, but it has been this way since the beginning. Windows users can feel free to skip ahead.

The purpose of this control is to add a drop shadow to an overlay element. You enable the Shadow option by clicking an overlay element to make it active and then checking the Shadow box. While the overlay element is active, you can adjust the opacity, offset, radius, and angle of the drop shadow in the same manner as the Cast Shadow control in the Options panel. Note that the opacity setting of the overlay element also affects the opacity of the element's shadow, so if the element itself has a low opacity setting, you'll need a high opacity setting to see the shadow.

You can create custom text templates that will be available to be used in the Slideshow module, as well as the Print, Web, and Book modules. The process starts with clicking the ABC button and choosing Edit from the drop-down menu that appears. From there:

1. **Delete any tokens that appear within the Text Template Editor, as shown in Figure 13-10.**

2. **Add tokens by clicking the desired token's Insert button.**

   This adds the token to the editing field, so the order in which tokens are added is important. You can also type directly into this field to include things like punctuation into the token.

3. **Click the Preset drop-down menu to save your template for reuse.**

   You can also use that menu to manage your templates over time. Saved templates appear in all the modules where they can be used.

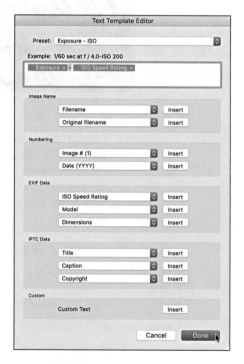

FIGURE 13-10:
The Text Template Editor.

BACKDROP PANEL

A good background supports and frames your photos but doesn't compete with them. The Backdrop panel, shown in Figure 13-11, offers three ways to adjust the look of the area behind your photos. I don't mind telling you that I wish the controls were arranged differently, and after I show you how to use them, I think you'll agree.

Here's how the controls work in the order in which I use them:

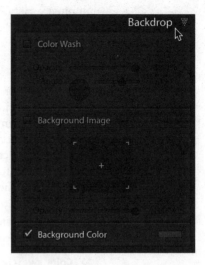

FIGURE 13-11:
The Backdrop panel.

» **Background Color:** Check the Background Color box to enable it and click the color swatch to choose a color. Keep in mind that your perception of color is influenced by surrounding colors. Because of this, you'll see black or neutral gray as the most common background color choices. Of course, you can use any color you want if that's what fits with your goals for a particular audience. Know the rules and then break them when it suits you!

» **Background Image:** As an alternative, you can add a background image to the slide. Check the Background Image box to enable it and then drag a photo from the Filmstrip to either the slide background or the Background Image box in the Background panel, as shown in Figure 13-12. After the background image is in place, you can adjust its opacity via the slider. **Note:** When you decrease the opacity of the background image, the background color increasingly shows through. Different background colors affect your background image in different ways.

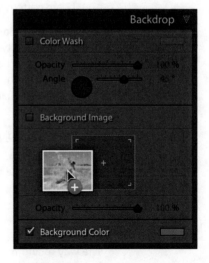

FIGURE 13-12:
Adding a background image to the slide.

» **Color Wash:** Each of the earlier options can be further enhanced by applying a color wash, which is why I use this control last. You use it to add an additional color, in the form of a gradient, across the background. You can adjust the opacity and angle of the gradient wash by using the respective controls.

As you can see, these controls can be used alone or in tandem to offer an almost unlimited variety of creative background possibilities!

TITLES PANEL

The Titles panel, shown in Figure 13-13, offers a simple bit of polish to your slide-show presentation by providing a means to add a nonphoto beginning and ending screen to your show. The Intro Screen appears before the first photo slide, and the Ending Screen appears after the last photo slide. These screens are entirely optional and function independently, meaning that you can add an Intro without an Ending and vice versa. The Titles panel is divided into two sections, with the Intro options on top and Ending options below. However, the type of controls for each screen are the same:

>> **Enable Screen check box:** Each screen type is enabled by checking the box at the top of each section.

>> **Color swatch:** Click the color swatch to set the color of that screen.

>> **Add Identity Plate check box:** Check this box to add an identity plate to either screen. This is the only means to add text or a graphic here.

>> **Choose/Create Identity Plate:** After you've checked the box to add the identity plate, you can choose to use an existing one or create a new one specifically for this purpose by clicking anywhere in the box with the checkerboard pattern and choosing from the menu that appears.

>> **Override Color:** This control allows you to override the actual color of a textual identity plate without having to alter the identity plate itself. In other words, if you have a custom identity plate that uses black text but want to add it to a black Intro screen, you can simply override the original color with this option and change it to white without affecting your custom identity plate. Make sense?

>> **Scale:** This adjusts the size of the identity plate.

Click and hold the handle on the Scale slider to see a preview of the screen in the content area.

MUSIC PANEL

The way to add music to a Slideshow has evolved over the years, and this current incarnation is the best so far. You can add up to ten music tracks (though that is very long) using .mp3, .m4a, or .m4b music files. The process is simple:

1. **Toggle the switch in the panel header to the up position to allow music to be added.**

2. **Click the + icon, navigate to the music file you want to add, and select it.**

   The track is added to the slideshow. The duration for the track is displayed alongside the filename. A running total duration appears at the top as you add more music tracks.

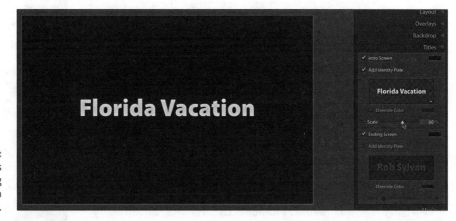

You can reorder the tracks by dragging and dropping them within the panel into the order you want. You can remove a track by selecting it and then clicking the Remove Music (–) icon at the top of the Music panel.

Music is not included in JPG or PDF outputs.

REMEMBER

PLAYBACK PANEL

After you design the look and sound of your slideshow, you are ready to configure how it plays. The Playback panel, shown in Figure 13-14, is divided into the seven (six if you have only a single monitor) sections:

>> **Slideshow Mode:** When set to Automatic, playback follows the settings configured in the duration section. When set to manual, you advance each slide manually with your arrow keys, and unsupported options will be hidden from the panel.

>> **Slide Duration:** Unless you have a one-photo slideshow (not likely!), you'll want to set the slide length and transition timing. The Slide Length slider controls how long each photo appears, and the Crossfades slider controls the duration of the transition from one photo to the next. If your slideshow includes music, try checking the Sync Slides to Music check box, which disables the previously mentioned sliders and tells Lightroom Classic to set the transitions based on the beats in the music. (Note that selecting Sync Slides to Music disables the playing of video within the slideshow.) Clicking Fit

to Music tells Lightroom Classic to adjust the Slide Length so that the duration of the slide-show is the same as the duration of the combined audio.

>> **Audio Balance:** If your slideshow includes video clips (with audio), you can use the Audio Balance slider to adjust the volume of the audio in the video clip so that it can either be silences (move slider toward Music) or be easily heard over the music (move slider toward Video).

>> **Pan and Zoom:** Commonly known as the Ken Burns Effect, when enabled, Pan and Zoom can add some movement to your stills by automatically panning and zooming into and out of each slide. The higher the setting, the more movement you will see (use in moderation to prevent motion sickness in your audience).

>> **Repeat / Random Order:** These two are pretty straightforward.

>> **Playback Screen:** If you have only one monitor hooked up to your computer, this section doesn't appear in your Playback panel. If you have multiple monitors, you use this section to choose which monitor to run the slideshow on. Click the icon representing your monitor choice, and the Play symbol appears on the icon. Check the Blank Other Screens box to black out the screen not running the show.

>> **Quality:** The options in the Quality drop-down menu — Draft, Standard, and High — control the quality of the previews used in the slideshow. The higher the quality, the longer it will take to build the previews. Use Draft when you tweak the presentation, and switch to High when you show it to others. If you run the slideshow through on High by yourself, the previews should be ready to go when you are in front of your audience. (You don't want them to sit in front of the Preparing Previews progress bar.)

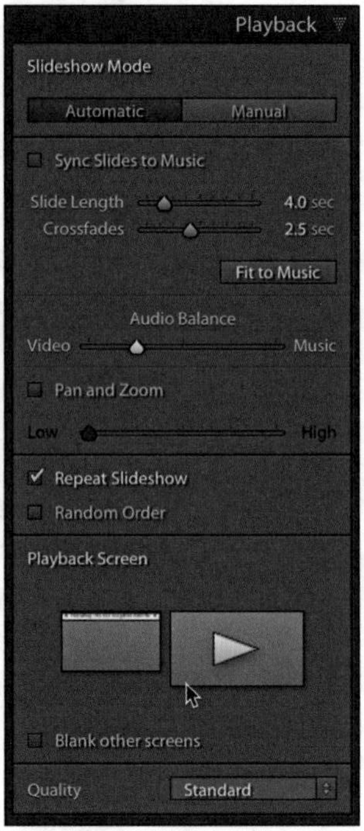

FIGURE 13-14:
The Playback panel showing two-monitor setup.

TIP

If you see an exclamation point next to an audio file, Lightroom Classic can't play it, and you'll need to select a different track.

Step 4: Save your settings as a template for reuse

You don't need to rely solely on the preinstalled templates after you get your feet wet. As you begin to customize slideshows to your liking, I recommend saving your preferred settings as templates. Here's how:

1. **Choose Slideshow ⇨ New Template Folder to create a new template folder.**

Give the folder a descriptive name and click the Create button.

TIP

Keeping your templates organized can increase your efficiency by providing order to your template collection. The Template Browser displays template folders and individual templates in alphanumeric order, right below the Lightroom Templates heading. Note that you cannot create template folders within folders.

2. **Go to Slideshow ⇨ New Template to create a new template from the settings you specified.**

Give the template a descriptive name, assign it to your desired folder, and click the Create button.

Step 5: Save your photos and settings as a special slideshow collection

Special collections, sometimes referred to as saved creations, are first covered in Chapter 12 (refer there for the steps), which covers creating books. In the Slideshow module, creating a saved slideshow collection saves all photos in the Filmstrip and your slideshow settings to this special collection with the icon for slideshow.

Playing the Slideshow for Your Audience

Showtime! Now, before you head onstage to show your work, do a few dress rehearsals to check your timing and make sure everything flows as it should.

Playback

To aid you in test-driving your show, Lightroom Classic can play the show right within the content area. Click the Preview button below the Playback panel. You'll hear the music (if enabled) and see the show just as it would play if you had it full screen, but you can also watch the progression of photos in the Filmstrip.

Consider this a preflight check to ensure you're ready for prime time. Click the content area or press Esc to stop the preview.

If you have a dual-monitor setup, you get to choose which monitor you want to run the show on by selecting its icon in the Playback panel. If you have a single-monitor setup, the choice is made for you. To start the show, click the Play button, sit back, and enjoy!

TIP

Lightroom Classic provides three keyboard shortcuts worth memorizing for running a slideshow:

>> Press Enter to start the show.

>> Press the spacebar to pause the show.

>> Press Esc to quit the show.

Export

Having options is nice. When you can't bring your computer to your audience or your audience to your computer, you can send your slideshow to your audience. Lightroom Classic's slideshow Export function can save your slideshow to a series of JPEG files, a single multipage PDF file, or as a video. The good news is that anyone with a simple image viewer can see JPEGs, the free Adobe Acrobat Reader is in such wide use that almost anyone can view a PDF, and every computer has some default video player installed. The thing to keep in mind is that music isn't included in JPEG or PDF exports, and the transition times are fixed in PDF, so if music is important you'll want to choose the video option. First, here are the steps to export your show to PDF:

1. **Click the Export PDF button at the bottom of the Left Panel Group.**

    The Export Slideshow to PDF dialog appears, as shown in Figure 13-15.

2. **Navigate to the location on your computer where you want to store the PDF.**

3. **Enter a name in the Save As field.**

4. **Choose a quality setting for the JPEG compression applied.**

    The higher the quality setting, the less JPEG compression, which results in a better-looking image but a larger file size.

5. Choose the Width and Height of the exported file.

This value should be based on the resolution of the monitor the presentation will be viewed on. The Common sizes drop-down menu can help pick a size.

6. Check the Automatically Show Full Screen box.

When the PDF file is opened, it appears full screen and begins the slideshow. Warn the people you deliver the file to that this will happen so they know what to expect. Also tell them to press the Esc key to exit when they're done.

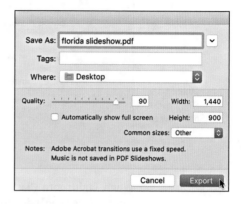

FIGURE 13-15:
The Export Slideshow to PDF dialog for Mac.

7. Click the Export button.

When Lightroom Classic's progress meter is complete, the file is ready to test (always test everything). If you're sending the file by email, check the final output size of the PDF and resave with either higher JPG compression or smaller pixel dimensions (or both) if the file is too large.

The Export to JPEG functions essentially the exact same way (right down to the dialog) with one logical difference: There is no Automatically Show Full Screen box. With the Export JPEG function, Lightroom Classic simply saves each slide out as a separate JPEG file. How the slides are viewed depends on what application the viewer opens them with. That said, the most common export option for a slideshow is as a video. Here's what that looks like:

1. Click the Export Video button at the bottom of the Left Panel Group.

The Export Slideshow dialog appears (see Figure 13-16).

2. Navigate to the location on your computer where you want the file saved.

3. Enter a name in the Save As field.

4. Choose a video preset based on where the video is destined to be played.

A helpful description appears at the bottom for each preset size to help you gauge the best choice for your intended purpose.

5. Click the Export button.

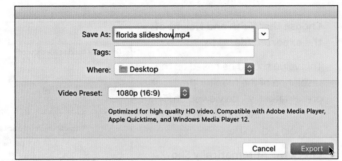

FIGURE 13-16:
The Export
Slideshow to
Video dialog
for Mac.

When Lightroom Classic's progress meter is complete, the file is ready to test. Double-click the video to open in it your computer's default player. Video files are much larger than PDF or JPG, so I don't recommend delivering them via email. Look into a free cloud-based file sharing service (such as Dropbox) to help facilitate the sharing of such large files.

TECHNICAL STUFF

Lightroom Classic's video export is intended to be played on a computer or mobile device. If your intention is to play in a DVD player, you must find software for authoring a DVD (that you could import this video into) and a device to burn the DVD (because optical media is fading from common use and not typically included on new computers), all of which is outside Lightroom Classic's skill set.

Chapter **14**

Printing Your Work

The goal of Lightroom Classic's Print module is to facilitate getting your digital work to paper in a color-managed environment with a high-quality output. (Say that three times fast.) Although originally geared toward sending data to a local inkjet printer, Lightroom Classic also makes it possible to save your print layouts as a JPEG (I prefer the shorter JPG) file that you can deliver to a print service.

Can I tell you what I think is one of the greatest things about printing from Lightroom Classic? It's that you can create a print right from your raw image data without first having to save a TIFF, PSD, or JPG copy of the original (most printing applications are unable to print raw files). Gone are the days of having to create and manage multiple versions of each file cropped, optimized, and prepared for each print size! Of course, you might need to render TIFF, PSD, or JPG versions of your raw files at times, and that's fine, but it sure is great when you don't have to bother!

Exploring the Print Module

I'd like to take a moment to reinforce that each Lightroom Classic module is structured essentially the same way, which means the interface behaves the same no matter which module you're working in. You can show and hide, and collapse and expand panels as needed to maximize your work area, and display only the controls you need. For a look at the Lightroom Classic interface as a whole, refer to Chapter 1.

WARNING

This is more of a heads-up than a dire warning, but the Print module is a place where minor visual differences exist in the interface depending on the operating system being used. Most of my screen captures throughout the book are on a Mac, but I do include Windows captures when needed to call out those differences. Assume that figures are showing the Mac interface unless the caption indicates that they show Windows.

Getting to know the panels and tools

As is typical for all Lightroom Classic modules, the organizational and preview panels are on the left side of the content area, and the right side holds the configuration panels. The Filmstrip is across the bottom and the Module Picker is across the top. Specific to each module are the tools provided for completing the task.

A unique aspect of the Print module is that it contains three different layout possibilities (Single Image/Contact Sheet, Picture Package, and Custom Package), and although I will go into each layout in detail, I want to point out that your choice of layout controls what configuration panels are available on the right side. To illustrate the difference, Figure 14-1 shows the Print module interface with the Single Image/Contact Sheet layout selected, and Figure 14-2 shows the Picture Package layout (Custom Package's panels are the same as Picture Package). It's like having three Print modules for the price of one!

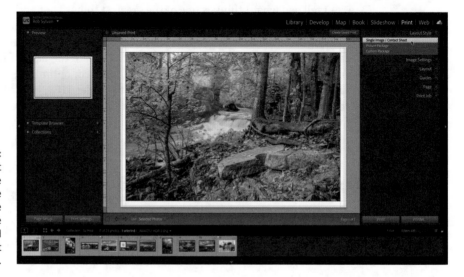

FIGURE 14-1:
The Print module interface showing the Single Image layout selected in the Layout Style panel.

An embarrassment of riches? Wait until you see the plethora of tools and panels Lightroom Classic lays at your feet. Admittedly, you never see all these panels at the same time, but I thought it would be a good idea to list all of them for easier reference:

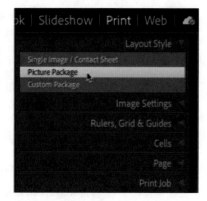

>> **Preview panel:** Displays a preview of each template layout as you move your cursor over the items listed in the Template Browser.

>> **Template Browser:** Provides controls for creating new — and managing existing — templates.

FIGURE 14-2:
The right side of the Print module showing the Picture Package panels.

>> **Collections panel:** Provides access to all the collections you've created, as well as the controls to add new ones that retain all the print settings. If needed, refer to Chapter 5 for a Collections refresher.

>> **Page Setup button:** Launches the Page Setup (Print Setup for Windows) dialog for choosing your printer and paper size. This is how Lightroom Classic communicates with your *printer driver,* which is the software that installs with your printer for the purpose of configuring printer settings and running printer maintenance. It's a very important part of the printing pipeline. In Windows, you click the Properties button in this dialog to access advanced printer settings. (I explain this later on in the "Setting Up a Print Job" section.) You might need to pull out your printer manual if you're not familiar with configuring its settings.

>> **Print Settings button:** (Mac only) Launches the Print dialog for configuring your printer settings. The options in this dialog vary based on your printer model; it's not a Lightroom Classic dialog. You might need to pull out your printer manual if you need guidance configuring its settings.

>> **Layout Style panel:** Provides access to the three types of layout options:

- *Single Image / Contact Sheet:* Create print layouts using a grid model where each cell in the grid has the same dimensions. You can print different photos on a single layout (a different photo in each cell, but the cells are all the same size).

- *Picture Package:* Create print layouts using cells of various dimensions, but only one photo can appear on a single layout (the same photo in each cell, but the cells can be various sizes).

- *Custom Package:* Create print layouts using cells of various dimensions and put different photos in each cell (different photos in each cell and the cells can be various sizes).

» **Image Settings panel:** Contains settings that affect the look of the photos appearing in the layout.

» **Layout panel:** Specific to Single Image, this panel provides options for creating the desired grid layout to be used.

» **Guides panel:** Specific to Single Image, this panel provides options for the configuration of these particular layout aids.

» **Rulers, Grid & Guides panel:** Specific to Picture Package and Custom Package, this panel provides options for the configuration of these particular layout aids.

» **Cells panel:** Specific to Picture Package and Custom Package, this panel controls the addition and configuration of new cells to a layout.

» **Page panel:** Allows for an identity plate, watermark, and supporting photo info text to be added to the print layout for output. Note that photo info text isn't available to either package style.

» **Print Job panel:** Controls output settings for sending data to a printer or saving it as JPG.

» **Toolbar:** Provides controls for navigating between print jobs containing multiple pages, an indicator of how many pages will be printed, and the Use controls for designating which photos will be used in the layout.

The layout style you choose determines which panels appear and the available options within panels for a given style. I continue to reinforce the differences as I cover the workflow throughout this chapter.

Becoming familiar with the menu options

The Lightroom Classic (Mac only), File, Edit, View, Window, and Help menus remain largely consistent throughout Lightroom Classic. You soon discover, though, that a couple of print options are located in the File menu. The Print command (same as the Print button) sends the current layout directly to the printer, using the existing settings without opening the printer driver — a great command to have when you're set up and just want to print. You also have access to other print-related submenus — Printer, Page Setup, and Print Settings (Mac only) — that function just the same as the previously mentioned buttons of the same name. Take note of the keyboard shortcuts!

The Print menu contains commands for creating new templates and template folders, navigating between pages in a multiple-page print job, and rotating the photos. The Create Saved Print command (note the button above the content area with the same name) allows you to create a special type of collection containing all the photos in the Filmstrip as well as the settings you've dialed into the Print module. This special collection appears in the Collections panel, and double-clicking its icon jumps you right to the Print module with all settings loaded up.

Setting Up a Print Job

Waiting to see a print for the first time can be a little bit like opening a birthday present — a mixture of hope and anticipation that it will be just what you want while bracing for disappointment if it isn't. Unless you're buying your birthday presents, you can't do much about that, but you can ensure the best possible print emerges from your printer.

Employing a print workflow

Although the three layout styles have some distinct differences and options, they still fit within the same place in the larger print workflow. I do my best to address their individual quirks and foibles, but for now, I just want to give you the big picture:

1. **Bring your photos to the Print module.**
2. **Configure the page setup.**
3. **Select a layout style for your starting point.**
4. **Customize the layout as desired.**
5. **Configure the output settings.**
6. **(Optional) Save your settings for reuse.**
7. **(Optional) Save your settings and photos as a saved print collection.**
8. **Print the layout.**

Step 1: Bring your photos to the Print module

The Library module is the most likely place you'll begin to gather your photos before moving to the Print module because it provides the greatest access to your portfolio and contains tools for finding, organizing, and grouping. Whether you select a folder or a collection, or create a grouping based on keywords or metadata, you need to identify and select the photos you want to print before you can print them.

TIP

One of the best ways to begin the process is to use a collection because it can contain photos from every corner of your imported portfolio. The other benefits of using a collection are

>> You can manually control the order in which the images appear in the layout.

>> You can create an infinite number of collections and sort them independently.

After you collect your photos for printing, you're ready to bring them into the Print module. Notice that the image grouping you created in the Library module is still displayed in the Filmstrip.

Step 2: Configure your page setup

Before you dive into creating your layout, you need to tell Lightroom Classic a few things about the page you want to create. Click the Page Setup button below the Collections panel or press Shift+⌘+P on a Mac (Shift+Ctrl+P for Windows) to launch the Page Setup (the dialog box is named Print Setup for Windows) dialog, as shown in Figure 14-3. The three things you want to do here are

1. Select your printer.

2. Select your paper size.

3. Select your paper orientation.

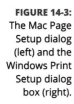
FIGURE 14-3:
The Mac Page Setup dialog (left) and the Windows Print Setup dialog box (right).

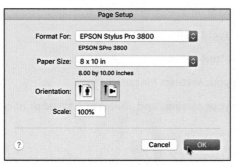
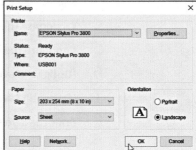

Click OK to close the dialog. Lightroom Classic uses this information to determine how the page displays in the content area as well as the document size and the minimum margins. Choose View ⇨ Show Info Overlay (if it is not already showing) to enable the display of a nonprinting indicator that shows you key information about your setup. You can also press the I key to toggle this overlay on and off. Keep Info Overlay on while you get familiar with Lightroom Classic to serve as a reminder of what you've configured.

Step 3: Select a layout style for your starting point

Expand the Layout Style panel (refer to Figure 14-1) and choose the style you want to use. Many of the panel options stem from this choice. Before I get into the details, I want to clarify the differences between these three layout styles so that you know which will best suit any given job:

>> **Single Image / Contact Sheet:** This style uses a grid to divide the paper into equal-size cells. The more cells you add, the smaller each cell becomes (because the paper size remains constant). This layout style is for when you want to print different photos on a single page within equal size cells (although it is possible to fill every cell on a page with a single photo), or you can use it to print a single photo, which requires just a single cell.

>> **Picture Package:** You use this style to create a layout for printing a single photo in a range of sizes on one or more pages. Think school portraits, where a single pose can be purchased in a package that includes prints from 8 x 10 down to wallet size, and in various quantities. This is a great feature for anyone needing to produce a set package of prints quickly. Just keep in mind that you can't create a single-page Picture Package that includes more than one photo. You can apply the same Picture Package layout to multiple photos, but each photo requires its own page.

>> **Custom Package:** This style provides the most flexibility in that you can use it to create cells of various sizes and then fill those cells with the same photo or a variety of photos. You can even overlap the cells to create poster-like layouts. The configuration options are basically the same as Picture Package, but many people use this option for all prints because it can print a single photo (one cell) or multiple different photos (multiple cells of various sizes) on a single page.

Step 4: Customize the layout as desired

This is the fun part! The rest of the panels on the right side of the window are arranged with an efficient workflow in mind, so keep working your way down. As I've said, you're going to see some differences in the options available, depending upon the layout style you choose. With Single Image, you have the Layout and Guides panels. With Picture Package and Custom Package, you have the Rulers, Grids & Guides panel and the Cells panel.

The rest of the panels appear in all styles, aside from a few minor differences in the Image Settings and the Page panels. In the next few sections, you get up close and personal with each configuration panel.

IMAGE SETTINGS

The controls in the Image Settings panel, shown in Figure 14-4, affect what happens inside each photo cell, regardless of the layout style used. Here's what the various controls do:

» **Zoom to Fill:** When this option is unchecked, your entire photo fits within each cell. If the aspect ratio of the cell is different from the aspect ratio of the photo, the photo won't fill the entire cell. When Zoom to Fill is checked, the photo is sized to fill the entire cell. If the aspect ratio of the cell is different from the aspect ratio of the photo, the photo appears cropped. Zoom to Fill doesn't appear in Custom Package because the photo will always fill the cell regardless of the cell's aspect ratio. Note that if your photo does appear cropped, you can reposition it within the cell by clicking and dragging while in Single Image layout or by holding ⌘ on a Mac (Ctrl key for Windows) and clicking and dragging while in Picture Package or Custom Package.

» **Rotate to Fit:** Check this box to have Lightroom Classic automatically rotate each photo to best fit the orientation of the cell. This is handy when printing a sheet of both portrait and landscape-oriented photos and you want each photo to fill as much of the cell as possible.

» **Repeat One Photo per Page:** This pretty much does what it says — fills every cell on a single sheet with the same photo. This option doesn't appear in Picture or Custom Package.

» **Stroke Border:** Adds a stroke around each photo. Click the color swatch to choose your color. Keep in mind that the stroke remains inside the cell, so increasing the stroke decreases the size of the actual photo. In Picture and Custom Package, this option is called *Inner Stroke*.

» **Photo Border:** Controls the width of the border around each photo in a Picture or Custom Package layout. The color of this border can't be changed and is always white. The option doesn't exist in Single Image.

» **Inner Stroke:** Adds a stroke around each photo in Picture or Custom Package. Click the color swatch to choose your color. Keep in mind that the stroke remains inside the cell, so increasing the stroke decreases the size of the photo. In Single Image, this option is named *Stroke Border*.

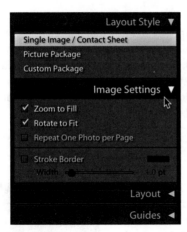
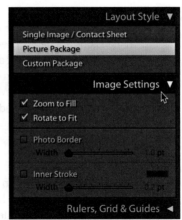

FIGURE 14-4:
The Image
Settings panel
with Single
Image layout
selected (left)
and Picture
Package
selected (right).

LAYOUT

The Layout panel, shown in Figure 14-5, appears only when the Single Image / Contact Sheet style is active because all the controls affect the layout of the grid on the page. The Layout panel has four sets of controls:

>> **Margins:** The Margins sliders function independently and control the edge of the printable area on the page. The smallest margin amount is determined by your printer driver settings, so if you want to print borderless, be sure to enable borderless printing in your printer driver (via the Page Setup button) before trying to zero out the margins. (Borderless isn't an option for every paper size and printer.) Set all margins to the same value to create centered prints.

>> **Page Grid:** Controls the number of cells in the layout. Rows are horizontal and columns are vertical.

FIGURE 14-5:
The Layout panel.

>> **Cell Spacing:** Adjusts the amount of spacing between cells. This option is grayed out when the grid consists of a single cell.

>> **Cell Size:** This determines the size of the actual printed photo. Maximum cell dimensions are determined by the size of the paper, margins, and the number of cells being used. Keep in mind that all cells in the grid are the same size. If you're interested in creating square cells, check the Keep Square check box, and the Height and Width sliders will be set to the same value and linked to each other when moved.

GUIDES

The Guides panel, shown in Figure 14-6, is also unique to the Single Image style. It contains a set of layout guide tools (under Show Guides) that can be enabled by checking their respective boxes. When the guides are enabled, you see them appear in the content area. Placing your cursor over any one of the guides and clicking and dragging allows another means to make layout adjustments. You can modify margins, cell size, and spacing this way. Checking the Dimensions check box displays the cell size dimensions as an overlay in each of the cells.

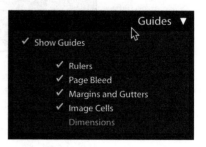

FIGURE 14-6:
The Guides panel.

RULERS, GRID & GUIDES

The Rulers, Grid & Guides panel, shown in Figure 14-7, is specific to Picture and Custom Package. It provides the following layout aids for creating your package layout:

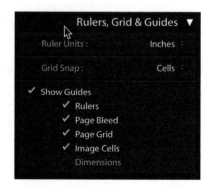

FIGURE 14-7:
The Rulers, Grid & Guides panel.

>> **Ruler Units:** Allows you to choose the unit of measurement.

>> **Grid Snap:** You might find it helpful to turn on snapping to Cells or Grid as you move the cells on the page. This way you'll feel a "snap" when you encounter either the background grid or another cell. Set to Off if it gets in your way. I find that snapping to cells helps prevent cells from overlapping each other when aligning them tightly.

>> **Show Guides:** This check box toggles all the visual guides on or off. Under that you can control each one individually:

- **Rulers:** This toggles the rulers on or off.

- **Page Bleed:** This check box toggles the shaded area showing the unprintable margin on or off.

- **Page Grid:** This toggles the layout grid on or off.

- **Image Cells:** This toggles the cell border on or off.

- **Dimensions:** This check box toggles the display of the cell dimensions within each cell on or off.

The problem with cells overlapping is that one photo will print on top of the other and cost you money in wasted paper and ink. Lightroom Classic warns you if two or more cells overlap in Picture Package by displaying an exclamation point inside a black circle in the upper right corner of the layout, as shown in Figure 14-8. Click the Auto Layout button in the Cells panel (see next section) to have Lightroom Classic rearrange the cells correctly.

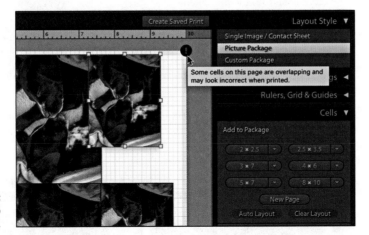

FIGURE 14-8: Cell overlap warning.

CELLS

The Cells panel, shown in Figure 14-9, is also specific to Picture and Custom Package. As the name of the panel indicates, all the controls contained here are for the creation and modification of Package cells. In the Add to Package section, you find the following controls:

>> **Cell buttons:** You use the cell buttons to add new cells to your layout — just click the button representing the size you want to add. The six buttons represent the default cell sizes, but you can click the drop-down arrow next to any button and choose a different cell size or click Edit to enter a custom cell

size. Every button click adds a new cell. Additional pages are added to the package as needed to accommodate new cells.

>> **New Page button:** As you might expect, clicking this button adds a new page to the package. You can create multiple new, blank pages before adding cells and then drag and drop cells between pages to create your layouts. Note that Lightroom Classic automatically adds a new page when you add a cell that requires a new page to fit in the layout.

REMEMBER

As soon as you have more than one page in a package, Lightroom Classic displays a black Delete Page button in the upper left corner of each page, as shown in Figure 14-10. Click that button to delete that page (and any cells it contains) from the package.

>> **Auto Layout button:** Click this button to arrange the cells to make the most efficient use of paper by rearranging cells in the layout across all available pages. Not available on Custom Package.

>> **Clear Layout button:** Removes all the cells from the layout.

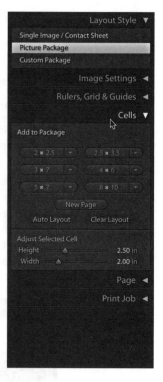

FIGURE 14-9:
The Cells panel.

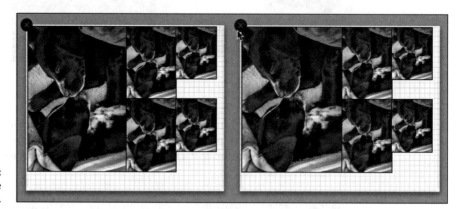

FIGURE 14-10:
Delete Page button.

After you add a cell to the layout, you can click and drag a resize handle to change the dimensions of the cell, or you can make height and width adjustments using the Adjust Selected Cell sliders. You can reposition a cell in the layout by clicking and dragging the cell to a new location, or even move cells between pages. To delete a cell, select it and press Delete on a Mac (Backspace for Windows). To duplicate a cell, hold the Option key (Alt key for Windows) while clicking and dragging a cell.

Keep in mind that each cell is simply a frame in which to place a photo. Your photo has a particular aspect ratio, but you could potentially create multiple cells with a range of aspect ratios. For example, a typical aspect ratio of an uncropped photo is 2:3 (also known as 1:1.5). A 4-x-6 print has an aspect ratio of 2:3. Therefore, if you place a photo with a 2:3 aspect ratio in a 4-x-6 cell, it should fill the entire cell without being cropped. Now, if you also want to include a 5-x-7 print in that package, you need to do some cropping because the 5 x 7 would have a 1:1.4 aspect ratio. However, you don't want to crop the source photo itself because then it wouldn't fit the 4-x-6 cell!

Here's where that Zoom to Fill check box comes in handy. After you check that box, you see the photo in the 5-x-7 cell appear to get larger and fill the available space in that cell; the 4 x 6 remains the same because it was already filling the cell. Now you can print a full 4 x 6 and a full 5 x 7 from the same source photo, and yes, the 5-x-7 print will be cropped, but the source photo will remain unchanged. You also can move your photo within that 5 x 7 cell to improve the default placement. Hold ⌘ on a Mac (Ctrl key for Windows) and click and drag the photo within the cell for better placement.

Note that you encounter a few minor differences when you use Custom Package. One is that there is no Auto Layout button, because I suppose the assumption is that in Custom, you put the cells where you want them. You'll find a Rotate Cell button for flipping the orientation of the cell. And finally, there is a Lock to Photo Aspect Ratio check box that keeps the cell's aspect ratio locked but allows you to resize the cell as needed.

PAGE

The Page panel contains the controls for background color (does what you expect), the identity plate, watermarking, as well as a few additional layout style–specific overlay elements. Figure 14-11 shows how the panel looks in each layout style.

Consider the identity plate section first because it functions the same way in all styles. The purpose of the identity plate is to provide a means to add either a textual or a graphical element to your printed page. This could be your graphical logo or simply a textual copyright notice and your name. You can apply it on each image or place it on a blank area of the page.

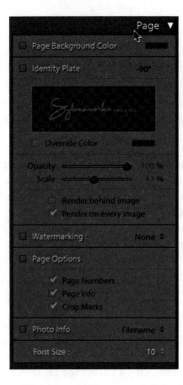
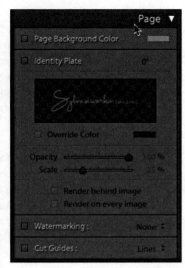

FIGURE 14-11:
Overlays panel
with Single
Image (left)
and Picture/
Custom
Package (right).

The identity plate appears in many places throughout Lightroom Classic. Here are the basic steps for using identity plate in the Print module:

1. **Click the Identity Plate check box to toggle it on.**

2. **Choose Edit from the Identity Plate drop-down menu.**

   Choosing Edit launches the Identity Plate Editor. If you previously created a custom identity plate, you'll see it listed in the menu and you can (obviously) choose it.

3. **In the Identity Plate Editor, select either a styled text or graphical identity plate.**

4. **Customize as desired.**

   Chapter 5 has bunches more on customizing your identity plate.

5. **Choose Save As from the Custom drop-down menu if you want to save your customized identity plate for future use.**

   Doing so launches the Save Identity Plate As dialog, where you can name this identity plate and click Save.

6. **Click OK.**

TIP

The identity plate appears in the content area. Click and drag the identity plate to reposition it. You can adjust opacity and size as desired with the provided sliders. The Override Color option allows you to change the color of a textual identity plate temporarily without permanently altering your saved identity plate. You can rotate the identity plate by clicking the rotation amount indicator (starts at 0 degrees) in the top right corner of the panel. Choose the amount and direction of rotation you require.

TIP

Check the Render on Every Image check box if you want to use the identity plate as a watermark for all images in the layout. Just keep in mind that when this option is enabled, the identity plate will be "rendered" to the center of each photo. You can still adjust its rotation, scale, and opacity, but it cannot be repositioned off the center.

Render behind Image is a little-used option that places the identity plate behind your photos. This can be used when you want your identity plate and photos to overlap but don't want the identity plate to print on top of the photos.

Further down the right side of the screen, you encounter Watermarking. I provide more in-depth coverage of watermarking in Chapter 15, because you are more likely to use it in a web gallery. However, you can check the Watermarking box to access your saved watermarks or create a new one from the Watermarking drop-down menu. Just remember the placement of the watermark is based on how you create the watermark in the Watermark Editor. From here, the remaining options are unique to each layout style. In Single Image you have

>> **Page Options:** Allows for the addition of page numbers, page information, and crop marks to be printed on the page with your photos. Page information includes

- *Sharpening Setting:* The amount of sharpening you choose in the Print Job panel.

- *Profile Used:* The color-management setting you choose in the Print Job panel.

- *Name of Printer:* The name of the printer you use.

>> **Photo Info:** Provides the ability to include a limited amount of textual information about the photos being printed. Click the check box to enable and then click the drop-down menu to choose a text template to apply, or click Edit to create a new text template. You can adjust the size of the font via the Font Size drop-down menu. You cannot change the font face and positioning.

In Picture and Custom Package, Cut Guides provide a printed visual to aid in cutting the photos after printing. Choose either Lines or Crop Marks.

Step 5: Configure the output settings

After you finalize your layout, as outlined in the previous sections, you're ready to prepare the data for output. This is the phase where you prepare Lightroom Classic to hand off the image data to the printer (or a JPG file to a print service). The prep work here involves configuring a few settings in the Print Job panel and/ or tweaking settings in the printer driver — if you're printing locally. The most critical component of this hand-off process is the color management of the image data. The next few sections take a closer look at each setting involved.

PRINT JOB

The Print Job panel, as shown in Figure 14-12, is where you configure your output image data so that it meets the specifications for the job at hand. The options are the same for both the Grid and Picture Package layout engines:

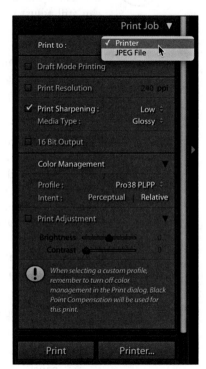

FIGURE 14-12:
The Print Job panel.

>> **Print To:** The Print To drop-down menu is where you choose whether you want to send your output to a printer or save it as a JPG file.

>> **Draft Mode Printing:** When Draft Mode Printing is checked, Lightroom Classic uses the image data from its preview cache instead of re-rendering image data from your source files. The benefit of this is purely speed. The trade-off is quality. The quality of the image data in the preview cache is usually good enough for thumbnails on contact sheets, which is when I am most likely to use Draft Mode printing. When in Draft Mode print resolution, the Print Sharpening and Color Management configuration options are disabled. The Color Management setting is set to Managed by Printer.

>> **Print Resolution:** When checked, you can set the resolution value for Lightroom Classic to use when it renders the image data you want delivered at output. Here's why I tend to leave it unchecked: If enough pixels exist in my source photo so that the native resolution is 180–480 PPI (or even higher),

TIP

I don't worry about it. Here's an easy way to see the native resolution at a given print size:

1. **Select your photo.**

2. **Choose the Single Image layout style from the Layout Style panel.**

3. **Create a cell that matches your desired print size in the Layout panel.**

4. **Check the Dimensions box in the Guides panel.**

5. **Uncheck Print Resolution in the Print Job panel.**

6. **Look at the Print Size overlay in the cell.**

   This little trick works in both layout engines, but I just picked Single Image for this example. The key is to have Dimensions checked and Print Resolution unchecked. Lightroom Classic displays the print size in the selected units as well as the native resolution for that size of print.

If you're in the 180–480 PPI window, you're good to go. However, if this setting makes you the least bit uneasy, go with the default setting of 240 PPI. If you're printing to a JPG and you're not sure what your print service requires, your safest setting is going to be 300 PPI.

» **Print Sharpening:** Adobe worked with the group of folks who wrote the book on print sharpening to create the sharpening algorithms that are applied to your image data. Now, you won't see any change in the content area because this sharpening is applied only after you click the Print button, when Lightroom Classic renders the image data from the source file and applies all your Lightroom Classic adjustments. The proof is going to be in the print, so I highly suggest you produce a set of test prints on each type of media you use with each sharpening setting to get a sense of which you prefer. Here's how you do that:

1. **Check the Print Sharpening box.**

2. **Choose the desired amount (Low, Standard, or High) from the Print Sharpening drop-down menu.**

3. **Choose either Matte or Glossy (depending on the paper type you're using) from the Media Type drop-down menu.**

You can also apply sharpening when saving your output in JPG format — you determine your settings the same way as when you're printing to your attached printer. Don't be surprised by how the image looks if you open it in Photoshop; the proof is still going to be in the print.

» **Color Management:** Possibly the most important setting in this module, simply because a bad Color Management setting can single-handedly ruin your output (and possibly your day). The goal of color management is to literally manage the conversion of colors between Lightroom Classic's working color space and the color space of the output device. The method for achieving the best output is to let Lightroom Classic manage the conversion. The alternative is to let the printer manage the colors (which arguably has improved greatly in recent years).

When the print job is configured to let the printer manage colors — select Managed by Printer from the Profile drop-down menu — Lightroom Classic sends the image data using its color space and leaves it up to the printer driver to convert those colors to the output color space correctly. The problem is that not all printers know how to handle ProPhoto RGB data and, therefore, are unable to convert the colors correctly. Feel free to test the Managed by Printer option, but know that older printers may not handle this as well as newer ones. That said, if you want to try it, here are the steps:

1. **Choose Managed by Printer from the Profile drop-down menu.**

2. **Configure the other Print Job settings as desired.**

    These settings are things like unchecking Draft Mode Printing, setting your resolution (or not), and applying sharpening.

3. **Click the Printer button and do the necessary stuff in the Print Settings dialog.**

    This stuff includes going into Advanced Settings and turning on the printer driver's color adjustment setting, setting paper type and print quality, and then clicking OK to return to Lightroom Classic.

If the colors look good, your printer can handle the data Lightroom Classic is sending. If you see a color cast, or the colors look washed out, your printer can't handle the data Lightroom Classic is sending, and you need to have Lightroom Classic manage the color.

TECHNICAL STUFF

You may be wondering why Managed by Printer is the default setting for Draft Mode printing. The reason is that with Draft Mode printing, the image data is sent from the preview cache in Adobe RGB space, which most printers can handle.

To let Lightroom Classic manage the colors, you need to have installed the ICC profiles for the paper and printer combination you're using. The manufacturer of the paper (which can also be the same company that makes the printer) typically provides these profiles. Go to the paper manufacturer's website and download the latest profile available for the specific paper and printer model you're using. After installing the profile with the directions provided by the supplier, do the following:

1. **Choose Other from the Profile drop-down menu.**

    The Choose Profiles dialog appears (see Figure 14-13).

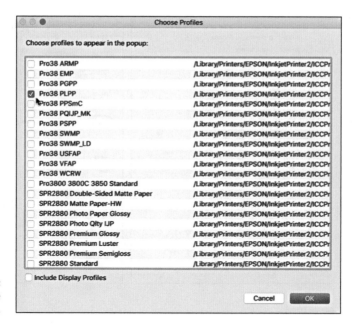

FIGURE 14-13:
The Choose
Profiles dialog.

2. **Check the box next to the profile for the paper you're going to use and then click OK.**

   Lightroom Classic returns to the Print module.

3. **Click the Print Settings button at the bottom of the left panel (Page Setup in Windows), go into the Print Settings (may also be called Color Matching on some printers) section of the printer driver (click the Properties button in the Print dialog box on Windows), and make sure color adjustment is disabled.**

   This is absolutely critical, or else the printer driver will also attempt to manage the colors, which typically results in light prints with a magenta cast. Access to these settings varies with each operating system and printer. Depending on your printer driver, look for a color management setting that appears disabled or reads "off," "no color adjustment," or "no ICM." Consult your printer manual if you're unsure where this setting is on your system. Figure 14-14 shows the location of this setting for an Epson 3800 on Mac and Windows. Fortunately, in recent years printer drivers have been configured to automatically disable color adjustment when Lightroom Classic has a profile selected.

4. **In the printer driver, select correct Media Type (based on the paper you are using) and desired Print Quality settings and then click Save (OK for Windows).**

   Lightroom Classic returns to the Print module.

WARNING

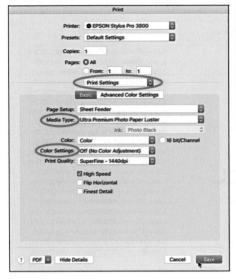
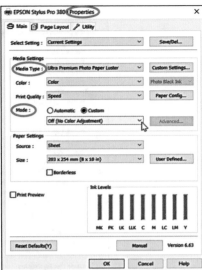

FIGURE 14-14:
Color
adjustment
setting on an
Epson 3800
on Mac (left)
and Windows
(right).

After you return to Lightroom Classic, you still need to choose a rendering intent. "What's that?" you ask. Well, when Lightroom Classic is set to convert colors to the output space by using the ICC profile you choose, it needs you to tell it how to handle colors that are beyond what the printer is capable of printing. In other words, it needs you to tell it what your "rendering intent" is. It gives you two choices:

- *Relative:* This option keeps all the colors that are within the gamut of the output color space and clips those outside it to the nearest reproducible color.

- *Perceptual:* This option remaps all colors in the source space to fit within the destination space. The downside is that colors within the gamut can appear desaturated, but the upsides are better gradation between colors and overall better color detail when many out-of-gamut colors are present.

Keep in mind that the goal of both Rendering Intent options is to preserve the original color appearance. For a rule of thumb, if a photo contains many out of gamut colors, try Perceptual; otherwise, go with Relative, but I would encourage you to make a few test prints to get a feel for any differences.

>> **Print Adjustment:** When the Print Adjustment box is checked, you have the ability to control Brightness and Contrast of the print. As with print sharpening, you won't see anything change in the content area. These adjustments are only applied to the image during output. One of the most common complaints in the early days of Lightroom Classic were of getting prints that were

too dark, which were often caused by the monitor being set too brightly. Adobe's solution for people who just couldn't get good prints through traditional color management workflow techniques was to just increase the Brightness slider to compensate. If this sounds like you, you'll need to conduct a few test prints to find the right setting, but then you can just leave it that way for all future prints.

If you're a Mac user and you're printing to a printer that supports 16-bit data, you can print in 16-bit from Lightroom Classic. The benefit is improved gradations, but it might take a keen eye to spot the difference between an 8-bit and 16-bit print. If you fit the above criteria, you can enable this feature by first checking the 16-bit Output box in the Print Job panel, and then enabling 16-bit printing in the printer driver. After you have a layout and your print settings are configured, it might be in your best interest to save them for reuse. Read on to find out how to do that.

Step 6: Save your settings for reuse

This optional step in the workflow has the potential of combining all the steps to this point into a single click. You just invested all that time creating the layout and configuring all your output settings, so if there's any chance that you'd repeat those steps with the same or different photos, then I highly suggest you save your work. Here's how:

1. **(Optional) Choose Print ➪ New Template Folder. Give the folder a descriptive name and click the Create button.**

TIP

This opens the New Folder dialog, where you can enter a name for your folder. Keeping your templates organized can increase your efficiency by providing order to your template collection. The Template Browser displays template folders and individual templates in alphanumeric order, right below the Lightroom Classic Templates default template folder. To keep my custom template folders organized, I name them with a number. Note that you can't create template folders within folders. Once you create your folder structure, you don't need to create a new folder each time.

2. **Choose Print ➪ New Template. Give the template a descriptive name, assign it to your desired folder, and click the Create button.**

This opens the New Template dialog where you can enter a name for your template, and even choose a folder to place it within.

Step 7: Save your photos and settings as a special collection

We first encountered these special collections, sometimes referred to as saved creations, in Chapter 12 (refer to Chapter 12 for the steps). Here in the Print module, creating a saved print collection saves all photos in the Filmstrip and your settings to this special collection with the icon for Print.

Step 8: Printing the layout

It took a bit of work to get here, but this is the moment you've been waiting for — clicking the Printer button (on the bottom of the right panel group). Doing so launches the printer driver (again) and gives you one last chance for a preflight check of your settings. Until you feel confident in your setup and configuration of everything, I strongly recommend that you double-check the printer driver settings. It just takes a few seconds, and it can save you both time and money. If all the settings are correct, click the Print button (OK on Windows) to complete printing (don't forget to load paper in the printer). You'll see "Preparing Print Job" appear (briefly) above the Identity Plate, and then Lightroom Classic hands off the data to the printer to complete the job.

When you feel like you have it down and you consistently get the expected results from the printer, click the Print button to bypass the printer driver's dialog and simply send the data directly to the printer.

Putting it all together

I'd like to walk through a few examples, including the process of Soft Proofing (simulating how your print will look in Lightroom Classic), to demonstrate how you'd set up a Single Image layout, a Picture Package layout, and a Custom Package layout. I'll send the Single Image layout to my inkjet printer and save the Picture Package as a JPG to deliver to a print service, just to highlight the key differences in output as well. The workflow scenarios can be accessed by going to http://lightroomers.com/L4D/printworkflows.pdf.

Chapter **15**

Creating a Web Gallery

t's an online world these days. High-speed Internet and digital photography go together like peanut butter and chocolate. Lightroom Classic's Web module offers a diverse range of photo gallery styles and configurations for creating professional-looking galleries without touching a bit of code. Seamless integration between your portfolio and Lightroom Classic's built-in FTP (File Transfer Protocol) software means you can take your photos from import to web gallery to web server in a matter of minutes!

Just like with a book or slideshow, you can create a web gallery from any grouping of images you can pull together in the Library module. You can start from a folder, keyword search, metadata browse, or collection. If you can group them, you can put them on the web!

Exploring the Web Module

If you've been reading this book from the start, you might be tired of hearing it by now (but at least you won't forget), but each Lightroom Classic module is structured essentially the same way to make your workflow more efficient. Here's the benefit from this consistency: The interface behaves the same way no matter where you are! You can show/hide and collapse/expand panels as needed to maximize your work area, and you can have Lightroom Classic display only the controls you need. To find out more about the Lightroom Classic interface as a whole, move it on over to Chapter 1.

TECHNICAL STUFF

This is totally unrelated to the Web module, but everyone with a Creative Cloud subscription gets a free online portfolio through Adobe's Portfolio product. Adobe Portfolio is simple to use and includes online hosting (no need to buy a domain or pay for hosting). It is outside the scope of this book, but head over to `https://portfolio.adobe.com` to get started.

Getting to know the panels and tools

Figure 15-1 shows the Web module interface. The organizational and preview panels are on the left side of the content area. The right side holds the configuration panels — the Filmstrip (across the bottom) and the Module Picker (across the top) are consistent across all modules. Keep in mind that the only elements that change from module to module are the tools and settings specific to that module. Small comfort, perhaps, when you're first trying to take it all in, but I'll guide you each step of the way.

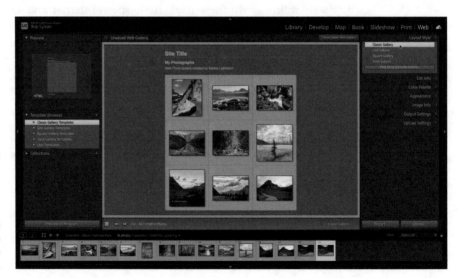

FIGURE 15-1:
The Web module interface.

Time to take a closer look and see what's here. Here's an overview of all the Web module components (minus the ones I cover in earlier chapters):

>> **Preview in Browser button:** Click this button to display the current web configuration in your default web browser.

- » **Layout Style:** Lists installed web galleries and is used to choose the active gallery (look at the About section under the Web menu for a description of the active gallery). The four preinstalled gallery types are

  - Classic Gallery

  - Grid Gallery

  - Square Gallery

  - Track Gallery

- » **Site Info panel:** Contains input fields for information about the gallery. Options vary with each gallery.

- » **Color Palette panel:** Allows for changing the color scheme of certain gallery elements. Options vary with each gallery.

- » **Appearance panel:** Configures attributes that affect the structural appearance of each gallery type. Options vary with each gallery.

- » **Image Info panel:** Allows you to display information about the images in the gallery. Options vary with each gallery.

- » **Output Settings panel:** Most galleries make use of a small thumbnail photo in combination with a larger version of the same photo. The main option in this panel controls the output size settings of the larger version. Other options vary with each gallery.

- » **Upload Settings panel:** Configuration and storage of your FTP settings.

- » **Export button:** Click this button to save all your gallery files to a location on your disk.

- » **Upload button:** Click this button to begin copying files to the web server you configured in the Upload Settings panel.

REMEMBER

Keep in mind that the contents of some panels change to reflect the options available in a given layout style. All the screen captures reflect the contents of the Classic Gallery because it reveals the most options.

Becoming familiar with the menu options

The one menu option unique to the Web module is the aptly named Web menu. It contains commands for creating new templates and template folders, reloading the content area (similar to refreshing your web browser), exporting the web gallery, and previewing the gallery in your browser. The Create Saved Web Gallery command allows you to save the custom settings of the gallery and the photos as a special collection. The Content command provides the option to choose which photos — within the active image grouping — will appear in the gallery. The About menu provides additional functionality details and a Feature list regarding the active gallery type.

Creating a Web Gallery

The look of your web gallery is going to be driven by your photos, your intended audience, the reason(s) you're putting these images online, and your own creativity. With that in mind, and knowing that new questions will emerge, you can enter into your web gallery workflow on the right footing.

Employing a web gallery workflow

Lightroom Classic is all about workflows within workflows! The creation of every web gallery follows the same basic steps. Here's an overview of the process:

1. **Bring your photos to the Web module.**

2. **Select a template or layout style for your starting point.**

3. **Customize as desired.**

4. **(Optional) Save your settings as a template for reuse.**

5. **(Optional) Save your settings and photos as a special web collection.**

Step 1: Bring your photos to the Web module

After you collect your photos for the gallery, it's time to bring them into the Web module by clicking Web in the Module Picker. Notice that the image grouping you created in the Library module is still displayed in the Filmstrip.

Step 2: Select a template or layout style for your starting point

A template is simply a way of saving unique combinations of settings for reuse. The preinstalled templates are helpful for seeing possibilities, but also serve as great jumping-off points for creating your own custom web galleries. You can see a thumbnail layout of any template in the Preview panel by moving your cursor over its name. The preinstalled templates (refer to Figure 15-1) are grouped by layout type. Alternatively, you could select one of the gallery types from the Layout Style panel, which applies the default template for that style as your starting point.

Step 3: Customize as desired

The controls for customizing your web gallery are on the right side of the module. The panels are arranged with an efficient workflow in mind, so start at the top and work your way down.

TIP

A nice feature of the Layout Style panel is that when it's collapsed, a drop-down menu appears in the header, which enables you to switch between gallery types without needing to expand that panel! Okay, let's roll up our sleeves and go through each panel in greater detail.

SITE INFO PANEL

The contents of the Site Info panel will depend on which gallery type you choose. However, all galleries share some form of Title field. This information is displayed in the title bar of web browsers visiting your site and can be displayed within the content area of the gallery, depending on the gallery type you choose.

TIP

Either you can enter the information into the fields in the panel, or you can click the text you want to edit in the Content area and edit it right in the live gallery preview!

Only the Classic Gallery makes use of the following fields, shown in Figure 15-2:

>> **Collection Title:** Think of this as a subtitle for your site title.

>> **Collection Description:** Enter a description of the contents of your gallery.

>> **Contact Info:** This field works hand in hand with the Web or Mail Link field below it to create a clickable link.

>> **Web or Mail Link:** Enter the link or mailto code to accompany the data you entered for Contact Info.

Although I did say at the start of this chapter that you wouldn't have to touch "a bit of code," here is one place you can. If you want to create a link to another page from your gallery, you use both the Contact Info and the Web or Mail Link fields to make it work. For example, say I want to link this web gallery to my site's home page, and I want that link to display the

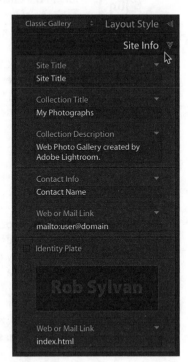

FIGURE 15-2:
The Site Info panel.

text, "Home." (Home is the text you would click.) To get all that to work, I'd start by entering **Home** into the Contact Info field. I would then enter the complete link to my home page in the Web or Mail Link field, so I'd enter `http://www.myWebsite.com`.

The other option is to create an email link, which when clicked opens that person's email program with a new message already addressed to me. This works the same way. First, enter the text you want visitors to click — **Email Me,** for example — in the Contact Info field, =, and then enter the `mailto:` code (this is what tells a web browser to open the email) followed by your email address. It would look like this:

```
mailto:me@myWebsite.com
```

The default text is formatted that way to remind you to always put `mailto:` before the email address.

Lightroom Classic remembers text you've entered in each field and provides you quick access to previous entries via the drop-down arrow above the field.

Only in the Classic Gallery can you add an identity plate in addition to the Site Title at the top of your page, as shown back in Figure 15-2. You won't see this in the Site Info panel for any other gallery type.

Check the box to enable the identity plate. You can choose an existing identity plate or create a new one. You can make the identity plate into a clickable link by completing the Web or Mail Link field that appears below it (see Chapter 5 for more on the Identity Plate).

COLOR PALETTE PANEL

As the name suggests, the Color Palette panel holds the controls for changing the color scheme of your gallery. Figure 15-3 shows the Color Palette panel for the Classic Gallery. Although the configurable elements in each gallery type vary, the color controls work the same way in each instance.

Click the color chip corresponding to the element you want to change to access Lightroom Classic's Color Picker (it's really cool), as shown in Figure 15-4. You can choose a color in a number of ways:

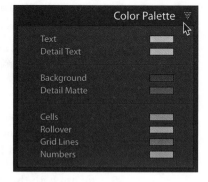

FIGURE 15-3:
The Color Palette panel.

- >> **Enter HSL values.** Uses the HSL (*H*ue, *S*aturation, *L*ightness) color model. You can enter specific values by clicking each H, S, or L field. Right-click the color bar to switch between HSL and HSB.

- >> **Enter HSB values.** Uses the HSB (*H*ue, *S*aturation, *B*rightness) color model. You can enter specific values by clicking each H, S, or B field.

- >> **Enter RGB values.** Uses yet another color model — this time the RGB (*R*ed, *G*reen, *B*lue) color model. You can enter specific values by clicking each R, G, or B field.

- >> **Enter Hexadecimal values.** The numbers used in HTML for defining color are commonly referred to as *hex* values. If you know the hex values used on your website, click the word Hex; this changes the RGB fields to a Hex field where you can enter the desired values.

- >> **Click a spot on the palette.** You can also simply choose a color by clicking the bar and adjusting the saturation with the ramp slider.

- >> **Use the eyedropper tool.** By far the coolest option! Click the color swatch, but do not release the mouse button so that you keep the eyedropper active. Move the eyedropper over any (and I mean any) area of your screen to select a color. This is great for pulling colors right from your photos to create the color palette for your gallery. While you move the eyedropper around the screen, you see the color of the element you're working on change. Release the mouse button to select the color.

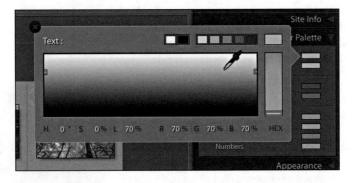

FIGURE 15-4:
The Color Picker.

You can use the swatches along the top of the Color Picker to save colors you like. Placing your cursor over each swatch displays a pop-up tooltip instructing you how to use that swatch. Close the Color Picker by clicking the color chip in the color palette you selected to open it.

APPEARANCE PANEL

The contents of this panel vary the most of any panel among the different gallery types. As you can imagine, each gallery type has a set of controls to alter its appearance. Figure 15-5 shows the Appearance panel for the Classic Gallery.

Despite the differences in the controls for each gallery, they're all rather straightforward in their purpose — you immediately see your adjustment's effects on the active gallery. For example, if you add more cells to the Classic Gallery, the live preview automatically updates before your eyes. Note that in the case of the Classic Gallery, the controls in the Image Pages section affect the page that displays the large version of the image. Click a thumbnail in the content area to switch to an Image Page to see the effects of the controls.

IMAGE INFO PANEL

This panel, shown in Figure 15-6, is where you find controls for adding a caption and title to go with the large image in your gallery. The main difference between Title and Caption is where they're located in each gallery (Title is always higher). You can display any type of textual information in either element (refer to Chapter 13 for steps to create custom text templates).

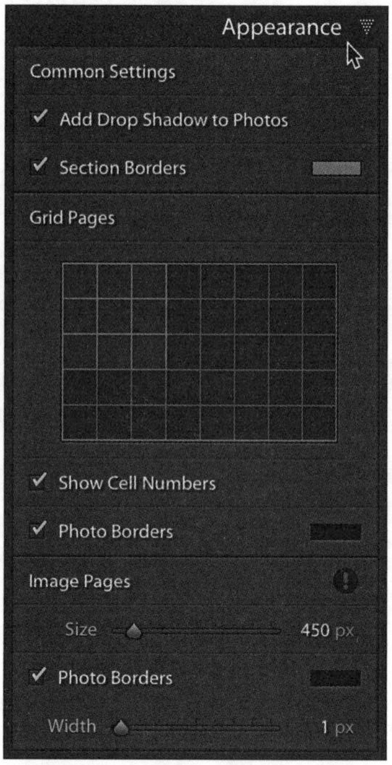

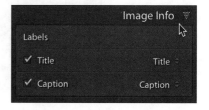

FIGURE 15-5:
The Appearance panel for the Classic Gallery.

Here's how to add a caption:

1. **Select the Caption check box.**

2. **Click the drop-down menu and either choose one of the text templates listed or choose Edit to create a custom text template.**

   After you choose a template, it immediately appears in the gallery. Note that Caption and Title only appear when viewing the large version of the photo; so if you're viewing the Classic Gallery grid, you won't see them until you click a photo to get to the large version.

FIGURE 15-6:
The Image Info panel.

REMEMBER

If you are using a Caption or Title template, you must enter an actual caption or title for each photo via the Metadata panel in the Library module. The text tokens pull that information from each photo's metadata to display in the gallery.

OUTPUT SETTINGS PANEL

The Output Settings panel, shown in Figure 15-7, contains the settings that affect the large image component of the gallery:

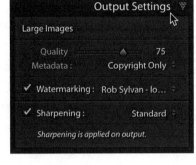

FIGURE 15-7:
The Output Settings panel.

>> **Quality:** This control sets the amount of JPG compression applied to the large image. The more compression, the smaller the file size, but the appearance can be degraded with too much compression. I wouldn't go below 50.

>> **Metadata:** Gives you the option to leave all metadata intact in the large JPGs (by selecting All from the drop-down menu), or stripping everything but your copyright (by choosing Copyright Only).

>> **Watermarking:** The Simple Copyright Watermark just pulls the copyright data you entered into the Copyright field of the Metadata panel in the Library module and displays it as a watermark on the photo. You can also choose existing custom watermarks or create your own (which I cover shortly).

>> **Sharpening:** Applies one of three levels of output sharpening (low, standard, or high) when the gallery leaves Lightroom Classic. Standard is a good default amount.

I want to take a closer look at how to create a custom watermark of your own. To open the Watermark Editor (shown in Figure 15-8), click the Watermarking drop-down menu, and choose Edit Watermarks. You can also get there from any module via the Lightroom ⇨ Edit Watermarks (Edit ⇨ Edit Watermarks for Windows) menu. From there, follow these steps to create a text watermark:

1. **Select the Text Watermark Style and enter your desired text in the field below the photo.**

   To create the © symbol, press Option+G (Alt+0169 on the numeric keypad for Windows).

2. **Expand the Text Options panel.**

   Select a Font from the drop-down menu; then configure its Style, Alignment, and Color.

3. **(Optional) Check the Shadow box if you want to apply a drop-shadow effect to the text.**

4. **Expand the Watermark Effects panel.**

Set the Size of the watermark first. There are three controls for sizing a watermark.

- *Proportional:* Enables the size slider so that you can set the watermark to a size that will remain constant (in proportion to the size of the exported photos) regardless of the photo's orientation.

- *Fit:* Expands the watermark to fit the entire width (or height depending on how the watermark is rotated) regardless of the photo's orientation.

- *Fill:* Expands the watermark to fill the width and height of the photo.

I recommend experimenting with each size setting to get a better feel for how they work. Proportional is likely to be the one used most often.

5. **Adjust the opacity with the Opacity slider.**

6. **Use the Inset and Anchor settings to control the exact placement of the watermark.**

For example, click the lower-left-corner Anchor point; then use the Horizontal Inset slider to bring it off the left edge of the photo and the Vertical Inset slider to bring it up off the bottom. You can rotate the watermark using the buttons to the right of the Anchor.

7. **Preview the watermark on different photos.**

At the top of the panel are left- and right-facing sets of arrows. These allow you to step through all the photos you selected before opening the editor. Go back and adjust sizing and placement as needed.

8. **Save as a preset.**

Click the preset drop-down menu in the top left corner and choose Save Current Settings as New Preset. Enter a descriptive name in the New Preset dialog and click Create. You can also use that same preset drop-down menu to access existing presets for editing, renaming, and deletion.

All the settings in the Watermark Effects panel work the same way for creating a Graphic Style watermark, except that the Text Options panel is unavailable. Here are the key things to know about creating a Graphic Style watermark:

>> Create the graphic in Photoshop before you launch the Watermark Editor.

>> Only JPG and PNG file formats will work.

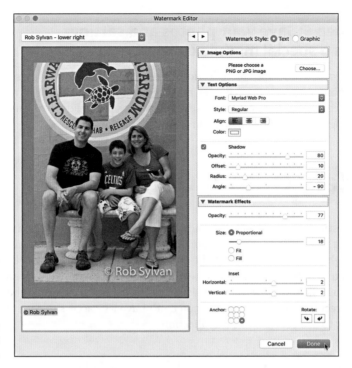

FIGURE 15-8:
The Watermark
Editor.

>> If you want to maintain transparent areas in your graphic, turn off the
   background layer in Photoshop and save as PNG.

With that in mind and your graphic on hand, you can click the Choose button in
the Image Options panel and create a new preset based on a graphic. From there
you can click the Done button to exit the editor. The next time your output needs
require a watermark, you can access your presets from any output module and
send your photos out in style.

Step 4: Save your settings as a template for reuse

You don't need to rely solely on the preinstalled templates after you get your feet
wet. As you begin to customize web galleries to your liking, I recommend saving
your preferred settings as templates. Here's how:

1. **Choose Web ⇨ New Template Folder to create a new template folder.**

   Give the folder a descriptive name and click the Create button.

2. **Choose Web ⇨ New Template to create a new template from the
settings you've specified.**

   Give the template a descriptive name, assign it to your desired folder, and click
   the Create button.

Step 5: Save your photos and settings as a special module collection

I cover these special collections, sometimes referred to as saved creations, in Chapter 12 (see that chapter for the steps). Here in the Web module, creating a saved web gallery collection saves all photos in the Filmstrip and your gallery settings to this special collection with the icon for web.

Web Gallery Output Options

Testing your web gallery locally (meaning on your computer) is standard operating procedure in web development, but the next phase is testing on a web server. Lightroom Classic has a built-in FTP (File Transfer Protocol) utility that enables you to upload your gallery directly to your web server without ever leaving Lightroom Classic! However, you also have the option to export all the web gallery files directly to your hard drive if you don't have FTP access to your web server or prefer to use your own FTP application.

Uploading your gallery with Lightroom Classic

To test your images on a web server, you need access to a web server. A web server is just a computer that "serves" files over the Internet. If you're just sharing your gallery with friends or family, you should check with your Internet Service Provider (ISP) support staff. ISPs commonly include web server space as part of your package. Just keep in mind that the link to this type of gallery will probably look something like this:

```
http://internetserviceprovider.net/~yourusername
```

Although people might look at you funny when you say "Tilde" (which is how you pronounce that symbol in front of *yourusername*), you're already paying for that web server space, so don't worry about the funny looks and learn to live with the tilde in order to save yourself some money.

Clearly, the professional solution is to get your own website. It doesn't cost as much as you might think (sometimes as little as a few dollars per month). Web-hosting companies are a dime a dozen, so ask your web-savvy friends whom they recommend.

I'm going to assume, then, that you've somehow secured access to a server. Nicely done. Now, you need to come up with three critical pieces of information to configure Lightroom Classic so that it can upload your files to your web host:

>> **Server address:** The FTP address needed to access the web server

>> **Username:** The username for your FTP account

>> **Password:** The password for your FTP account

To set up Lightroom Classic's FTP configuration dialog, follow these steps:

1. **Choose the Web module from the Module Picker and expand the Upload Settings panel, as shown in Figure 15-9.**

2. **Choose Edit from the FTP Server drop-down menu.**

   The Configure FTP File Transfer dialog appears, as shown in Figure 15-10.

3. **Enter your FTP server information in the Server field, along with the username and password you were given for that server.**

   Check the Store Password in Preset check box if you're the only person using that computer.

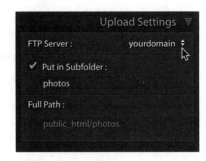

FIGURE 15-9:
The Upload Settings panel.

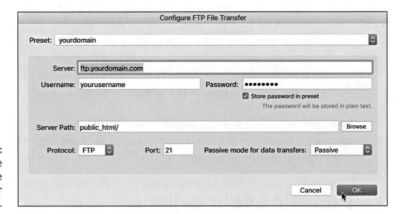

FIGURE 15-10:
The Configure FTP File Transfer dialog.

4. **Configure the Server Path field.**

   What you enter here will vary based on the web server. *Server path* refers to the folder on the web server where Lightroom Classic stores the files you upload. In some cases, you leave this field blank; in others, it might be something like `public_html/`. Ask your web hosting provider if you're not sure what to enter. Unless you're instructed otherwise, leave the Protocol drop-down menu set to FTP, the Port menu set to 21, and the Passive Mode for Data Transfers drop-down menu set to Passive.

5. **Choose the Save Current Settings as New Preset option from the Preset drop-down menu.**

6. **In the new dialog that appears, give the Preset a name and then click Create.**

   You return to the Configure FTP File Transfer dialog.

7. **Click OK in the Configure FTP File Transfer dialog to close it.**

   In the Upload Settings panel, you now see the name of your preset listed as the FTP Server. Now, all you need to do is decide where on your web server you want to store your gallery.

8. **In the Upload Settings panel, check the Put in Subfolder check box, enter a name in the field below (refer to Figure 15-9), and then press Enter.**

   The Full Path that appears at the bottom of the panel shows where your folder sits in relation to the Server Path field you configured in Step 4. **Note:** Do not use spaces in your folder names because spaces in links can be problematic.

   This subfolder becomes part of the path or URL (Uniform Resource Locator) to your gallery. Therefore, if you're uploading a gallery of flower photos (and who doesn't have a gallery of flower photos?), you might name the subfolder "flowers," which would result in the following path to your gallery:

   `http://www.yourdomain.com/flowers/`

9. **Click the Upload button in the bottom right of the panel.**

After the progress meter has done its thing, navigate to your new gallery in your web browser and give it a test drive! If you make changes to the gallery in Lightroom Classic, be sure to reupload it.

Exporting your gallery

If you have preferred FTP software, or if you don't have FTP access to your hosting environment, you can click the Export button, save your web gallery to your hard drive, and then upload the files outside Lightroom Classic.

Here are the steps:

1. **Click the Export button (bottom of right panel group, as shown in Figure 15-1).**

   It's next to the Upload button.

2. **In the dialog that appears, navigate to the location on your hard drive where you want to save the gallery files.**

3. **Enter a name for the folder containing the gallery and click Save.**

Wait for Lightroom Classic's progress meter to complete before attempting to upload the gallery to your web host. Be sure to upload the entire contents of the folder. You can change the name of the folder holding all the files, but do not change the name of any files within the folder unless you update the HTML code within the files to reflect that change. At this point, Lightroom Classic's job is finished and it's up to you to complete the job. If you make changes to the web gallery in Lightroom Classic, you need to reexport the entire gallery.

5

The Part of Tens

Chapter **16**

Ten Things to Know About Using Lightroom Classic and Lightroom Together

In Chapter 1, I explain the differences between Lightroom Classic and the (newer) Lightroom ecosystem based on cloud storage, with the goal of helping you choose the right product for your needs. I still believe that Lightroom Classic offers the best combination of editing power, library management, and output options for the price, which makes it the path I recommend for most people. That said, there's a lot to like about the new cloud-based Lightroom, and it makes a lot of sense for Lightroom Classic users to learn its capabilities and how the two programs can be used together. There may even come a day where you find that the new Lightroom ecosystem has all the features you want and you switch over to it completely.

WARNING

To avoid confusion, Adobe does not recommend installing the desktop version of the cloud-based Lightroom on the same computer running Lightroom Classic and then turning on the sync function between them. If you are using Lightroom Classic, you don't need to install the desktop version of the new Lightroom too. These next three chapters cover using Lightroom Classic in conjunction with the Lightroom app for mobile devices (iOS and Android).

Why Would You Use Them Together?

As much as I love my DSLR, I must admit that I have my iPhone with me all the time, and as a result, I use that mobile camera a lot. Regardless of whether I capture a photo with my iPhone, DSLR, drone, or point-and-shoot digital camera, I want to manage all my photos with Lightroom Classic on my computer. The Lightroom app for mobile provides me the following:

>> **Sync with Lightroom Classic:** Syncing means that I can automatically share photos and edits from Lightroom Classic to my mobile device and vice versa. I explore this capability further in the section "Syncing Collections from Lightroom Classic."

>> **Powerful Camera:** The camera module in Lightroom for mobile is so awesome that I devoted an entire chapter to it (see Chapter 18).

>> **Familiar Editing Tools:** You've got almost the entire Develop module in your pocket (see Chapter 17).

>> **Familiar Flagging/Rating Tools:** Flags and star ratings applied to synced photos are visible in both apps (see Chapter 17).

When I sync these apps, I can designate photos in Lightroom Classic that I want to see in the mobile app, and any edits, ratings, or flags I apply to those photos (in either app) are kept in sync. Any new photos I add or capture in the mobile app are automatically downloaded (via the cloud) to my computer running Lightroom Classic. At the most basic level, I gain a portable portfolio of my work that is always in my pocket and an automated system for downloading all mobile photos back to my main computer for storage and backup. As great as all this sounds, there are some things to be aware of before you dive in.

Know Before You Go

Lightroom Classic synced with Lightroom for mobile workflow is where this new Lightroom got its start. Even so, when Adobe created the desktop version of the cloud-based Lightroom, things got a little weird. As I explain in Chapter 1, Adobe created a self-contained Lightroom workflow with cloud storage at its center. The new Lightroom for desktop and mobile are designed specifically to work together, and as such, all things are kept in sync between those apps. Unfortunately, when this happened, Lightroom Classic became the local-storage-only workflow option for anyone not wanting to go all in on cloud storage, and this event created a rift in how the syncing features were developed from that point forward between Lightroom Classic and the new Lightroom cloud-based apps.

Basically, everything that could sync (at the time of the rift) between Lightroom Classic and Lightroom for mobile remained in place (like the features I mention previously), but any new syncing features were only added to the new Lightroom cloud-based apps. That means that there are some things that cannot sync between Lightroom Classic and the other Lightroom apps, such as

>> Keywords

>> Color labels

>> People tags

>> Organizational structure for grouping collections (more on this later)

>> More to come?

Although I feel it is unfortunate that there is a partial (and growing) list of things that do not sync between Lightroom Classic and the new Lightroom ecosystem, I use it only for keeping certain photos (and their edits) synced between Lightroom Classic and Lightroom on my mobile devices. To me, those benefits outweigh the limitations, as long as you know what you are getting yourself into.

Setting It Up

Here's how to get your Lightroom Classic catalog to sync with the Lightroom app on your mobile device. The key to syncing is your Adobe ID, so when the time comes, you just need to be logged in with the same Adobe ID on your computer and on your mobile device. Follow these steps to enable sync in Lightroom Classic:

1. **Open the Lightroom Classic catalog you want to sync with Lightroom for mobile.**

You can only sync one Lightroom Classic catalog, and most people only have one anyway.

2. **Click the Cloud icon in the upper right corner to open the syncing pop-up dialog.**

3. **Click the Start Syncing button (see Figure 16-1).**

   Once sync has been enabled, the Start Syncing button changes to a Pause Syncing button, which you can click to pause syncing if ever needed.

4. **Grab your mobile device and install the Lightroom app from the App Store on iOS or Google Play store on Android.**

   Log into the mobile app using the same Adobe ID and password that you use on your computer. When prompted during set up, uncheck Auto Add to avoid all photos on your device importing into Lightroom at this time.

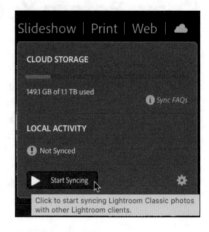

FIGURE 16-1:
Click Start to enable sync between Lightroom Classic and the cloud-based Lightroom.

Lightroom Classic Preferences

Once you have sync enabled, you can tweak your preferences to suit your needs. In Lightroom Classic, head to Lightroom Classic ⇨ Preferences for Mac (Edit ⇨ Preferences for Windows) and click the Lightroom Sync tab. In the Location section, check the Specify location for Lightroom's Synced images box and then click Choose to navigate to the folder on your system where you want all photos downloaded from the cloud to be stored. This folder is where photos you take using the Lightroom for mobile camera or photos directly imported into Lightroom for mobile will be downloaded locally. You also have the option on that panel to have Lightroom Classic create subfolders based on capture date of the downloaded photos.

I chose a folder within my Pictures folder on my internal drive because that location is always available. From there, I use Lightroom Classic to move those folders to my external drive when it is connected. Choose a location that works best for your system and needs. If you don't set up a specific folder, you'll see the name of your mobile device appear in the Folders panel as though it were a connected drive, but it is really just a local folder that Lightroom Classic creates in the absence of your specifying a location.

Syncing Collections from Lightroom Classic

The primary vehicle for syncing photos from Lightroom Classic to the cloud-based Lightroom is regular collections. When you sync photos from Lightroom Classic, a smart preview for each synced photo is created, and it is this smart preview that gets uploaded from Lightroom Classic to the cloud. There is no way to upload full-resolution copies of your photos from Lightroom Classic to the cloud.

The upside of uploading only Smart Previews is that these Smart Previews do *not* count against your cloud storage limit. When you consider that the standard Creative Cloud Photography Plan comes with only 20GB of cloud storage (the All Apps subscription plan gives you 100GB), this is a huge benefit, because it enables you to theoretically have unlimited photos synced from Lightroom Classic to the cloud.

Here's how to sync existing collections using Smart Previews:

1. **Expand the Collections panel.**

2. **Check the box to the left of the collection name.**

   If you don't see the box to the left of the collection name, as shown in Figure 16-2, go back to the Cloud icon and enable syncing as described previously in the "Setting It Up" section.

Unchecking that box removes the collection from being synced, but it may leave synced photos in the All Synced Photographs collection, which I cover in the upcoming section "All Synced Photographs."

TIP

When you create a new collection, you can sync your collection right from the start by selecting the Sync with Lightroom check box in the Create Collection dialog.

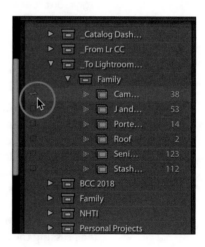

FIGURE 16-2:
Check the box to the left of the collection name to sync it.

Making Collections Public

When you view a synced collection in the Library module, you may notice the button labeled Make Public in the upper right corner above the thumbnails. Because all synced photos are stored in the cloud (even if just a Smart Preview), you can view those photos through your web browser. Adobe refers to this as Lightroom for the Web (and has no relation to the Web module in Chapter 15), which is a bit of a mouthful. The core feature that we are concerned with here, though, is being able to share that link with other people so that they can view and interact with a gallery of photos.

After you click the Make Public button, a link is generated and displayed above the thumbnails. Clicking that link opens Lightroom in your default web browser, or you can right-click the link and copy it to your clipboard for easy pasting into an email or text message to share with others. You can learn more about this feature on my blog: `https://lightroomkillertips.com/lightroom-cc-webs-gallery-feature`.

All Synced Photographs

New collections appear in the Catalog panel labeled All Synced Photographs, which keeps a running tally of all photos synced between Lightroom Classic and the Lightroom ecosystem. You can drag and drop photos from other places in Lightroom Classic into this collection to have those photos sync, although doing so can get unmanageable, seeing as how those photos may not appear in any individual collections.

You can also remove photos from being synced by selecting them in this collection and pressing the Delete key. You'll see a prompt warning you that those photos will be removed from all synced devices (and all synced collections) but not removed from the desktop catalog. I use this option to remove photos from being synced because that also removes them from being stored in the cloud without removing them from my local storage. Doing so is useful for managing how much data you have stored in the cloud. You can read more about this over on my blog: `https://lightroomkillertips.com/managing-adobe-cloud-storage-space-classic-users`.

Collections or Albums?

Brace yourself for a bit of confusing lingo you need to understand. *Collections* in Lightroom Classic are referred to as *albums* in the cloud-based version of Lightroom. In Lightroom Classic, collections are organized with collection sets. In the cloud-based version of Lightroom, albums are organized by putting them into folders. To further complicate matters, collection sets cannot be synced to cloud-based Lightroom; you must manually organize your albums in the cloud-based app to group them into folders. This is one more place where the rift between Lightroom Classic and the new cloud-based Lightroom is apparent.

Lightroom for Mobile Interface

Although this app does get updated frequently with new features, and it looks slightly different on the two supported platforms (iOS and Android), the core layout, shown in Figure 16-3 appears the same across platforms:

>> **A:** Folder icon, which contains albums

>> **B:** Album icon, which contains photos

>> **C:** Add Photos icon, for adding photos from a mobile device's camera roll

>> **D:** Camera icon, to launch Lightroom camera (more in Chapter 18)

>> **E:** Create New Albums and Folders icon

>> **F:** Settings icon

Be sure to bookmark the Lightroom Learn & Support page to learn more: https:// helpx.adobe.com/support/lightroom-cc.html.

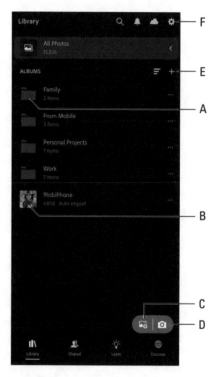

FIGURE 16-3:
The Lightroom for Mobile interface on an iPhone.

Change Is a Constant

Adobe is clearly committed to continually evolving its products to meet the needs and technologies of the future, and it can pose challenges for users to keep up with the changes. This is a strength and a weakness of the times we live in. My hope is that this book provides a good foundation for you to build on no matter what changes occur. However, if you ever encounter something in your software that doesn't quite match what you see in the book, this is most likely due to something that changed after the book was published. Stay up to date by visiting me at https://LightroomKillerTips.com.

Chapter **17**

Ten Things to Know About Organizing and Editing in Lightroom

Chapter 16 was devoted to getting you set up with syncing your Lightroom Classic catalog with Lightroom for mobile. This chapter builds on that chapter with a look at the top things you need to know about using Lightroom for mobile to organize and edit your photos. Keep in mind that although Lightroom Classic is the ultimate home base for all of our photos in this workflow, there is still a lot we can do while we are on the go. I use Lightroom on my iPhone as my primary mobile camera app (see Chapter 18), but I also use it to import photos from a memory card while in the field. No matter where my photos are coming from, I can leverage all the key editing tools in Lightroom Classic's Develop module to edit those photos and have it all sync back to my Lightroom Classic catalog.

There's no way I can fit everything there is to know about Lightroom for mobile in these last three chapters, so be sure to check out the resources I've provided throughout the book to keep up to date with new changes and to learn more. My goal here is to whet your appetite and get you started.

Note that I'm writing this from the perspective of a mobile phone user because those devices are better for using the built-in camera. However, all these functions are available on mobile tablet devices, but the interface for tablet screens may look slightly different from my phone screen captures shown in the book.

Help & Support

You can get some help in the form of FAQs, access to the Adobe support forum, and guided tutorials right from within the app itself. Tap the Settings icon in the upper right corner of the Home screen to enter the app Settings. On the Settings screen, find the menu for Help & Support along with a great deal of other useful features to help you get the most out of the app. Take a moment to explore each option to see what's available. Check out the What's New section after each app update to see what was added. At the bottom of the Home screen, tap the Learn icon to delve into hundreds of step-by-step editing tutorials that happen right inside the app itself or tap Discover to learn and be inspired by your peers.

All Photos and Filtering

The All Photos album that appears at the top of the Home screen gives you single-tap access to all photographs that have been synced with Lightroom. This includes all photos that were synced from Lightroom Classic and all photos you've captured in the app or imported from your camera roll.

You can filter what is displayed by tapping the Funnel icon at the top of the screen. I find it helpful to filter what is displayed when viewing All Photos, but the feature works the same in any album you are viewing. Tapping the Funnel icon displays the following (and growing) list of criteria you can use to filter your photos:

>> **Rating:** Star ratings applied here or in Lightroom Classic can be used to refine what is visible.

>> **Flags:** As with ratings, flags applied in either app can be used here.

- » **Type:** Can filter by HDR, photo, panorama, raw, or video.

- » **Camera:** Filter by the camera used to create the photo.

- » **People:** If you've used the face recognition functionality within the cloud-based Lightroom, you can filter on those results. Note that people tags do not sync between Lightroom and Lightroom Classic.

- » **Location:** Photos can be filtered based on their geolocation data.

- » **Keywords:** If you've applied keywords in the cloud-based Lightroom app, imported photos that had keywords applied to them previously, or migrated a Lightroom Classic catalog (where you import an entire catalog into the Lightroom cloud), you can filter on those keywords. Note that keywords don't sync between Lightroom and Lightroom Classic.

- » **Edited:** Filter based on whether a photo has been edited.

Segmentation and View Options

Tap the three-dot menu in the upper right corner of the screen to access the menus for changing how the photos are segmented (grouped), change the sort option, and access additional view options. When used together, they are a set of powerful tools for displaying just the photos you want to see and how they are shown.

Adobe Sensei Search

Due to the fact that all photos in Lightroom are stored in the cloud (even if just a Smart Preview), Adobe employs their proprietary technology that uses machine learning and artificial intelligence (referred to as *Adobe Sensei*) to identify the contents of your photos and automatically tag them with relevant keywords that you can use to search within Lightroom. Note that this functionality does not exist in Lightroom Classic.

Using Adobe Sensei, you can search your library in the cloud-based Lightroom without having to manually add any keywords at all. Just tap the Search icon (it looks like a magnifying glass) when viewing the source you want to search (start in All Photos to search everything) and then enter the words you want to search on. As you type you'll see a list of facets ranging from keywords, locations, camera metadata, and more that you can tap to see the results (or just keep typing to enter your criteria). You can enter multiple terms (facets) to further refine the results, as shown in Figure 17-1 (where I searched on Red and Leaf). Tapping the x on any search facet will remove it from the results. I expect this will only continue to improve in time.

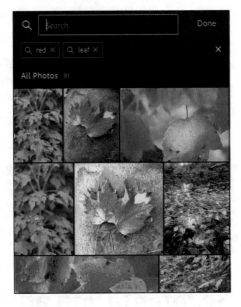

FIGURE 17-1:
Explore your library using Adobe Sensei.

Adding Photos from Camera Roll

If you're like me, you're bound to have a multitude of other photo editing and camera apps on your mobile device, and you've probably got more than a few photos already on the camera roll. You can certainly keep using any other apps, but I would urge you to consider importing everything important on your camera roll into Lightroom to copy those photos to your computer and back them up. Here's how:

1. **Tap the blue Add Photos icon on the bottom right of the screen.**

   The left side of the blue button is for adding new photos, and the right side opens the Camera module.

2. **Choose the source where your photos reside.**

Your device's camera roll will be the most likely location, but you may see other options based on your device and what is connected to it.

3. **Select the photos you want to add.**

You can single-tap any photo to select it, or tap-drag across a range of photos. The three-dot menu in the upper right gives you access to commands for selecting all and even filtering by photos, videos, raws, or screenshots. Any photos that had previously been added to Lightroom display a Lr logo in their upper left corner, as shown in Figure 17-2. You can deselect photos by tapping them a second time.

4. **Tap the Add button that appears at the bottom of the screen to complete the process.**

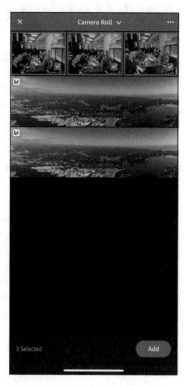

FIGURE 17-2:
Adding photos from the camera roll.

You can add photos to a specific album by first entering that album and then tapping the Add Photos icon to start the process. You can import photos from a memory card from any camera in the same fashion. (You may need an adapter with a card reader, depending on your device.)

Apply During Import

While you can't do as much from cloud-based Lightroom as from the Import window in Lightroom Classic, you can automatically add a few things to photos as part of the import process. Tap the Settings icon on the Home screen to go to the Settings screen. From there, tap Import to access its options, as shown in Figure 17-3. Here you can enable and disable the automatic adding of photos, screenshots, and videos from your camera roll (I recommend disabling all of these right away to avoid your entire camera roll getting dumped into Lightroom), have a simple copyright statement applied to photos, and customize the Raw Default setting (go here to learn more: https://lightroomkillertips.com/customizing-camera-raw-defaults-in-lightroom-classic).

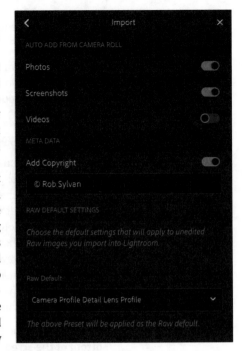

FIGURE 17-3:
Import settings you can configure.

Creating Albums and Folders

As you add more photos to Lightroom, you may want to organize them using albums and folders. Refer to Chapter 16 to see how albums and folders map back to what you use in Lightroom Classic for organization in the Collections panel. The key thing to know here is that albums hold photos and folders hold albums.

In my case, I created a single album that I use as my working camera roll within the app, which is where I put all new photos at first until I can go through them and decide which I will keep. Because all photos I import into Lightroom are uploaded to the cloud and then downloaded to my computer, I don't keep any photos in my device's camera roll at all (at least not for long). This has allowed me to regain a lot of storage space on my device without losing the ability to view my important photos within Lightroom. Once photos are imported into Lightroom and I've confirmed that they were downloaded to Lightroom Classic, I delete them from the device's camera roll.

Here's how to create a new album:

1. **Tap the Create New Albums and Folders icon (+) to the right of the Albums header on the Home screen.**

   This reveals the options for creating a new album or folder.

2. **Tap the Create New Album icon.**

   This reveals the Create Album pop-up window.

3. **In the Create Album pop-up window, enter a meaningful name, and tap OK.**

   This adds the new album.

The steps for creating a new folder are the same, except that you tap the icon for Create New Folder instead. Once you create a few albums, you can add (or move) photos between albums. Here's how:

1. **Start in All Photos so that you have access to your entire library of synced photos.**

2. **Select a photo you want to add to an album.**

   A long press on a photo selects it and puts you in the mode for selecting more.

3. **Tap any additional photos you want to include.**

   You can tap-slide your finger over multiple photos to select them faster.

4. **Tap the Add To icon at the bottom of the screen.**

   A list of your existing albums appears.

5. **Tap the check box to the left of the album to which you want to add the selected photos and then tap Add.**

   The photos you selected are added to that album.

The albums you create here sync to Lightroom Classic and appear in the Collections panel within a collection set named *From Lightroom*. Remember that folders in the cloud–based Lightroom do not sync (nor do collection sets from Lightroom Classic).

Applying Ratings and Flags

One of the first uses for the Lightroom on mobile workflow was a way to apply ratings, flags, or both to your photos while on the go. One scenario might be to import a shoot into Lightroom Classic while in the field and then add those photos to a synced collection/album. After the sync is complete, you can leave Lightroom Classic, and while on the flight/ride home pull out your phone, open Lightroom, and review the photos to start the flagging and rating process. Note that data charges may apply when not on Wi-Fi.

To start applying ratings or flags, you need to switch to Rate & Review view. Single-tap a photo to have it fill the screen, tap the drop-down menu in the upper left corner of the screen, and choose Rate & Review. Quickly apply a star rating by tap-dragging up or down on the left side of the image and stopping when you reach the desired star rating that appears onscreen. You can quickly change the flag state by tap-dragging up or down the right side of the photo to access the flagging options. Then swipe left or right to move to the next photo. With a little practice, the process moves along pretty quickly. Those settings are then automatically synced back to Lightroom Classic. There are also star and flag icons below the photo that you can tap to apply ratings and flags that way as well.

Edit Photos Anywhere

With each update to Lightroom, Adobe has brought it closer to feature parity with the Develop module in Lightroom Classic. I don't have enough room in this book to delve into each of the options, but I can provide a map of the tools in Lightroom for mobile back to the relevant descriptions of the same tools from when I covered them as being part of the Develop module. Remember, everything you can do in Lightroom Classic can be rendered correctly in Lightroom for mobile and vice versa. The differences in the interface are largely due to using a touch-based device as opposed to a keyboard and mouse, but Adobe did also rename and regroup some adjustments with the move to the cloud-based Lightroom. As a Lightroom Classic user, I think you'll find the tools to be intuitive and familiar once I get you oriented.

To enter editing mode, tap the drop-down menu in the upper left and tap Edit. If you hold your device in portrait orientation, the editing tools appear along the bottom of the screen. If you rotate your device to landscape orientation, the editing tools appear along the right side of the screen (remember that the larger screens on a tablet will look slightly different than on a phone). Whichever way you hold your device (and depending on its screen size), Lightroom has more tools than can appear in one screen, so be sure to swipe the toolstrip to the left or right to see them all. I recommend starting in portrait orientation, as shown in Figure 17-4, because it displays a name under each tool's icon to help you get to know them. Most of the tools are a straightforward match to what you know in the Develop module, but I want to point out a few that are less obvious:

>> **Auto:** Tap the icon labeled Auto to automatically adjust tonality and color saturation.

>> **Light:** Tap the icon labeled Light to access the tonal value adjustments found in the Basic panel as well as the tone curve.

>> **Color:** Under Color, you find the white-balance adjustment tools, the Vibrance and Saturation sliders, and the B&W, Color Grading, and Color Mix (HSL) controls.

>> **Effects:** Texture, Clarity, Dehaze, Vignette, and Grain are all nested under here.

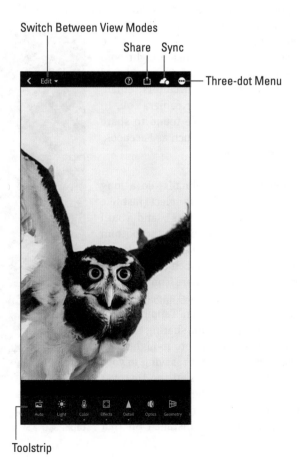

FIGURE 17-4: Get familiar with the editing tools in Lightroom for mobile.

- » **Detail:** Sharpening and Noise Reduction are nested under here.

- » **Optics:** Remove chromatic aberration and enable lens corrections.

- » **Geometry:** This contains the controls found under the Transform panel in the Develop module.

The best way to learn here is to play. All your edits are nondestructive, and at the far right of the Toolstrip, you find the Reset button, which you can use to get back to where you started. Be sure to check out the tutorials inside the Learn area that I mention in the beginning of the chapter.

Export Copies

After doing all the work to get your photos into the app, sort them, rate them, and edit them, you're probably ready to share them with the world. Sure, you can wait until it all syncs back to Lightroom Classic and use the Export function, but there's no need to wait. You can select photos inside Lightroom and share edited copies to your favorite social media platforms, other photo editors, email, text messaging, or even your camera roll. In fact, this is the best way I've found to share photos to social media apps such as Facebook, Twitter, and Instagram.

If you are looking at thumbnails, do a long press on the photo you want to select (just like when adding photos to albums), and you'll see the Share icon appear along the bottom of the screen (look for the Share label). If you are viewing a single photo (such as when you apply ratings or editing), a Share icon (a square with an upward pointing arrow) appears in the upper right corner of the screen. Tapping either Share icon reveals options for sharing to other apps, getting a link to the photo in Lightroom for Web, opening in other apps, saving to your device, or sharing your edits in the Discover section (see Figure 17-5). The available options depend on your device's operating system and what other apps you have installed on that

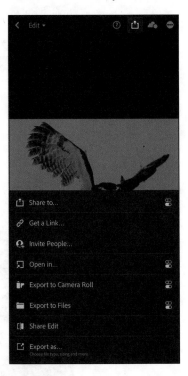

FIGURE 17-5:
Output options available after tapping the Share icon.

device. Tap Export as to configure export settings for the copy that is created. Note that if the selected photo was synced from Lightroom Classic, you'll be working only with a Smart Preview, which is limited to 2560 pixels on the long edge, so you won't be able to export anything larger than that.

This is only the tip of the Lightroom for mobile iceberg, so explore, check out the resources I've shared, and have fun.

» **Shooting modes**

» **Shoot-through presets and overlays**

» **More ways to press the shutter**

» **Launching the camera**

Chapter **18**

Ten Things to Know About Using the Lightroom Mobile Camera

The camera module within the Lightroom app for mobile (iOS and Android) has become my absolute favorite camera when I'm on the go. When you sync your Lightroom Classic catalog with Lightroom for mobile, all the photos you take in the mobile app are automatically uploaded to the cloud and then eventually downloaded to the computer running Lightroom Classic. To me, this is an unbeatable combination just for that alone, but there's a lot more in the Lightroom for mobile camera to love.

Some of the features found in the camera module will depend on the mobile device you are using at the time. Be sure to check out the minimum requirements mention in Chapter 1 to ensure that your mobile device is compatible. (Note that these screen captures were made on an iPhone 13 Pro Max with multiple lenses, so they may vary slightly from what you see on your device.) Remember that this app undergoes rapid development, so there will be new features added that are not covered in this book. Keep up with all Lightroom news at `https://Lightroom KillerTips.com`.

Shooting in Raw Mode (DNG)

Sure, you can shoot in the standard JPG file format, but why not shoot in Raw mode and take full advantage of the editing power inside the Lightroom app? Refer to Chapter 3 for a discussion of file formats to see the benefits of each. Keep in mind that photos captured in the app are not saved to the local camera roll (they are stored in a temporary cache until they can be uploaded to the cloud — data charges may apply — and then removed from the device) so these photos won't clog up your device's local storage.

Tap the Camera icon (it looks like a blue camera) to open the camera. You can change file format between JPG and DNG (raw) by tapping the File Format icon in the top center of the screen, as shown in Figure 18-1. This opens the File Format Selector, where another tap will switch you DNG (if not there already).

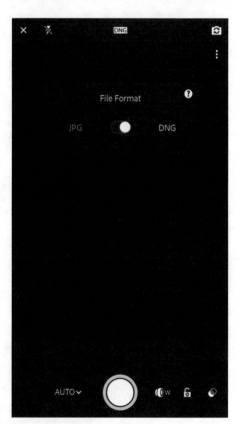

FIGURE 18-1:
Switching to shoot in DNG file format.

TECHNICAL STUFF

Note that for iOS, DNG raw image capture is supported on any iPhone or iPad device that has at least a 12-megapixel camera and is running iOS 10.0 or later. For Android, DNG raw image capture is supported on devices running Android versions 5.0 and later (though support for DNG capture is enabled and set solely by the device manufacturers).

Shooting in Professional Mode

When you first open the camera, it will probably be set to Auto mode, which lets the camera control shutter speed, ISO, focus, and white balance automatically. That's fine for snapshots or when you are in a hurry, but try taking back a little more control by switching over to Professional mode. Tap Auto to expand the Mode Menu and tap Professional, as shown in Figure 18-2.

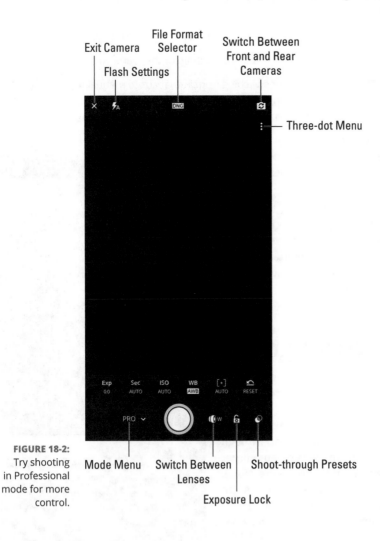

FIGURE 18-2: Try shooting in Professional mode for more control.

In Professional mode, you can choose from the following controls (or leave them in auto mode):

>> **Exp:** This is the control for exposure compensation, which allows you to override the camera's meter and increase or decrease the exposure value to better match the scene.

>> **Sec:** Control shutter speed if you are trying to stop motion or play with creative blur.

>> **ISO:** Manually control ISO setting to avoid noise or work in low light.

>> **WB:** Choose the right white-balance setting for the scene you are in.

>> **[+]:** This is the control for switching from auto focus to manual focus. Note the green highlight appearing along in-focus edges is called *focus peaking*. The area highlighted in green is in focus.

>> **Reset:** One tap sets all the previously mentioned controls back to automatic modes.

Tap the icon representing the aspect you want to change to access its options (usually represented by a simple slider except in the case of white balance). Double-tapping an icon resets it to its default settings.

Using Shoot-through Presets

If you like to visualize creative effects while shooting, tap the Shoot-through Presets icon in the lower right corner of the screen (refer to Figure 18-2). There are five built-in presets (in addition to none) to choose from: High Contrast, Flat, Warm Shadows, High Contrast B&W, and Flat B&W. To help you visualize the scene in B&W, for example, choose either of the B&W presets and the live scene changes to match, as shown in Figure 18-3. These

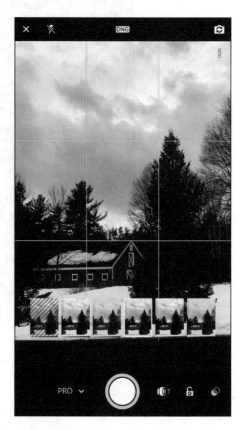

FIGURE 18-3:
Shoot-through presets add creativity to your shooting.

presets are completely non-destructive, so you can modify the settings applied to the photo or completely reset the settings when editing.

Helpful Overlays

There are a number of overlays that you can invoke to help compose the photo and avoid overexposing the highlights. Tap the three-dot menu in the upper right corner of the screen (refer to Figure 18-2) to expand the options. From left to right, as shown in Figure 18-4, the options are

>> **Aspect Ratio:** This will show the default aspect ratio for your device at first, but you can switch between 16:9, 3:2, 4:3, and 1:1. You'll get a live preview of the aspect ratio you choose for taking the photo, but you can always revert to the full (uncropped) image in the Crop tool by choosing Original from the list of aspect ratios.

>> **Self Timer:** Set a 2-, 5-, or 10-second timer before the shutter trips. I cover this more in the next section.

>> **Grid & Level:** You can switch between three grid overlays to help with composition and even enable an electronic level indicator to help you avoid crooked horizons.

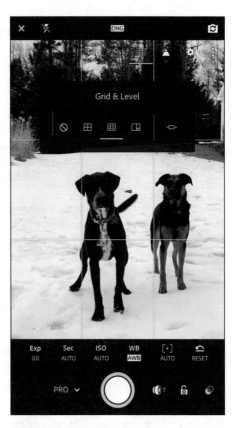

FIGURE 18-4:
Access additional tools that help you get the best shot.

>> **Highlight Clipping:** Enable this option to easily see any area of the photo that the highlights are being overexposed. Any highlights in danger of being clipped will show a series of diagonal lines called *zebra stripes*. Use that exposure compensation mentioned in the previous section to recover those highlights before taking the photo.

>> **Settings:** The Settings panel contains controls for maximizing screen brightness to help you see in bright daylight conditions and to enable/disable geotagging photos. If your camera supports HDR mode (covered in the upcoming section "In-Camera HDR Mode") you can have the app save the normal unprocessed photo in addition to the HDR version.

Self Timer, Burst Mode, and Remote Trigger

You can trigger the shutter within the app by tapping the big shutter button within the app interface or by pressing the volume control on the side of your device. Note that on Android, you need to first click that Settings icon I mention previously and enable capture from the Volume Keys Function menu. This is very handy when you hold the device in landscape orientation.

You can also leverage that volume control trigger by turning your headphones (with volume control) into a remote camera shutter. This can be useful for slow-shutter scenes when your device is on a stable platform (like a tripod). There are even Bluetooth-enabled volume control buttons that you can buy for a true handsfree remote shutter trigger.

On the iPhone (and I hope coming to Android), you can fire the shutter in burst mode by pressing and holding the volume control button on the iPhone (not headphone), which is very useful for capturing fast-action scenes. One final tip, switch your phone to silent mode to disable all sounds, including the fake camera shutter sound.

Last Photo Preview

You can quickly see a preview of the last photo taken by tapping the small thumbnail to the left of the shutter button. This is useful for things like making sure everyone's eyes are open in a group photo. Just tap the preview photo to dismiss it, return to the camera, and keep shooting.

Exposure Lock

When faced with a tricky exposure situation, you may want to ensure that the camera doesn't change its exposure settings due to changing light (such as on a partly cloudy day). To do so, you can frame up your photo, dial-in any desired exposure compensation, and then tap the Exposure Lock icon (refer to Figure 18-2) to lock in your settings. The camera will hold those settings until the Exposure Lock icon is tapped a second time.

In-Camera HDR Mode

A very cool feature in the Lightroom camera is the ability to shoot in HDR (High Dynamic Range) mode on supported devices. This allows you to shoot in raw (DNG), and when you press the shutter button the camera takes three photos exposing for the highlights, shadows, and midtones, automatically aligning and blending them into a single DNG photo. This photo will have a much higher dynamic range than any single photo but all the benefits of a raw photo for editing purposes. You can even shoot these handheld, so no tripod is needed.

Use this mode when photographing a scene that has bright highlights (such as clouds in the sky on a sunny day) and dark shadows (such as shaded areas on the ground). It is not ideal for moving subjects, but don't be afraid to experiment and see what is possible.

Take a Selfie or Switch Lenses

You can switch between the rear- and forward-facing cameras on your device from within the Camera app by tapping the Camera icon in the upper right corner of the interface (refer to Figure 18-2). Selfie is also an option in the widget and 3D touch options I cover in the next section for faster access. If you have a dual-lens device, you can switch between the wide and telephoto lenses by tapping the Lens icon that appears to the right of the shutter button.

Camera Launch Shortcuts

Beyond tapping the Camera icon in the app to open the camera, you can use any of the alternative shortcuts when you want to open the camera quickly. These shortcuts do vary with your operating system, so let's look at iPhone first. If you have a device that supports 3D touch, you can do a long press on the Lr app icon to access a shortcut for jumping right to the camera. Additionally, on iOS you can configure a Lightroom widget on the Home screen to allow fast access to the camera. Head here to learn more about configuring widgets on iOS: `https://support.apple.com/en-us/HT207122`.

In a somewhat similar fashion on Android, you can add a Lightroom camera widget to the Home screen. Head here to learn more about adding widgets on Android: `https://support.google.com/android/answer/2781850?hl=en`.

Once you have the options configured, you'll be ready to capture anything that comes your way!

Index

About the Author

Rob Sylvan is a photographer, educator, and aspiring beekeeper. He is the author of many Lightroom, Photoshop, and photography related books, e-books, and videos. Rob also authors and curates tutorials found within the Photoshop and Lightroom applications, is an adjunct faculty at NHTI, a Canon Product Educator, regularly contributes to *Photoshop User* magazine, and teaches at photography industry conferences such as Adobe MAX, Photoshop World, PHOTOPLUS, and more.

Dedication

To Dad.

Author's Acknowledgments

The fact that you're holding this book right now is more a testament to the multitude of people who made it possible than just the person who put the words to paper.

My deepest thanks go to Pete Bauer, for not only taking me on to the NAPP/KelbyOne Help Desk all those years ago, and mentoring me, but for opening doors to new worlds of opportunity. Of course, without KelbyOne I would not be where I am today, and so I would also like to extend my thanks to Scott and Kalebra Kelby, Jean Kendra, and all the rest of the amazing staff for creating and maintaining the most amazing professional resource I have had the pleasure of being associated with. I am also grateful to all the KelbyOne members who have sent in their Photoshop and Lightroom questions over the years; you served as the voice in the back of my mind as I wrote.

My undying gratitude goes to the awesome team at Wiley. To the folks I worked with directly, Steven Hayes, Jennifer Yee, Scott & Maureen Tullis, and Doug Sahlin, as well as all those behind the scenes, many thanks for your patience, support, professionalism, and most of all, for making this all come together!

Thanks to the Lightroom team at Adobe for mixing your passion and brilliance into this fantastic tool for digital photographers.

All my love to my wife, Paloma, my son Quinn, and the rest of my family and friends for keeping the coffee flowing, putting up with late nights, making me get out of my chair at regular intervals, and generally taking such good care of me. We did it!

Publisher's Acknowledgments

Executive Editor: Steve Hayes

Development/Copy Editor: T-Squared Services

Technical Editor: Doug Sahlin

Production Editor: Mohammed Zafar Ali

Project Manager: T-Squared Services

Cover Image: © Rob Sylvan